Tourism Social Science Series
Volume 16

The Discovery of Tourism Economics

Tourism Social Science Series

Series Editor: **Jafar Jafari**

University of Algarve, Portugal
University of Wisconsin-Stout, USA
Tel: +1 (715) 232-2339; Tel: +34 659 75 45 59; Email: jafari@uwstout.edu

The books in this Tourism Social Science Series (TSSSeries) are intended to systematically and cumulatively contribute to the formation, embodiment, and advancement of knowledge in the field of tourism.

The TSSSeries' multidisciplinary framework and treatment of tourism includes application of theoretical, methodological, and substantive contributions from such fields as anthropology, business administration, ecology, economics, geography, history, hospitality, leisure, planning, political science, psychology, recreation, religion, sociology, transportation, etc., but it significantly favors state-of-the-art presentations, works featuring new directions, and especially the cross-fertilization of perspectives beyond each of these singular fields. While the development and production of this book series is fashioned after the successful model of *Annals of Tourism Research*, the TSSSeries further aspires to assure each theme a comprehensiveness possible only in book-length academic treatment. Each volume in the series is intended to deal with a particular aspect of this increasingly important subject, thus to play a definitive role in the enlarging and strengthening of the foundation of knowledge in the field of tourism, and consequently to expand the frontiers of knowledge into the new research and scholarship horizons ahead.

Published TSSSeries titles:

Volume 15: The Study of Tourism: Foundations from Psychology, *Philip Pearce*

Volume 14: Modern Mass Tourism, *Julio R. Aramberri*

Volume 13: The Discovery of Tourism, *Stephen L.J. Smith*

Volume 12: The Sociology of Tourism: European Origins and Developments, *Graham M.S. Dann and Giuli Liebman Parrinello*

Volume 11: Explorations in Thai Tourism: Collected Case Studies, *Erik Cohen*

Volume 10: Identity Tourism: Imaging and Imagining the Nation, *Susan Pitchford and Jafar Jafari*

Volume 9: The Study of Tourism: Anthropological and Sociological Beginnings, *Dennison Nash*

Volume 8: Contemporary Tourism: Diversity and Change, *Erik Cohen*

Volume 7: Empowerment for Sustainable Tourism Development, *T.H.B. Sofield*

Volume 6: Exporting Paradise: Tourism and Development in Mexico, *Michael Clancy*

Volume 5: Tourism and Modernity: A Sociological Analysis, *Ning Wang*

Volume 4: Tourism Community Relationships, *Philip L. Pearce, Gianna Moscardo and Glenn F. Ross*

Volume 3: Tourism and Religion, *Boris Vukonić*

Volume 2: Leisure Migration: A Sociological Study on Tourism, *József Böröcz*

Volume 1: Anthropology of Tourism, *Dennison Nash*

179907

UCB
University College Birmingham

Tourism Social Science Series
Volume 16

The Discovery of Tourism Economics

LARRY DWYER
University of New South Wales, Australia

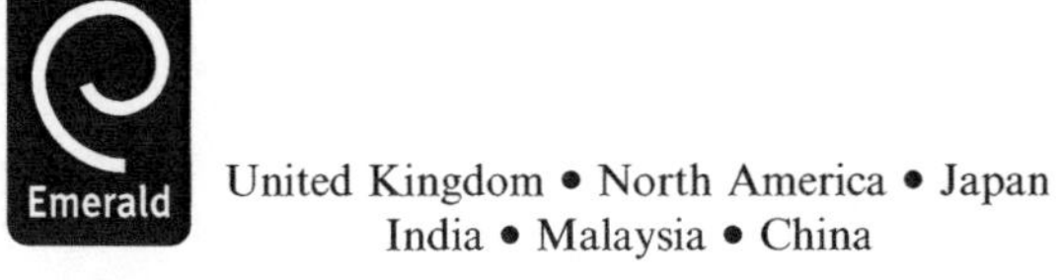

Emerald Group Publishing Limited
Howard House, Wagon Lane, Bingley BD16 1WA, UK

First edition 2011

Reprints and permission service
Contact: booksandseries@emeraldinsight.com

British Library Cataloguing in Publication Data
A catalogue record for this book is available from the British Library

ISBN: 978-0-85724-681-3
ISSN: 1571-5043 (Series)

Emerald Group Publishing Limited, Howard House, Environmental Management System has been certified by ISOQAR to ISO 14001:2004 standards

Awarded in recognition of Emerald's production department's adherence to quality systems and processes when preparing scholarly journals for print

INVESTOR IN PEOPLE

Contents

List of Contributors

Brian Archer	School of Management Studies, Surrey University, UK
Nevenka Čavlek	Faculty of Economics and Business, University of Zagreb, Croatia
Larry Dwyer	Australian School of Business, University of New South Wales, Australia
John Edward Fletcher	International Centre for Tourism and Hospitality Research and Graduate School at Bournemouth University, UK
Peter Forsyth	Department of Economics, Monash University, Australia
Douglas C. Frechtling	Department of Tourism and Hospitality Management, School of Business, The George Washington University, USA
William (Bill) Gartner	University of Minnesota, USA
Thomas J. Iverson	Sustainable Development Institute, the University of Guam, USA
James Mak	University of Hawaii Economic Research Organization; University of Hawaii at Manoa, USA
Tanja Mihalič	Faculty of Economics, University of Ljubljana, Slovenia
Pauline J. Sheldon	International Academy for the Study of Tourism and School of Travel Industry Management, University of Hawaii, USA
Egon Smeral	Austrian Institute of Economic Research, Austria

Haiyan Song	The Hong Kong Polytechnic University, Hong Kong
Clement A. Tisdell	School of Economics, The University of Queensland, Australia
Timothy Jay Tyrrell	School of Community Resources and Development in the College of Public Programs; Center for Sustainable Tourism at Arizona State University, USA
Norbert Vanhove	Katholieke Universiteit Leuven, Belgium
Boris Vukonić	University of Zagreb, Croatia
Stephen Wanhill	University of Limerick, Ireland; Bournemouth University, UK

Introduction

This book is the fourth in a mini-series and began with an invitation from Jafar Jafari, the editor of the *Tourism Social Science Series* (to which this book belongs). Other volumes in the mini-series address the discovery of tourism by sociologists (Nash 2007), geographers (Smith 2010), and psychologists (Pearce 2010). Following in this tradition, the present volume provides the personal histories of many of the world's leading tourism economists, many of whom pioneered the field.

One can, of course, look at the emergence and development of any field of study by describing and analyzing the evolution of ideas relating to that discipline as revealed in published works. But as Dennison Nash (2007) has emphasized in his volume, scientific ideas do not only exist in a disembodied world of their own. He sees them as created and maintained by human beings dealing with a mix of social forces while engaged in purposeful, subjectively meaningful action. Using this perspective, we can try to comprehend more fully how economists have addressed the issues in this (for them) new context of tourism.

Tourism has been a major growth industry globally for over five decades. Factors underpinning this expansion include the increase of incomes and wealth, improvements in transport, changing lifestyles and consumer values, increased leisure time, international openness and globalization, immigration, special events, education, information and communication technologies, destination marketing and promotion, attractive core resources, improved general and tourism infrastructure, and so on. Since there are economic aspects to all of these factors, it is not surprising that research in the area of tourism economics has increased substantially during the same period. At the same time, field of investigation has attracted relatively few research economists compared to other topics within the mainstream discipline.

The autobiographies appearing in this volume suggest the importance attached by these tourism economists to improving the welfare of people. It seems fair to say then that the primary concern of these pioneers has been with "applied" rather than "pure" economics. As they have seen it, the role of tourism economics is to improve the quality of decisionmaking by stakeholders in both the private and public sectors. All the contributors have been driven by a passion for "making a difference" to people's lives. Most have been involved to some extent with tourism in developing countries. It is possible to glean a few patterns. The first tourism economists were primarily concerned with this industry as a tool for economic development. This led to an emphasis on it as a potential catalyst for economic growth, particularly in developing countries. While policymakers in developing countries often had (and still have) overly optimistic views of tourism's potential to enhance the welfare of residents, economic analysis has indicated that this view must be heavily qualified. From an early emphasis on the "leakages problem," which was identified as limiting tourism's multiplier effects, there evolved a growing recognition over the years that the economy-wide effects must be taken into account in determining the impacts of increased tourism expenditure in a destination. An expanding industry tends to "crowd out" other sectors of economic activity. The extent of these "crowding out" effects depends, in turn, on factor constraints, changes in the exchange rate, the workings of labor markets, and the macroeconomic policy context. By implication, tourism growth generates "losers" as well as "gainers," an understanding of which is of crucial relevance to policymakers.

The earlier contributors to the discipline also faced the challenges of applying economic analysis in a rather unfamiliar context. There was an ongoing debate about the nature and scope of the tourism industry, the boundaries of which were considered by many to be artificial (Leiper 1979; Smith 1988). The development of tourism satellite accounts has helped to defuse this debate. The application of economic concepts to tourism was made especially difficult given the differences between tourism products and services and the types of goods and services that are normally the domain of economic analysis. For one thing, tourism has a "complex product," in the sense that comprises a set of different goods and services demanded by visitors during their time in the destination. For another, most tourism experiences are based on the consumption of a (tangible) product and an (intangible) service. These facts alone make the economic analysis of tourism different from analyses of the outputs of other industries that are the standard purview of the economist. Further, other aspects of tourism supply make it difficult to analyze, including issues of intangibility, irreversibility, inseparability, heterogeneity, perishability, interdependence, seasonality, spatial fixity, and so on. The challenges to analysis associated with the relative complexity of tourism products remain to the present day.

Tourism economics has become increasingly quantitative over time, paralleling developments in the mainstream economics literature. Critics have argued that the emphasis on positivist/postpositivist epistemologies renders the economics of tourism less relevant than it might otherwise be in addressing real-world issues and problems. As Jennings (2007) has argued, quantitative-based research has become the "orthodoxy" for tourism economists and has prevented them from addressing tourism problems in a more holistic, interdisciplinary way appropriate to the complexity of these phenomena. Jennings' view is that new and different methodologies and methods must be employed for theory development, to better serve the industry, and for policy formulation. This reflects the debate in the wider literature concerning the continued adherence to positivist, quantitative-oriented orthodoxy in the face of tourism's complexity, rapidly changing characteristics and instability. The point is well taken, as many fear that the use of ever more sophisticated econometric and other techniques is rendering tourism economics inaccessible to the majority of researchers across the other disciplines relevant to a detailed understanding of tourism and its effects.

While some critics have argued that current economic analytical frameworks are too narrow to address tourism realities, the concerns inevitably call into question the attitudes of the economists who employ such narrow approaches. Most would freely admit that no economic model is able to capture all of the dimensions and effects of tourism activity. At the same time, existing models and concepts can provide a useful starting point for the development of new frameworks (Tisdell 2000b). A discussion of the topics that have been addressed in tourism economics reveals, however, that the range of issues addressed is perhaps much wider than the criticisms might imply. A reading of the issues that have been addressed by the contributors to this volume will confirm this. It is fair to say, however, that tourism economists, like their mainstream colleagues, largely continue to work within the traditional positivist paradigms of micro- and macro-economics, emphasizing the attainment of equilibrium outcomes. Mainstream economics has long been criticized for its restrictive assumptions that have narrowed the accepted orthodoxy, leading to a progressive divorce of the discipline from real-world issues and problems.

The concern is that the social context of tourism is being ignored when a narrow economic focus is adopted. The range of different approaches in the discipline suggests that a pluralistic attitude is required, with cross-fertilization of concepts, theories and methods, both within and from outside the subject. However, as pointed out by Stabler, Papatheodorou and

Sinclair (2010), within the mainstream discipline there are signs of pressure to broaden its perspective coming from psychology, social psychology, and sociology, which can inform tourism demand modeling the newer fields of ecological and environmental economics. In particular, the ecological research field has widened the scope of economics by acknowledging the relevance of and embracing the natural sciences; sociology; cultural, ethical, and political studies; and welfare economics, which recognizes the normative elements of the subject. By implication, tourism economists will need to better embrace mixed (quantitative and qualitative) methodologies within interdisciplinary research agenda to advance knowledge in tourism.

Given its fairly recent birth, it is not surprising to be able to identify some areas that tourism economics has relatively neglected. New economic growth theories, which have helped to bring spatial issues more into the agenda of mainstream economics, have been relatively neglected by tourism economists. With some exceptions, labor market theories and tourism employment are also underresearched (Baum 1996). Moreover, there is a lack of attention to the contribution that growth theories can make to our understanding of tourism development (Stabler et al 2010). In particular, insufficient attention has been paid to issues of how international trade, both in goods and services, coupled with globalization, affects the structure, development, and growth of destinations and consequently their natural, human-made, and human environments. Drawing on examples concerning branding, niche and segmentation marketing, Stabler et al (2010) argue that the Ricardian and Ohlin–Heckler theories applied in mainstream economics do not fully accord with what is required to analyze tourism. In particular, there are problems in relating them to how trade influences infrastructural investment and strategies. The theories by Linder (1961) and Porter (1990) that concern market structures, emphasizing the relevance of interindustry trade that is a feature of tourism, have not received sufficient attention from tourism economists. Issues relatively new to economics, such as experimental economics, the effects of information and communication technologies, and a host of issues that arise from climate change pose new challenges to researchers.

The directions for further research highlighted above are just some of those that arise in the topics covered in the wider literature. Changing global trends (economic, social, demographic, political, technological, and environmental) will continually pose challenges to economic theory and policy and the ways we analyze tourism activity. Consider how the complexities of human behavior have affected forecasts of the effects of the global financial crisis on tourism. Our lack of knowledge about the possible consumer responses to the crisis has placed great impediments in the way of forecasting its effects on the tourism industry.

Thus, consumers may spend less and travel less given the ongoing crisis, but to what extent do they shift to other products? Or reduce debt? Or save more? Estimates of the income elasticities of demand for tourism are typically based on data over several years and are not applicable to the sharp falls associated with the crisis. Do tourists switch to closer destinations? Do they exhibit shorter lengths of stay? What is the extent of any shifts to domestic tourism? Is there some "trading down" (e.g., toward lower cost carriers, lower standard hotels, business class to economy, and so on)? Do such crises make consumers become more sensitive to price signals and differentials, thereby increasing the elasticity of demand for tourism products? What are the implications for particular destinations? What are the implications for particular tourism market segments (e.g., seniors tourism vs. business tourism vs. visiting friends and relatives vs. cruise tourism)? Will remote areas be differentially affected? To what extent do price level and exchange rate falls offset income falls to maintain tourism flows? There are many other related questions that could be asked. The point is that we simply do not know enough about consumer travel behavior and pattern to give definite answers to these questions. A comprehensive analysis of the economic dimension of the economic crisis necessarily implies input from other disciplines. Many other examples could be offered to support the view that an overly narrow economic perspective will not provide an adequate understanding of the economic effects of shocks to tourism demand.

Whatever the specific topics that researchers will address in the coming years, it is clear that tourism economics provides a fertile ground for research with the potential to inform policymaking to improve socio-economic prosperity in all destinations worldwide. The contributors to this volume were among the first to plow this fertile ground, providing the basis upon which the edifice of tourism economics continues to be constructed.

THE MAKING OF THIS BOOK

After accepting an invitation from the series editor, Jafar Jafari, my first tasks were to prepare a formal proposal for review and decision by him and the publisher and, concurrently, decide who would be invited to contribute. In consultation with other tourism economists, I made up a list of those who are widely thought to be among the world's foremost tourism economists, and invited each to contribute a chapter to this volume. Given that the contributors had been directly involved in the evolution of tourism economics, they could, therefore, help to construct for the reader as full a picture as possible of the discipline of tourism economics from an insiders' point of view. These discoverers of tourism economics were asked to prepare a loosely structured written narrative (personal history) about themselves and the contexts in which they acted as they came to be interested in and involved with the subject.

Following the approach adopted by Steve Smith in his geography volume (Smith 2010), contributors were given prompts: how did your interest in tourism develop?; who were the influential people in your academic career; significant events (personal, professional, community, social, political) that drew tourism to your attention?; did you start out intentionally studying tourism or did your interest slowly evolve over time?; what are/have been the joys and frustrations of working as a tourism economist; what was your significant field work?; where and how it was influential in your development or research career?; how has your view of tourism as a research field evolved?; how would you describe your research epistemologies, ontologies, preferred methods?; are there particularly significant intellectual trends that have shaped you or that you see as important to the discovery of tourism?; what do you consider to be some of your most significant accomplishments?

Each author was encouraged to discuss her or his particular interests as well as how these interests have evolved over time. While these "prompts" were helpful to the contributors, I emphasized to all that they had substantial discretion in terms of how they presented their personal histories. Each has discussed how she or he "discovered" tourism and why she/he chose to devote her/his career to the subject. The focus of each contribution is on the experience of being a tourism economist. Asked to think of themselves as informants, they were asked to provide an account about their discovery of, and subsequent involvement with, the subject of tourism. The intent was to have their voices and personalities come through as well as the specific details of their contributions to scholarship. Many contributors voiced their concern that the content may be too personal and not sufficiently "academic," but as editor I emphasized the importance of the relating of their "journey" in tourism economics. I received feedback from a number of the contributors that they enjoyed this exercise. A reading of the chapters confirms the pleasure that many experienced in sharing their journey with the reader.

Only one invitee declined to contribute. Another, unfortunately, was too ill to participate. I fully realize that there are other fine tourism economists who could have been invited to contribute and who I appear to have overlooked. I beg them not to take their omission personally. In truth, the volume could have been twice as large taking other important contributors to the field into account, but space limitations precluded additional invitees. All of those selected for the sample have been involved in the field of tourism study since its beginnings and have left a recognizable mark in it by their writing, teaching, or other scholarly actions. The contributors are based in eight different countries on four continents. Some began their careers in communist societies and have very different stories to tell from their colleagues in the West. Of the 17 contributors, only 3 are women. This reflects the relative scarcity of female economists who have addressed tourism issues. The challenges faced by female scholars of balancing a career and family are well known. In my view, the balance is slowly but surely changing and a new generation of female tourism economists is emerging.

All of the contributors to this volume have worked in the university environment, although often not exclusively. Many have also worked as consultants and in private and public sector employment. Of course, tourism economists do not work only in departments of economics but in other academic units such as business or tourism schools. This dispersal of economists among different academic departments reflects their broad intellectual curiosity, capacity, and contributions. It also implies that these personal histories should be of interest to scholars outside the field of tourism economics.

Each of the draft chapters was read by me and Associate Editor Leo Jago. I wish to acknowledge my appreciation for his involvement in this task and for the valuable insights that he provided. In most cases, we had suggestions for improvements which the authors were happy to adopt. The problem with many first drafts was that the author focussed more upon ideas, not injecting enough of their own personality into the text. Some participants succeeded better than others in accomplishing this in their redrafts, but most of the participants ultimately adapted to this requirement reasonably well. I then submitted the revised chapter versions to Jafar Jafari who performed an important role in providing additional feedback on each chapter contribution. In most cases, I was able to handle the required revisions myself without the need to go back to the author.

The result is a series of stories that relate the career journey undertaken by many of the "discoverers" of tourism economics. The study of tourism economics is a global phenomenon. Not surprisingly, this collection presents the stories of scholars working in many different countries. The different stories reveal the diverse personalities, passions, and special circumstances behind the authors' choice of tourism as a specialization within the economics discipline. Such experiences are worth reporting as a celebration of the global community of economic scholars—current and future—working in tourism. Hopefully the opportunity to read the histories of senior scholars may help emerging ones as well as students, whether in economics or other social sciences, appreciate the challenges and rewards of scholarly activity associated with tourism.

Larry Dwyer
University of New South Wales, Australia

Chapter 1

Musings of a Multiplier Man

Brian Archer
Surrey University, UK

Brian Archer is professor emeritus at Surrey University, United Kingdom, where for 17 years he was professor and head of the School of Management for the Service Industries (formerly the Department of Hotel, Catering and Tourism Management) and for the following nine years pro-vice-chancellor of the university. During the 1970s and 1980s, he developed a series of regional multiplier models, some based on macroeconomic and others on input–output analysis. These were used for a variety of studies, some such as the impact of a nuclear power station, the introduction of new industries into a region, and the impact of tax-haven companies showed the wide scope of the models, but the largest use was for the analysis of the impact of tourism in various countries and regions. Indeed, some 40 studies were undertaken over a range of different countries. As part of his work, he has been a consultant to the World Bank, UNDP, World Tourism Organization, and the Commonwealth Secretariat, as well as a special advisor on tourism to a House of Commons Select Committee. He is the author of more than 100 articles, reports, and books and has given papers at conferences, colloquia and seminars in 60 different countries. Email <brian@brianarcher.force9.co.uk>

INTRODUCTION

I was not destined to become a farmer, a classical scholar, a geographer, an army officer, or a schoolmaster, yet at various stages during my early years these were alternative career choices available to me.

The Discovery of Tourism Economics
Tourism Social Science Series, Volume 16, 1–13

ISSN: 1571-5043/doi:10.1108/S1571-5043(2011)0000016004

I was born in 1934 on a dairy farm in the southern suburbs of Liverpool. My family on both sides had been farmers for at least 500 years, yet I showed no inclination to follow this tradition. My father subsequently sold the dairy farm and, in cooperation with 50 or so other farmers, he opened and became managing director of a milk processing company. Again I showed little interest in making this my career, a decision that my parents respected. I attended a private school in Liverpool where, at the age of 13, I was channeled into the classical stream, which involved the study of Latin, Greek, and Ancient History at the expense of the various science subjects. It soon became apparent that I had no aptitude whatsoever for the classics, but it took several years to withdraw from this ill-advised line of study and to concentrate upon areas that were of interest to me. In my final two years, I was permitted to study subjects of my own choice: English, history, and geography. Economics was not available on the curriculum at that time.

In 1953, I was conscripted into the army for two years of national service. In many ways, this was the most intense period of my life. Initially I was posted as an Englishman to a Scottish Highland regiment where, as a "foreigner," I was an object of interest and some suspicion. I worked hard to gain acceptance. In so doing, I achieved one of the most difficult tasks in my life: to be promoted to Corporal within a year of joining the regiment. I also represented my regiment at cricket and field hockey. Selection for officer training followed and, after four tough months at Eaton Hall Officer Cadet School, I was commissioned into an English regiment. At this stage, I seriously considered the army as a career. Fortunately, I decided to defer the decision until after I had completed my degree at Cambridge University. I maintained my military connection, however, through the Territorial Army in which I served for 12 years, retiring finally in 1967 with the rank of Major. I was fortunate to have been able to continue on a part-time basis what had nearly become a full-time career.

Cambridge

Cambridge was a revelation. The atmosphere was vibrant, whether for work or play, and there was plenty of time for both. At this point, I must make a confession: I studied geography not economics. Please do not regard me as a renegade. Economics arrived at a later stage to dominate my life. I was admitted to study geography with a strong dose of history and I thoroughly enjoyed the program. I would make the same choice if the opportunity arose again. The geography staff were approachable and included many who were world authorities in their particular specialities. They included several PhD students whose work later altered the direction, shape, and content of geography as a field of study. It was the most stimulating period. During my final year at Cambridge, I developed a serious interest in economics, but too late to make a change of direction at that stage. The first of two strands that shaped my future career was now evident. The second, tourism, grew out of my love of travel. Over the next 10 years I visited most of the countries of western, and some of eastern Europe, as well as destinations in Africa and Asia. The United States and Canada I became familiar with thanks to the $99 for 99 days Greyhound bus pass. Using the overnight buses as dormitories, I managed to visit 47 of the states over a period of three years.

In 1958, with my university days behind me, I had to make a choice of career. Farming was definitely out; the army was a possibility but I could continue my connection on a part-time basis through the Territorial Army. What I needed was useful and enjoyable employment that would give me the time to embark upon a thorough study of economics on a part-time basis. School teaching was an obvious answer. This would give me plenty of teaching experience, the opportunity to continue my interest in sport through coaching and playing, and the long holidays in which to continue my traveling and embark upon a part-time economics degree. A post was vacant at Monmouth School and I was fortunate enough to be offered the job.

Monmouth

Situated in the Wye Valley, Monmouth School proved to be an excellent choice and I enjoyed 10 interesting and productive years there. In those days, it was a school with 450 boys and had a fine academic and sporting reputation. I kept fit by coaching rugby and cricket and in the summer I played cricket for the staff team and the Monmouth town XI. During the school holidays I traveled extensively, including one memorable visit to an African country that coincided with a civil war.

I was marooned in the outback of the country together with five other persons, each unknown to the others, in a local hotel with a grand view of the main town square in which people were being hanged daily. After several days with no news, one of the travelers, an Australian bush pilot and a veteran of World War II, decided to fly out by "borrowing" the old DC3 that had flown us in and was waiting on a nearby air strip. The rest of us decided to join him and, after distracting and disarming a lone sentry left to guard the plane, we embarked on our escape. I sat by the pilot and, with a tourist map of the country on my knee, helped to guide him as he flew through the mountains. We landed at the country's second international airport, now closed, but outside the main war zone. We helped each other over the perimeter fence and then, with the aid of several underemployed taxi drivers, we moved to a nearby hotel where we sat out the final two days of the war. We left the plane by the perimeter fence for the authorities to make what they could of its location.

I went to Monmouth as a junior geography master to share the teaching of the subject at all levels from 11- to 18-year-olds. At that time, only a small number of boys studied economics under the supervision of an elderly economic historian. On learning that I had registered at London University as an external student to study economics and politics, the headmaster agreed that I could introduce economics on a trial basis for students in their final two years. The response from the boys was overwhelming and eventually my final two-year group exceeded 50.

The next step was to introduce the subject throughout the school and, within a few years, economics was available as a subject from the age of 13. Meanwhile, a lot of time and effort had been devoted to my own studies. In 1962, I was able to graduate with a London University degree in economics and politics. I had benefited considerably from teaching the subject which, of necessity, demanded that I understood the theory in order to be able to explain difficult points to intelligent and demanding 18-year-olds.

The two separate strands of tourism and economics were now both present but had not yet come together to determine my eventual career path. For this to happen, a most unexpected case of serendipity was required. On one of my occasional visits to Cambridge, I met Jack Revell whom I had known as the economics tutor at my college. He had just been appointed professor and head of the Department of Economics at the University College of North Wales, Bangor, and was in Cambridge to recruit staff for two research units that he intended to form.

The proposed work sounded very interesting and I visited Bangor for a formal interview at which I was offered the post of senior research officer in the then newly formed Economics Research Unit. Three years later, this was renamed the Institute for Economics Research of which I eventually became the director.

TOURISM RESEARCH

Bangor

Once again I had made an excellent choice to develop my research experience and to further my career. Bangor is a city of about 15,000 on the coast of northwest Wales and the university is the main source of employment. Although not a tourist center in its own right, it is conveniently near both Snowdonia National Park and also the sand beaches of north Wales which attract over 2 million visitors or tourists annually.

My most immediate task was to undertake a detailed study of the Isle of Anglesey to assess the impact made on the island of the introduction of a large aluminum smelter.

Anglesey for many years has been the principal arable farming area of north Wales and is also an area where the sheep and cattle from the Welsh Mountains are fattened up before sale. It possesses many attractive beaches and is a major holiday destination, especially for day-trippers from northwest England.

The work involved the construction of an input–output model incorporating several unique features, including a number of feedback mechanisms. Under the guidance of Peter Sadler, a senior lecturer in economics, who took responsibility for the mathematical development and subsequent computerization of the model, the embryo research team of Christine Owen and me, began the herculean task of constructing an input–output table with initially blank cells. All the data that could not be processed from existing information, and that meant the majority, had to be gathered by undertaking detailed surveys. Some of these were onerous. In particular, Christine visited about 500 farms which, for someone afraid of farm animals, was quite brave. At the same time, I had the less onerous task of visiting each of the 105 public houses on the island. An idea of the magnitude of data gathering required can be gleaned from the "Sources and Methods" appendix to "Regional Income Multipliers," the first in the *Bangor Series of Occasional Papers in Economics* published by University of Wales Press. It was a physically and mentally exhausting task, which sometimes made me wonder whether I had made the right choice of career.

The Anglesey study, however, was crucial in helping to bring together the two strands of tourism and economics into a meaningful relationship. Anglesey was very much a tourist destination, and tourism expenditure formed a significant part of the economy. Early in the study, I was faced with the twin problems of identifying the magnitude and nature of tourist expenditure and of trying to mesh this into an input–output table. The first was solvable by undertaking further surveys to assess the number and nature of tourists. No original methodology was needed for this task, but the problems of fitting tourist spending into an input–output table initially appeared insurmountable; input–output tables are normally constructed on the basis of industrial classification with earnings from tourism entered as an invisible export to the most convenient service sector. Fortunately, since the

Anglesey input–output table was being constructed without any preconceived ideas as to the nature of its rows and columns, it proved possible to add specific sectors for the different parts of the economy that received tourist expenditure. For example, rows and columns were added for tourist accommodation establishments, caravan sites, shops, transport, and so on to create a total size matrix of 33 × 33.

It was while planning this work that the notion of undertaking a PhD to examine the state-of-the-art in tourism economics and to adapt, develop, and compare different models to analyze the impact made by tourism on an economy became increasingly attractive. The two strands in my career had now fused together. With Anglesey near at hand and with the data from the Anglesey study gathering in my files, I duly registered for a part-time higher degree. To a considerable extent, particularly data collection, my doctoral work could proceed in parallel with the Anglesey study. A lot of effort and time was required, however, to read into and critically evaluate the literature and research findings in the field. Unfortunately, it was not until a few years later that recognized authoritative journals in the field appeared and, in consequence, many of the articles on tourism economics at that time were dispersed across a wide spectrum of mainstream journals. Nor was the internet available to aid the search.

Meanwhile, the Anglesey study was completed within the original time scale and my contract was extended for another year. My new task was to develop a model to assess the present demand for housing in the county of Gwynedd and to forecast changes in this demand over the forthcoming 10 years. This was not an easy task given that at that time no such model existed, that I should be working entirely on my own, and that the work was financed partly by a local consortium of builders. My first task was to build an appropriate model from first principles.

Perhaps not surprisingly, I chose a matrix approach showing the number of dwellings occupied with a separate matrix for each of 10 socioeconomic groups of householders. The number of dwellings occupied by each group was defined in terms of their size and their quality. Changes in demand were assessed as people moved from one socioeconomic group to another as real incomes changed through time. A very considerable effort was needed to undertake the fieldwork necessary to acquire the data and I was relieved when the study ended. However, it was not well received by the builders' consortium who considered it "too academic." However, I had the last laugh when 10 years later the findings of the study proved to be surprisingly accurate.

Three years after joining Bangor, I was appointed to a tenured post as a lecturer in the Department of Economics, but I maintained close contact with the developing Institute of Economic Research as its deputy director. From my first year at Bangor, I had been involved in teaching. Initially I gave a second-year lecture course in macroeconomics and also a third-year tutorial group in regional economics. Now with my tenure secured, I was able to extend my teaching to encompass a new first-year lecture course called Practical Economics to replace the original microeconomic and macroeconomic lectures, which were replaced by small group tutorials, tutored by the growing number of keen young researchers in the institute. Also I introduced a new third-year tutorial class in the Economics of Tourism and Recreation, which incorporated also the growing literature on the economics of leisure. During the summer, I was able to visit Winnipeg, Canada, to teach a course of macroeconomics in the University of Manitoba Summer School, which gave me the opportunity to search their library for any references to tourism research in North America.

Despite the heavy workload, I was beginning to enjoy my time at Bangor. I moved into a Hall of Residence as a tutor and I played cricket for the university staff team and the Bangor City Cricket Club. In the winter, I helped with the coaching of the university rugby team; and for two years I was solely responsible for coaching the University 1st XV—an activity which kept me very fit.

I still spent much of my time in the growing Institute of Economic Research, although my work became increasingly supervisory. Among the studies carried out at this time was the extension of the Anglesey research to cover the whole of Gwynedd (of which Anglesey is a part), some work for the Zuckerman Commission on Mining and the Environment, a study of the possible impact of a second nuclear power station on the economy of Gwynedd, and a project appraisal mission in Nigeria. Several staff were involved in the latter study, and I visited Nigeria twice for periods of eight and nine weeks, respectively. Both visits produced memorable incidents. On the first occasion, accompanied by my colleague Steve Wanhill, we arrived at Ibadan airport to find no driver waiting for us and no means of journeying onwards. Nor was there any chance of making early contact with our hosts in Ile-Ife, since the telephone wires between the two towns had been down for at least a year and sections of the wire were used to make bangles and other ornaments.

We were rescued, however, by a vehicle from Ibadan University where we were housed for several days while contact could be made with our hosts. In return for this hospitality, we were requested to act as external examiners for their economics program. It appeared that the original external examiners had been killed in a road accident the previous day while traveling to the university. On the second occasion, Steve Wanhill and I brought with us bolts of cloth under the mistaken impression that we could easily have well-tailored tropical suits made in Lagos. Unfortunately, the outcome was bizarre. My suit was so heavily padded that the jacket would stand upright on its own. I brought it back home where not even Oxfam would accept it as a gift. Steve Wanhill fared equally badly because the tailor did not realize that on a pin-striped suit, all of the stripes are intended to run vertically.

Tourism economics was starting to dominate my research time and as my thesis neared completion, so the number of requests to carry out tourist studies of various types increased. Notable among these were an investigation on behalf of Wales Tourist Board of the supply of, and demand for, labor in the industry over the whole of Wales, an analysis of the economic effectiveness of government grants to tourism projects, and a series of different multiplier studies in Wales, the English Lake District, and East Anglia to measure the local impact of tourism on particular cities, towns, and even villages. Essentially, these latter studies involved placing one or more of the institute's researchers on the ground in the area for periods of weeks or months to gather the data required for the model.

In 1972, with my thesis completed, PhD awarded, and findings published, I made what proved to be the most fortuitously fortunate decision in my life so far by accepting an invitation to present my multiplier model at a session of the Travel Research Association's annual conference held in Colonial Williamsburg, Virginia. I was uncertain how an account of a tourist study carried out in north Wales would appeal to an international audience, but I was in for a pleasant surprise.

I was allocated a 30-minute slot, including question time, followed by a coffee break. During the latter, I was approached by a steady stream of people asking the same question: "Would this model work in our country?" to which my answer was "Yes, provided that the data are available." Invitations followed to carry out tourism impact studies in several locations. The Hong Kong Tourist Association wanted a fairly quick multiplier analysis, and the work was completed in 1975–76. The Bahamas Ministry of Tourism, supported by a grant from the Commonwealth Secretariat, wanted a more detailed input–output study that I undertook in 1975. This led to further work until 1981, including its updates and also a study of the effectiveness of the country's training facilities in producing employees for the tourism industry.

Bermuda, on the other hand, marked the start of a longer-term commitment. Initially, Steve Wanhill and I carried out a very detailed input–output analysis to assess the overall impact of different categories of tourists on the economy. Subsequently, the study was updated annually with a major report produced every four or five years.

In 1986, the scope of the work expanded when the Ministry of Finance in Bermuda requested me to include the impacts on the economy made by international companies and foreign military stations. This work was updated annually. My contact with Bermuda lasted for about 28 years. Working in the Bermudian environment was idyllic and was a justification and reward for the long hours I had previously devoted to my research.

In the mid-1970s, Peter Sadler moved to the University of Aberdeen to be the first professor of the economics of sparsely populated areas. This left a vacancy for a senior lecturer at Bangor, which I was fortunate to obtain after a formal interview. About the same time, I was appointed to the directorship of the Institute of Economic Research. This small but burgeoning unit had been strengthened by the arrival of two economists, Steve Wanhill and John Fletcher, who later became luminaries in the field of tourism economics.

In 1977, I worked with Steve Wanhill on an Airport Location study in Cyprus to assist in the selection of an optimum site for a new airport. This introduced me to the practicalities of the technique of social cost-benefit analysis, which proved an interesting diversion from multiplier analysis.

The same year, the University of Wales Press published my principal publication *Tourism Multipliers: The State of the Art* (1977). I was interested to note recently that this book, which has been out of print for many years, and which sold originally for £3.25, is available on the internet for prices ranging from £7 to £439. Unfortunately, I neglected to hoard a stock when they were new!

At this stage, a major shift occurred in my career. The retirement of Rik Medlik left a vacancy at the University of Surrey for a professor and head of Department of Hotel, Catering and Tourism Management. The post offered new challenges, and I duly applied and was appointed to start in January 1978.

Surrey

The University of Surrey is situated in Guildford, a city 35 miles south of London. Hotel and catering subjects had been taught at the university and its predecessor institution for more than 100 years, and the department had acquired an international reputation. Tourism, on the other hand, was relatively new and had been introduced in 1972 as a Masters course by Rik Medlik. I was pleased that the tourism staff included such people as Fred Lawson (planning and design), Victor Middleton (marketing), David Airey (economics), and John Westlake (geography). Over the next few years, this team was strengthened by the arrival of Chris Cooper (geography), David Gilbert (marketing), and my former economist colleagues from Bangor, John Fletcher and Steve Wanhill.

The department had many well-established contacts in the hotel and catering sector at all levels from senior decisionmakers to working chefs. From my first year in the post, I received invitations to lunches and dinners in various parts of the country. Conscious of my growing waistline, I accepted these invitations selectively. I was invited also to speak at industry-based conferences and to sit on various panels and boards. In my first year, I was rash enough to accept invitations to help judge two competitions. The first of these was to join a wine-tasting panel in London. Wine is not my forte, and I was apprehensive on discovering that the audience consisted of wine merchants and wine buyers, plus a large number of hotel and catering students. Fortunately, the other two panelists were experts in this field and I positioned myself last in the line as we passed before the 69 bottles on the table and the audience. This gave me the advantage of hearing what the two experts had said and, with the aid of this limited knowledge, I was able to make my own comments together with original remarks such as, "you can almost taste every individual grape" and, "what a presumptuous little wine." The students duly copied my comments into their notebooks and the organizer seemed pleased with my contribution.

On the second occasion, I was asked to help judge the "Young Waiter of the Year" competition at the Savoy Hotel, London. Invited guests at tables for four were served by contestants who were each responsible for the service of a five-course meal at a single table. The five judges circulated to see the work of each contestant. Fortunately, the judges all selected the same winner and everyone was satisfied that justice had been done. At this point, the judges were thanked, shaken by the hand, and dismissed without even the offer of a sandwich or the reimbursement of their expenses.

Several members of the department had acquired an international reputation through the publication of textbooks, but the urgent need was to increase the output of research. Over the next 10 years, the number of research studies and resultant articles increased significantly particularly in the fields of hotel management, food science, and tourism. In 1981, however, progress was temporarily halted by the government's ill-considered and ill-timed attack on the university system in general. Savage financial cuts made it no longer economic to accept British students without dramatic changes being made in the methods of teaching. Small group tutorials became rare and were replaced by lecture courses given to larger numbers of students.

Although less time was available for staff research, many members of staff still found the energy to continue their research efforts.

With over 12 students applying for every place, the department was able to maintain its high standards during this period of uncertainty; but as part of its own plans for growth and expansion, the department introduced three additional postgraduate courses to complement the existing Masters in tourism. They were tourism planning and development, tourism marketing, and international hotel management. From the beginning, these courses attracted high-quality candidates both from overseas and the United Kingdom. My own teaching on these courses was to assist with economic analysis, cost-benefit analysis, and demand forecasting.

At the same time, my own overseas research continued with work in various countries including St. Lucia, jointly with Fred Lawson, to assess the island's manpower and training requirements; Egypt, on behalf of the World Bank, to contribute to a development plan for the Suez Canal region; Mauritius and Seychelles, to undertake tourism impact studies over a number of years, funded initially by the World Bank and the Commonwealth Secretariat, respectively, and then by the governments concerned. Ireland to advise Bord Failte on aspects of tourism economics; Fiji and Vanuatu, with John Fletcher, to evaluate the impact of export industries, including tourism on the economies of the two countries and the People's Republic of China, to give a series of lectures and seminars during a three-week tour. In addition, I continued my work in Bahamas and Bermuda. Other long-term commitments were with Korea and New Zealand, to speak at conferences, give seminars, and provide advice where relevant. In each of these countries, I was able to travel widely to visit the principal destinations; over a 10-year period, I met and discussed issues with leading politicians and other decisionmakers.

My work, however, did not always find universal acceptance. Indeed in one Caribbean country, it was the cause of a general strike. The national newspaper reported (erroneously) that I had recommended an increase in the level of income tax. The union members paraded in thousands and marched through the city behind their band. The leaders chose a circular route, which brought the front of the procession in contact with the rear, thereby creating a continuous parade. Each time the parade passed my office, the bass drummer announced his presence, accompanied by chants from the crowd of "Archer OUT, OUT, OUT." Since I was leaving the country the next day, this advice was superfluous. I have revisited the country on several occasions since then and have encountered no residual rancour among the population.

By 1990, the department had doubled in student numbers, but the number of staff had increased by only 50%. Somewhat surprisingly, but very pleasingly, the output of research work and the number of publications had increased considerably and the department had emerged with credit from the government attack.

The nature of my own workload had started to change. Alongside the problems and headaches of managing quite a large department was added a progressive load of university committee work. In addition, in 1987, I was appointed a pro-vice-chancellor of the University of Surrey, with particular responsibility for personnel, continuing education, and enterprise. By 1990, I was a member of 22 university committees, of which I chaired 12, and 4 industry-based ones, including 2 for the British Tourist Authority. For three years, I tried to combine this work with the headship of the department, but the strain became too great and I reluctantly relinquished the headship. In recent time and since my retirement, the department has gone from strength to strength. It is now the School of Management, with over 2,200 students and a wide portfolio of courses of which hotel management and tourism are a relatively small part.

CONCLUSION

I have no regrets about my choice of career. Tourism economics gave me the opportunity to work in a new and developing field, to travel widely, and to meet a number of political and industry leaders. Although I have been dubbed "the multiplier man," my work has covered a fairly wide spectrum of tourism economics, including project appraisal, manpower planning, development planning, and general economic analysis. It has also sometimes brought me into contact with criminal elements.

On one occasion, for example, I was trying to discover why the revenue of a country's principal casino had fallen by several million dollars, with consequential effects on casino tax and the balance of payments. I traced the ownership of the casino through several holding companies, and finally I obtained an address in Miami. I wrote and received a courteous reply inviting me to meet with the president of the company in the penthouse suite of a prestigious hotel in Miami. I had a concise list of questions to put to him, but instead I had to undergo a detailed interrogation designed to discover exactly who I was and for whom I was working. At the end of 20 minutes, the president excused himself to attend another meeting. As I left the apartment, I heard someone mention his name, which confirmed my suspicions that I had been interrogated by one of the top mafiosas in Florida. I returned to England and informed my clients about the casino's true ownership and the destination of the revenue. I left the methods of retrieving the missing money to the imagination of my client and made no offer to help any further in this regard.

A newspaper correspondent once described one of my reports "...as boring as reading Shakespeare." I still do not fully understand the nuances of this comment, but if one finds what I have written boring, then I apologize, but if one finds it like Shakespeare, then I shall be amazed.

Chapter 2

My Fascination with Tourism

Nevenka Čavlek
University of Zagreb, Croatia

Nevenka Čavlek is professor and head of postgraduate studies in tourism management at the Faculty of Economics and Business, University of Zagreb, Croatia, currently serving as vice dean for international relations. She publishes widely on topics of tour operators and distribution channels in tourism. Her book tackling impacts of tour operators on international tourism development presents pioneering research in this field. She is editor-in-chief of *Acta Turistica* and editorial review board member of three international tourism journals. She is a member of the International Association of Scientific Experts in Tourism and of the Scientific Council for Tourism of the Croatian Academy of Science and Arts. Her research interests and expertise include tourism economics, tourism management, and international tourism. Email <nev@efzg.hr>

INTRODUCTION

If it is true that all is written in the stars, then I must have been bad at reading the signs. Coming from a small tourism resort, one would think that pursuing a career in tourism would have been the obvious choice. On the contrary, my future occupation in tourism was not clear to me until the very

The Discovery of Tourism Economics
Tourism Social Science Series, Volume 16, 15–28

ISSN: 1571-5043/doi:10.1108/S1571-5043(2011)0000016005

last moment. I was born in the small spa resort of Krapinske Toplice, some 50 km northwest of Zagreb, Croatia. My father was a small entrepreneur in machine engineering and my mother was a housewife holding together house and home, taking care of my older sister, my younger brother, and me. As an entrepreneur responsible for several employees, my father had to struggle to survive. In the socialist system of that time, being a "private owner" of a firm was more of a disadvantage than an advantage, given that this was associated with "capitalist rudiments."

FROM INDECISION TO COMMITMENT

In contrast to my sister and my brother, I had always been inclined toward higher education that required deeper studies. As early as primary school, every new subject led me to identify myself with the corresponding career opportunities. I saw myself pursuing a career in literature, geography, biology, physics, chemistry, classical music, or drama. The more books I read and the more school competitions I attended, the more fascinating dreams I had about my future calling. When I finished primary school, my parents decided to enroll me in a grammar school, since that kind of secondary education would open the way to a wide choice of studies. I thought that after completing grammar school, I would have a clear idea of what degree to study for. But right up to the end of grammar school, I kept the same multifocused interests. In the end, I decided to try my luck by taking entry exams for three different faculties of the University of Zagreb, including the Faculty of Foreign Trade that offered a major in tourism, and to enroll in the one where I would score best. By chance, it was the Faculty of Foreign Trade that first announced that I had been accepted and so I decided to enroll there. I persuaded myself that this was a good choice. The faculty had a program in tourism that would broadly satisfy my diverse interests in geography, foreign languages, entrepreneurship, communication skills, etc. It was also important for me to look at the employment opportunities—coming from a small tourism resort I already had a very good idea of what kind of jobs were on offer in tourism and hospitality.

Why did not I decide to study pure economics at the Faculty of Economics, within the same university? At that time, this faculty primarily had a macroeconomic approach related to general economic knowledge, and I was seeking more applied business economics that was in fact offered by the Faculty of Foreign Trade in its "Tourism and Hospitality" program.

I was immediately absorbed by the courses I took and was thus spotted by my professors as a student ready to participate in discussion on the discrepancies between tourism theory and practice. I was well prepared for this task, since during the summer holidays I worked as a receptionist at the hotel of the Krapinske Toplice spa. This was very useful experience in many ways: overbooking was not a term I learned in school; it was an issue I had to deal with during the high season on a daily basis. I was acquainted with the principles of yield management long before I learned the term. I will never forget the overbooking case when a guest was accommodated in the hotel director's office instead of in a booked room. I used all my communication skills to persuade the person to take the offered alternative. After three days, when the guest was finally able to take up the originally booked room, he decided to remain in the office until the end of his seven-day stay. This very modest alternative supplemented with extra special attention and communication resulted in a nice thank-you postcard from the guest and in his return visit some years later.

My curiosity to discover in practice what I had learned at the faculty and to challenge practice with theory pushed me to apply for more challenging summer jobs. I was the only student of tourism in my generation to work on the Croatian seaside for five months as a representative for foreign tour operating companies. Most of my colleagues opted to spend the holidays in more comfortable and stress-free surroundings.

Since I was fluent in German and had all the other necessary qualities, I easily found a summer job for a German tour operating company. The job was much more demanding than my previous reception-desk work. I can sum up this time of my life as the period of "growing up very fast." I became a mother and father to my guests in all pleasant and unpleasant situations, and stayed at their disposal seven days a week. This was the job where leadership qualities, excellent communication skills, and strong nerves were crucial. I learned a lot from the clients' complaints and became a specialist in solving them, irrespective of whether they were justified or not. I soon realized that a successfully resolved problem was much more appreciated by clients than any other kind of task, no matter how well done. I also became aware of what a successfully resolved complaint meant economically for the company. The job broadened my horizons. I experienced the tourism system from the perspective of the clients, and also from the side that is far beyond the clients' eyes.

I held the position of representative for German tour operating companies for three years, always in a different tourism resort every year. This was at my own request. Usually, representatives wanted to stay put, since things were easier once you had become familiar with the place and the people you needed to cooperate with—but not in my case. I wanted to work in new places for two reasons: to get to know different resorts and at the same time see more of my beautiful country, and to deal with different people and problems. An additional motive was to learn something new and not to get overfamiliar with the same type of complaints.

In the meantime, in January 1982, I successfully completed my undergraduate studies in tourism by defending my diploma paper, with Boris Vukonić as my mentor. When I tried to find a permanent job in tourism, I experienced the problems I only used to hear about. Knowing that there was a lack of staff with appropriate qualifications in tourism, I was hoping for a suitable job in the spa resort. Unfortunately, I was offered a position at the reception desk, the same as I had had as a student. When I politely refused, I was invited for a talk with someone higher up. He was impressed with my qualifications and the experience I had, and when discussing with me other employment opportunities, he asked me in a casual manner if I was a member of the Communist Party. At that moment it became clear that in such an environment I would never be offered a permanent job in line with my qualifications. This lesson of life did not discourage me. On the contrary, I decided never to stop learning, since this was the only capital I had and nobody could ever take it away from me. I knew that one day I would find a permanent job, but definitely not in the place where I was born.

For five more years following my graduation, I could not find a permanent job and became an expert in packing suitcases (advice on which I could have offered any number of tourists). At the same time, I wanted to continue my education in tourism at graduate level. Since in 1982 the Faculty of Foreign Trade merged with the Faculty of Economics, I was hoping to be able to continue my studies in this enlarged faculty. Unfortunately, a postgraduate program in tourism was not offered that year and I enrolled in the "Theory and Policy of Economic Development" masters program. In order to finance my studies, I continued my summer job with the German tour operator, but at the same time, I was seeking new challenges: to work for a British tour operator. However, there were two main obstacles before me: first, I was not fluent in English and, second, I had never visited Great Britain, which I thought was equally damaging if I wanted to be as successful as I had been with the German clients.

To remedy this, during the 1983 tourism season I saved money for an intensive English language conversational course in Great Britain. In 1984, I spent a month living with a young English couple, speaking, reading, and listening only to the English language (and even dreaming in English).

Subsequently I decided to apply for a job as representative of a British tour operator specialized in inclusive holidays to what was at that time Yugoslavia. Ten days later I started working as a Phoenix Holidays representative for British holidaymakers on the Adriatic coast.

Although I thought that I had learned all about cultural differences among German and British clients, I soon realized that there was a lot more to it than meets the eye. I used to talk to my British clients as politely as I would to any other client. However, after a month the first written complaint was sent from Phoenix Holidays for my attention. I could not believe my eyes when I read it—everything had gone wrong all holiday long for the writer and his wife. Fortunately, I had learned how useful it was to keep a record of my conversations with clients. I immediately checked what I had written about the couple: for their entire holiday, they had not complained to me about anything. How then was it possible that they were so dissatisfied with their holiday? Actually, according to my notes, I had several pleasant chats with them and they were always very kind and polite in return. This would hardly happen with German clients. If something was wrong, they would always search for the representative and complain on the spot!

After this lesson in cultural differences, discovering any problems my clients might have became a kind of exercise in solving puzzles. No wonder that I was soon among the top three representatives of Phoenix Holidays. This resulted in an invitation at the end of the season to work in its office in London and help out during the winter holiday booking period. This was another challenge that I gladly accepted. To work in Great Britain, the cradle of inclusive holidays, to see the process of creating a package tour in a leading tour operating company, to sense the atmosphere of launching the new holiday brochure, to worry about whether the price range was competitive on the market, to struggle to fill empty seats on flights, to redirect bookings to destinations and flights with higher commitments, and the like. I finally found myself where I wanted to be. It was as if my dream had come true. Economics of scale, pricing, yield management, marketing, finance management, liquidity in the tour operating business, human resources management, and so much more. All this became clear to me, and I was like a sponge! Here I could actually see where tourism theory was lagging behind practice.

I continued to work for Phoenix Holidays for another two seasons: between April and October on the Croatia coast, during the winter as a helper in London. In between, I prepared for my exams in the graduate school. My mentor was Dragutin Alfier—one of the doyens of tourism theory in Croatia. He was the only professor to offer elective courses in tourism at Masters level: I chose all four of them. Thanks to this, I was able to write my thesis in the field of tourism economics. Since my mentor and I had had some bitter debates during his lectures on some of the positive and negative effects of tourism development, he actually proposed "The stabilizing and destabilizing impacts of tourism activity on the economy and on society" for my thesis, which I enthusiastically accepted. However, I realized that I could not complete my work if I was away from the university and the library for most of the time. Comparing the efforts involved in preparing for the exams and in writing a thesis, it was the latter which fully revealed to me the new tourism dimensions. Despite my economics background, I became an advocate of the interdisciplinary approach in tourism studies.

The End of my "Nomadic Life"

In spring of 1987, I started looking for a permanent job in Zagreb, but I found it difficult to give up the "nomadic life" I had somehow got used to. The recently established Institute of Kinesiology in Zagreb was looking for a research assistant with an economics background. Since my CV corresponded to the official competition conditions and given that I was recommended, I finally got the long-awaited permanent job. The next year I was able to successfully defend my thesis. I will never forget saying to my parents that a Masters degree was as far as I wanted to go and that a doctoral degree was meant for somebody else. How much truth is there in the old saying: never say never?

I successfully worked in the Institute of Kinesiology, but never with the same passion as in tourism. Occasionally we would get projects linked to sport and recreation in tourism. Still, even then I would nostalgically think of "proper work in tourism." Out of the blue, I learned that Bemextours, the mother company of Phoenix Holidays, based in Switzerland, was considering opening a representative office for its seven European tour operating companies in Zagreb. The managing director of Phoenix Holidays from London would take the new position. I was determined to return to "real life" and to stay, if possible, for good in this high adrenalin business. Although the managing director of the Bemextours Representative office in Zagreb could have chosen many other offered names as his "right hand," he stuck with me. It was a privilege to work and learn from a person who was happy to pass on to me his knowledge and lifelong experience in tourism without any hesitation.

The Zagreb office was responsible for over 180 tourism representatives of the Bemextours Group, along the Adriatic coast and on Lake Ohrid in Macedonia. My job was to organize the work of the Bemextours Group representative network. Because I knew all the secrets of this job, I had no difficulties with this task. I was also responsible for controlling the financial results achieved by all seven tour operating companies in former Yugoslavia. Every year I was involved in the selection process for new tourism representatives, including conducting training seminars for the future representatives. Soon came another challenge: to write reports for a domestic tourism trade journal about major events and trends on the leading European generating markets. My first report was returned with numerous corrections in red. I was not discouraged or offended, but grateful, since I was again able to learn about something I had not done before. The following reports came back with fewer red marks. The next step was to write a report and critically observe the possible consequences of the developments on the observed markets abroad and their consequences on tourism both in our country and on our companies in the respective markets. This sharpened my economic analytical approach, which I hope I have kept acute ever since.

I could not have wished for a better job. It was very well paid, but I still would never leave the office until the work was done. I was perfectly happy in this job and probably I would never have left, had it not been for the tragic war aggression on Croatia in 1991 that changed the lives of most of its population.

Every Cloud has a Silver Lining

In 1992, the company I worked for was sold, the managing director of the representative office retired, and I accepted a job in the same office that was turned into a representative office of an Italian shoe trading company. The job was not challenging. Compared to the very dynamic and demanding job in the tour operating business, with the new job I had a lot of free time. Therefore, I started to learn Italian, I became a regular columnist for Croatian tourism trade journals, and a contributor of international news on tourism for the Croatian TV, analyzing and critically commenting on its developments and events on the European markets affecting Croatia. In this way, I found an outlet for my fascination with tourism and never lost touch with this industry.

At the beginning of 1993, I learned about a kinesiology conference, to be held in Rovinj—a picturesque town on the Istrian peninsula not affected by the war in Croatia. One track of the conference was devoted to "Tourism and Recreation." I decided to prepare a paper for the conference, not knowing that this decision would change my career forever.

Among the participants of the conference was Boris Vukonić. I was very excited when presenting my paper, since I felt I was again in a very important exam in front of my former professor. I expected his "sharp comments," as always. At the end we were both proud: he of his former student, and I about his positive remarks on my presentation. Then I learned that he was searching for an assistant at the faculty. Immediately I felt that this job would mean the fulfillment of my life mission in tourism. With this position I could always stay at the forefront of knowledge in tourism, I could transmit the knowledge I had gained in practice, and dedicate my research to the field in which I was so much absorbed. I asked him if he had found anybody suitable as his assistant; he simply said that it was not easy to find a person who would meet the necessary requirements. The next day I dared to ask him for the requirements he had in mind, and he mentioned everything that corresponded to my qualifications. I finally bucked up courage to ask him if he would consider me for the job. To my surprise he said that I would be more than suitable, but he knew I would never leave my job that was almost 10 times better paid than the one he could offer at the university. I proved him wrong.

My Tourism Academic Path

My academic career at the Faculty of Economics and Business of the University of Zagreb started in November 1993, as a teaching and research assistant. Something I had told my parents I would never do (pursuing doctoral studies) suddenly became my priority. Once again in my career I was privileged to work with somebody who was willing to open for me all the academic doors and I was committed to doing everything to push through those gates. My first task was to write and defend my doctoral dissertation. It was natural to focus my research on tourism economics, as this represented continued discoveries in the field to which I had so far devoted my education and practical experience. I was encouraged to use economics theories in the field I knew most about from the practical side, but which was neglected in tourism theory: the role and significance of tour operators in the tourism system. I found myself in an area that was challenging enough and for which I was prepared to fight any scientific battle. I selected "The Impacts of Tour Operators on International Tourism Flows" as the title of my dissertation.

The deeper I went into the research, the more open questions I found. In revealing the economic conditions of tourism development, most theoreticians avoid the topic of tour operators. Observing the problem from my practical experience, I did not realize how difficult it would be to assess the business from the perspective of tourism theory and to objectively prove something that was almost obvious to me. I found several obstacles in conducting my research: official data on the movement and total flow of world inclusive holiday travel are incomplete and in most cases are based on different forms of assessment; the methods of data collection have not been standardized and hence not comparable; and academic articles and books dealt with organized travel from the point of view of a single generating market and not from a broader international perspective. It was even a greater challenge for me to find other ways to correlate the impacts of tour operators with the development of international tourism.

By analyzing the ownership structure of the most powerful European tour operators, I came to the conclusion that the leading tour operators were only a segment of large multinational concerns that usually control foreign direct investment in tourism. Consequently, they direct tourism flows to those destinations and countries in which the investors who support them have a financial interest. I found myself facing another challenge: to test the relevance of my scientific work within the international academic field. I was warned that many scientists might assume that I was in an area that represented simply a matter of practice and not a field that needed a theoretical approach based on the solid principles of tourism economics. In 1994, my mentor informed me about an international conference that was going to be held in the summer of 1995 in Istanbul and suggested that I submit a paper to it. He expected a good attendance from academics engaged in international tourism.

Even before the presentation of my paper on "Global Tendencies in the Development of the Tour Operating Business in Europe," I was excited to be introduced to lead authors whose works I had used for my literature review (William Gartner, Richard Perdue, Muzzo Uysal, and Frank Go, among others). My adrenalin was running high when the time came to present my first paper at an international conference abroad. The authorities on tourism in the audience actually were an extra inspiration for me. I thought if I passed their exam (the questions after my presentation), this would be real proof to me that I was ready to continue my journey of discovery in my particular field. The encouragement I received was inspiring. My doubts began to subside that, although I was the right person in the tourism business field, my scientific research capabilities and my results might not be relevant enough for the international academic audience. My mentor's positive reaction to my capacity for lifting practice to a higher theoretical level, which I showed in my answers to questions from the audience, was a good sign for me. Any thoughts I might have had that William Gartner's very encouraging words after my debut were only a courtesy were settled by his invitation to contribute a chapter on "The Role of Tour Operators in the Travel Distribution System" to his coedited book with D.W. Lime ([26]2000).

In February 1997, I defended my doctoral dissertation and started giving lectures on the management of travel and tourism intermediaries, partially in tourism economics. In 1998, I published my first university course book in the Croatian language *Turoperatori i svjetski turizam* (*Tour Operators and International Tourism*). The critics were very positive and I received my first award from the University of Zagreb—the Mijo Mirković Award—two years later.

In 1998, I met William Gartner again in Zagreb when he was making a visit to inspect the venue of the International Academy for the Study of Tourism Meeting to take place in 1999. He was very much interested in hearing about my research. I updated him on the directions I was following on the consolidation processes of the European tourism market. This was the period of very intensive integration processes, and I wanted to study the consequences of these processes on structural changes of the tourism market. When he asked me about my publications, he made me aware of the need to publish articles not only in *Acta Turistica* but also in journals with a higher impact factor. His advice helped me to overcome the fear and my apprehension about setting my goals too high.

In the coming years, I no longer needed encouragement to prepare conference papers. International conference encounters in the Republic of Korea, Greece, the Dominican Republic, Costa Rica, Canada, Ireland, and many others followed. I got in touch with tourism researchers all around the world, found out about their own studies, and received comments relevant to my scientific interests and even support in publishing work on the topic. I had a unique opportunity to see the places I had not visited before. At the same time, I was able to discuss different models of tourism development with tourism experts from different fields. My analytical approach was very much complemented by these international examples. My horizons broadened and I became even more devoted to my field of research and more assured that I was filling the right research gap.

In 1999, I was invited as a keynote speaker at the "Tourism Industry and Education Symposium" in Jyväskylä (Finland). My address "The

Concentration Trend on the European Tourism Market: Opportunities and Challenges" intrigued the audience with an overview of a vertically integrated tour operating multibillion dollar industry, highly dependent on economic movements on the respective markets, on safety and all kinds of security risk, and, moreover, a very fragile low net-profit business that makes managers in this field feel as if they are dancing on thin ice almost every day. My research on consolidation processes in the European tourism market resulted in several articles on the topic.

In the same year, the International Academy for the Study of Tourism had its biannual meeting in Zagreb and I was involved in organizing the event. I proudly took over all operational tasks, since not only could I easily do the job given the experience from my former practice, but more importantly this was a unique opportunity to meet in person renowned authors I admired for their contributions. I wanted our distinguished guests to experience Croatian hospitality. No wonder that when it was my turn to speak on "The Position of Croatia on the International Tourism Market," during the technical preparations of my PowerPoint presentation, some members of the audience thought I was preparing the presentation for somebody else. However, when my name, affiliation, and the topic appeared on the screen, I could see the surprise in the eyes of many, since they thought I was just one of the operational staff from the faculty. Why had I not introduced myself assistant professor when I first met them? How could I? It would have been inappropriate in my eyes. Our guests were all the highest authorities on tourism and they had not introduced themselves by their titles to me. So I thought I needed to earn their respect first.

After my presentation, I was invited to consider becoming a member of the teaching staff at Bournemouth University. Although I very much appreciated the offer, which meant a lot to me in many respects, I could not accept it for family reasons. However, in 2000 and 2001, I delivered lectures to postgraduate students at Bournemouth University on tour operations management. Although I had already had experience as visiting professor in Finland at undergraduate level, I was really surprised when I entered the class at Bournemouth University. I expected mostly students from the United Kingdom, but instead I had a minority from the country, with the majority from Asia. By the following day, I was happy to give the students examples related to their countries of origin.

This kind of international experience resulted in a strong stimulus for me to publish my research in top-ranking tourism journals. Since at the turn of the new millennium, the hot topic (and not only in tourism research) was safety and security issues, I decided to prepare a paper for *Annals of Tourism*

Research. I was very much aware of the rejection rate of the journal and hence I was even more determined to succeed. The paper on "Tour Operators and Destination Safety" was published in *Annals* in 2002 and reappeared in [28]*Tourism Security and Safety: From Theory to Practice* (Čavlek 2006). I focused my research on the behavior of tour operators toward destinations hit by different types of crises.

The study revealed that their approach to the crisis-hit destination depends highly on the tour operator's own business interests there, and particularly on their financial involvements in the country. Analyzing the crises that Croatia was exposed to, I was able to assess the importance of tour operators in creating the image of destinations. Findings suggested that potential clients rely heavily on organic images and that the successful rebuilding of the destination image after a crisis should first start with organic, rather than induced images (Čavlek 2002:489). What an honor it was for me to receive the issue of *Annals of Tourism Research* with my article in it from the hands of Editor-in-Chief Jafar Jafari, a person of endless inspiration in my academic work. He continues to be my role model as I admire his devotion to tourism research and his enthusiasm for innovative projects.

For somebody who is a native English speaker, who had been educated at the world's best-known universities, and who comes from one of the well-known countries, this would probably be a very natural academic achievement. For me, it was far more than that. Even in my home institution, some of my colleagues were teasing me that in the time I had spent preparing the article for *Annals* I could have published several articles in Croatia. If I had taken that attitude, I would never have traveled on the roads of discovery in tourism economics and would not have experienced the joy for a woman to succeed in the international academic world.

The article also resulted in additional invitations to be a keynote speaker at conferences abroad. At some conferences, I had to convince academics that tour operating was not only a practice, but also an important field of study at university level. I knew that the attention of the audience can be drawn best through a provocative approach. The keynote speech in Finland, "Tourism Development under the Influence of Tour Operators: Well-being or Hell-being?," was well received. Since the lack of research in this particular field has also created some biases toward tourism development under the influence of tour operators, my aim has always been to critically evaluate these prejudices and to confront them with facts that have been neglected in research. Work in this area is a never-ending story for me. Tour operators, as the main representatives of mass tourism development, are blamed for bringing to destinations tourists with low purchasing power. I would always claim that it is the destination itself with the possibilities it offers that determines the category of clients to visit it, and not just the price of the package set by the tour operators.

The more international academic recognition I gained, the more challenging tasks at my home institution I was entrusted with. In 2006, I was appointed editor-in-chief of *Acta Turistica*, an honor that became my commitment to persevere in *Acta*'s long-established scientific reputation. Even in its hardest days of the most recent Croatian history, *Acta Turistica* has not ceased publication and has not strayed from its planned course in spite of the countless Scylla and Charybdes—hence reaffirming its motto that science must not be stopped by obstacles but has to find solutions for the most difficult challenges. Today *Acta* is facing new challenges, constantly competing with the favored Western journals, as well as reaffirming its relevance in the dissemination of scientific positions on crucial issues of tourism development of interest both to Croatian readers and global audiences. *Acta Turistica* continues to publish simultaneously in both Croatian and English, thus promoting linguistic diversity, updating the Croatian scientific terminology, and focusing on multiculturalism through a multidisciplinary approach.

As much as I enjoy research and presenting conference papers around the globe, I approach lectures to students with the same passion and devotion. Being committed to advancements in tourism studies, I have always been searching for better learning opportunities for my students. Knowing from my own experience the importance of being exposed to different ways of thinking, different methods of learning, different cultures, and a real tourism business environment which is usually impossible to achieve in traditional or even cyber education, these all inspired me to try to develop a unique eight-day intensive international study module on tourism for future experts in tourism (named International Tourism and Hospitality Academy at Sea, or ITHAS). The intention of all the delivered programs since 2005 has been to combine the theoretical and practical parts of tourism, giving students the chance to experience triple roles: to offer experience in the internationalization of tourism studies through the involvement of five other partner universities from Europe and Canada, to undertake the role of a tourist, and to practice the role of a tourism expert.

The study module is set up to give its students the opportunity to experience, at least for a week, the true tourism business in action while sailing. Since tourism is imbedded in a multicultural and international environment, the multinational encounter of students and renowned scholars has been the natural requirement for the success of the project. Every year another sailing route and another topic are set for an international group of 100–130 students, plus 20 professors and assistants. Through this kind of experienced learning, students not only explore the heritage, culture, and tourism development of the countries visited, but also acquire new knowledge and experience from the international scholars and the local experts, as well as from each other. My greatest reward for the time invested in organizing the event every year is the determination of all partner institutions and students to continue this kind of network building for the future (careerwise and friendshipwise), as the students experience it as the highlight of their studies.

CONCLUSION

If I was born again, would I change anything in relation to my decisions regarding my career? I consider myself lucky to have been able to gain a thorough education in tourism from undergraduate to graduate and doctoral level with a strong economics background. I have been privileged to gain a lot of experience in tourism practice since theory needs practice as much as practice needs theory. I am proud to be a part of a tourism research network that encourages me to continue my discovery in the field of tourism economics.

Enhancing education in tourism has become my mission, researching into travel and tourism intermediaries is my passion, and tourism practice will stay forever in my heart. So, how could I not but follow the same path of discovery?

Chapter 3

Curiosity Made the Tourism Economist

John Edward Fletcher
Bournemouth University, UK

John Fletcher is professor of tourism, director of the International Centre for Tourism and Hospitality Research (which he founded in 1996), and head of the Graduate School at Bournemouth University (since 2002). He started his academic career at the University College of North Wales, Bangor (1970–85), where he was director of the Institute of Economic Research, before he moved to the University of Surrey, where he was head of Postgraduate Studies and CEO of Surrey Research Group from 1985 to 1996. His career prior to academia was rich and varied, ranging from engineer to police officer, before setting out on his academic career as an economist. He has undertaken tourism research for many national governments and international agencies such as UNWTO, USAID, EU, and development banks. Over the past three decades, he has developed interactive economic and environmental impact models, particularly for island economies in the Caribbean, the South Pacific, the Mediterranean, and the Indian Ocean. He was one of the founding authors of *Tourism Principles and Practice* (now entering its fifth edition) and is editor in chief of the *International Journal of Tourism Research*. Email <jefletch@bournemouth.ac.uk>

The Discovery of Tourism Economics
Tourism Social Science Series, Volume 16, 29–42

ISSN: 1571-5043/doi:10.1108/S1571-5043(2011)0000016006

INTRODUCTION

My journey into tourism economics was not one that could have been predicted by either me, any member of my family, or the poor teachers (pun intended in some instances) that had to endure my reluctant presence throughout my schooling period. I was not a natural scholar at school and rarely became engaged in any of my lessons, unless they involved experiments in the laboratory. The fun parts of the day were always the break periods or when it was time to jump on my bike and ride.

Having spent my primary school days being told that I was not as focused or enthusiastic as my older brothers who had progressed through the same school previously, I lost whatever motivation I may have had and saw the challenge as being one of surviving rather than thriving in my schooling. This was a recipe for cooking up a rebel and a rebel was what I became. So much so that during one of my years at junior school, aged 9 years, I spent a year locked into conflict with the teacher, a Mr. Evans, who was almost as determined to break my spirit as I was to maintain it. Each day would bring a new opportunity for me to be punished. In this school the instrument of torture was a leather strap that had five or six thinly cut tails, which the victim had to retrieve from the headmaster's office before receiving two or three lashes across the hand. The routine was soon so well established that Mr Evans only had to call out my surname for me to acknowledge I was on the way to get "the strap." This particular year took an age to pass, and my movement to the next class up probably brought as much relief to me as it did to Mr Evans.

However, although not the natural scholar, I was blessed with an unusual level of curiosity—about the world around me and how things in it worked. This curiosity was a primary motivator for me then as a young boy, as it is now. As a child, I was not content to simply play with any toys I had been bought for Christmas or birthday. I had to pull them apart to find out how they worked (if they did in fact work). Thus, during the early days of my childhood, instead of being surrounded by loved and cherished toys, my bedroom took on the landscape of a factory or garage with half-dismantled/assembled toy cars and planes everywhere. I vividly remember one Christmas morning taking out the clockwork motor from a wind-up car and managing to get my left hand tangled up in its gears. So my father's early morning Christmas treat was to try and work out which way to turn these gears in order to release the flesh of my palm in a way that did not increase the pain I was in!

Even inert toys, such as the lead soldiers children were bought (who mentioned health and safety?), did not escape my curiosity. While my friend and colleague Stephen Wanhill, whom I later met as a student, was keeping his newly acquired lead soldiers in pristine condition, complete with their original boxes, only letting them out into natural daylight on odd occasions, I decided that I would melt all mine down in a crucible (read old OXO tin on a bonfire) in order to see if I could mold them into something more exciting such as a single, huge soldier. Unfortunately, this "experiment" was not a success and I was left with a rather bizarre landscape of half-molten heads, arms, legs, and rifles that looked like a modern depiction of Dante's Inferno. The world of economics was a long way off and little did I realize just how much value I was adding to Steve Wanhill's current day collection by taking my soldiers permanently out of the market place.

It will not come as a surprise to hear that I did not wish to stay at school one day longer than required by law. By the age of 16, I had already been attracted into the world of motorcycles and racing. It was a struggle to persuade my parents into letting me have my first motorbike, a Velocette, but a worthwhile struggle and I started a relationship with fast motorbikes that I still have today. Brokering a deal with my parents allowed me to wave goodbye to school at the age of 16 and take up an engineering apprenticeship with W & T Avery Ltd. based in Altrincham. By nature, I am a competitive person and soon I found a fundamental flaw in my skills as a motorcycle racer, in that I had to either win a race or fall off. Unfortunately, I managed to achieve the latter rather more frequently and so my active participation in races was somewhat short-lived.

Rather than provide a blow-by-blow account of my experiences on either motorcycles or my apprenticeship, I will skip to the next key point in my journey toward tourism economics, which was a departure from the route I had been taking, when I joined the police force. I did this to realize a young childhood ambition, which probably came from watching too many episodes of a popular TV series during my formative years. After recovering from a serious motorbike accident, I gradually moved toward four-wheeled transport by buying one of those ludicrously dangerous three-wheeled cars. I am still to this day unsure as to what sort of engineering mind could have thought that three wheels on a car, particularly when the single wheel was placed at the front, was better than either two or four wheels. The major problem with the Bond three-wheeled car (which was nothing like the car used by the spy with the same name) was that I regularly used to turn it over on sharp bends, much to the amusement of passersby in Coventry City Centre who got used to seeing a group of policemen, in full uniform, climbing out of the upturned car, putting it back onto its three wheels, returning inside, and driving off.

Two years in the police force proved that TV was not always accurate in its portrayal of life, and I was back into the world of engineering again, first in Southampton, training a group of young apprentices (my first foray into education, although I probably did not see it as such at the time) and then later back to Coventry to work for Triumph Motor Cars. The motor industry in the United Kingdom was not one of the most stable ones at that time, and there were as many days spent out of work through industrial disputes than there were spent building cars. Soon I decided it was going to be either them or me and to the horror of my friends I elected to give up a relatively well-paid post to go to university as a mature student and study economics. I chose economics out of a hat (literally) scrunching up a dozen pieces of paper and placing them into a hat, economics was the one that came out. Thus, my journey toward tourism economics had now taken its first significant step.

My next thoroughly researched decision was to identify where I should study economics. This one was relatively easy; the University College of North Wales at Bangor was the only place that I could afford to live and study at my age and with a wife and, by then, two children. A quick visit to Bangor, an interview with Alwyn Hopkins (to whom I am most indebted for seeing potential in me when many could not), and I had secured an offer as a mature student, sold my house in Coventry, and moved to a small bungalow in the foothills of Mt. Snowdon in Wales. Living some 12 miles from the university meant that the property prices were in my favor, there were hurdles to overcome, as I moved my family into a village where we were virtually the only non-Welsh-speaking people.

My first year at Bangor was a revelation. Having been out of the educational system for some years, the fact that none of my brothers had previously been taught by my lecturers, combined with the maturity that comes with being a father, I found that I did, after all, enjoy education. Bangor students had to choose three subjects in their first year of study (my choice being economics as my major, and psychology and history as my minors) and then carry on with economics plus one of the minors into the second year. Although doing well in psychology and history, I did not feel that they gave me what I needed to contribute to what was rapidly becoming a major passion in my life: economics. Therefore, I dropped both subjects in my second year and in their place took up mathematics, much to the alarm of my personal tutor. This was the first time I had come across matrix theory and its application, again serendipitous in view of the area of economics I would eventually embrace.

I thoroughly enjoyed studying economics, "the essence of life," particularly macroeconomics and found so many synergies between this subject and engineering. The areas that really absorbed me were those where one was looking at models of the economy, and my newly acquired knowledge of matrix algebra only served to enhance that enjoyment. My second year at Bangor was also a revelation in other respects, because there were several people who would come to play a large part in my future life as an academic: Steve Wanhill, a fellow student, and Brian Archer who had come to Bangor as a research officer and was working on his PhD. Not one of us, at that point in time, knew that we would eventually become what we now refer to as "tourism economists."

Following the completion of my first degree at Bangor, I was offered a post as a research officer to undertake a project for the British Library, which involved calculating the optimal level at which a library should move from a handwritten issue system to a computerized system. Although more micro than macroeconomics, it was a project that I found immensely entertaining, and I enjoyed working on a real-time project that could have such far-reaching consequences. The project involved the categorization of libraries by size, structure, and type of lending. From this, a sample frame was established and I found myself traveling the country armed with stopwatch, pen, and calculator. I think that the British Library project started my fascination in trying to measure the intangibles of life, a fascination that is well suited to the study of tourism.

A year on and I had completed the project and also completed a Master's thesis, which examined the financial support that was provided from central to local governments in England and Wales. I was now standing on the edge of the cliff that I had only momentarily considered when I started out on my economics degree: what do I do when I have finished? I considered the post of economic development officer with Cornwall County Council, but was then offered an interview at Swansea University for the post of lecturer in economics. Again, serendipity stepped in and a lectureship became vacant at Bangor. Following my application and interview, I was appointed and subjected to the ritualistic game of snooker with Jack Revell, the renowned financial economist who was head of the Economics Department. Thus, my academic career was underway as a macroeconomist. I was looking forward to working with Steve Wanhill who had been appointed as microeconomics lecturer the year before, and with Brian Archer who was, by now, senior lecturer in regional economics and director of the Institute of Economic Research.

I survived the rather unusual and somewhat traumatic introduction to life as a lecturer where the only tools provided were the names of the programs for which one would be responsible and the timetable showing when one's teaching slots would be. The rest was very much doing what comes naturally. I feel quite sorry for those students who had to endure my lectures and seminars as I learned the craft of writing and delivering lectures in a way that would instill passion to those listening. This was a very steep learning curve.

The early research projects I brought into the university were very much impact related, including transport and investment projects on the regional economy, together with my first foray into an explicitly tourism-related project that was to look at the likely impacts of marina development in Wales. Academic life at Bangor was rewarding. I was fortunate to share my early academic life with a group of fascinating characters at a time when academia really did give one the time to reflect on issues of importance, where student numbers were small, and there was encouragement to be innovative and radical in one's research. In this environment, I immersed myself in model building and was developing ones to reflect the findings of my Masters degree (soon to be my PhD) that examined the financial relationships between central and local governments, which in turn provided evidence to the debate on devolution in the United Kingdom. As a result of this research, I was invited to present a paper at the British Association for the Advancement of Science, which was to be my first major conference paper.

TOURISM RESEARCH

I took over as director of the Institute of Economic Research in 1978; Brian and Steve moved to the University of Surrey where the former had been offered the chair in tourism and head of department. We had worked closely together and shared the same passion for economic research. Thus, I briefly considered moving with them, but did not feel at that stage of my academic career that I wanted to move out of a mainline economics environment. There were several areas of research I was pursuing, and I did not wish, at that time, to close off those avenues. I continued to develop the institute. Over the following seven years, the institute grew into a sizeable body of researchers, with PhD students and attracting projects internationally. While the director of the institute, I inadvertently slipped a little further into the mold of a tourism economist. The UK government Foreign and Commonwealth Office (FCO) asked me if I would visit Gibraltar and meet with the governor and his chief financial secretary to discuss some economic research to assist them in their planning and policymaking. This visit started my relationship with the government of Gibraltar that still exists today. I am fortunate enough to be still building models for them and providing economic advice to members of the house, who are the sons and daughters of the ministers who were in place when I first visited Gibraltar.

As a result of my preliminary visit, I set myself the task of constructing my first input–output model for Gibraltar. It was new for them and it was the first time I had attempted to build such a model. Upon reflection, Gibraltar was a good place for an economist to cut his "input–output teeth," because the economy—although relatively small—was wonderfully complex. The late George Clayton was the incumbent economic advisor to the government of Gibraltar when I made my initial visit. He took me to a restaurant in Catalan Bay for dinner and briefed me on the structure of the economy. I ordered "Fresh Tuna Steak Salad" and, as I was enjoying it, came across a sharp triangle of metal in the tuna. Clearly the meat had been fresh at some point in its life, but this particular piece had come out of a tin.

My host, not wanting to make it look as if we were trying to get out of paying our bill, duly settled the account for our meal. When the waiter returned with his change, he handed him the piece of metal and asked him to get the manager to come and explain how this piece of steel was found in the supposedly "fresh" tuna. A few minutes passed by when a man came to the door, looked out at George and me, decided we were not going to be too much trouble. The manager went back inside his restaurant, locked the door, and switched all the lights off, leaving George and I sitting there in the veranda in complete darkness. This did not bode well for businesses in Gibraltar that were reliant upon good levels of tourist satisfaction. Clayton's comments about the Gibraltar economy included the interesting fact that the country did not grow tobacco, yet the exports of tobacco products exceeded more than was imported. This summed up the Gibraltar of the 1970s: complex, dominated by the UK Ministry of Defence and somewhat unusual. It also explained the number of high-speed power boats that were based there at that time. Although its complexity remains, Gibraltar is a much more robust and well-structured economy. Through the strength and leadership of its government and the resourcefulness of the business minds, it is truly an economy of the 21st century.

The Gibraltar study introduced me to some of the more challenging aspects of foreign tourism. As part of the study, I was required to visit the minister of labor in Rabat to discuss the large Moroccan labor force that worked in Gibraltar's dockyard. The journey was fraught with unplanned events, starting with the absence of the hired car that I was supposed to pick up from Tangier Airport (which was quietly waiting for me somewhere in Algiers).

My arrest on the ferry between Algeciras and Tangier was for a supposed passport irregularity, but when I was given the opportunity to escape across a port barrier, a civil riot erupted on the dockside in Tangier. The ferry on its journey from Tangier to Gibraltar rocked so violently that many passengers were vomiting across the food hall. Finally, I was attacked by a pair of Alsatians, which had escaped from the scrap metal yard they were supposed to be guarding, on Devil's Tower Road as I walked to the Caleta Palace Hotel late at night following my tortuous ferry trip from Morocco.

The Gibraltar economic model was the first step down a one-way highway and my journey into tourism economics, because input–output models are highly addictive. The fact that the Gibraltar model was so well received by both Gibraltar and the UK governments, resulted in another contact from the FCO asking if I would build a similar model for the Seychelles. But before I set foot in the country, Brian Archer had been commissioned to do the research from a different funding source. However, the roll of the academic dice had already been thrown and I was invited by the World Tourism Organization (WTO) to visit Jamaica (1984) and explore the possibility of building an economic impact model for them. The opportunity to build an input–output model for the Seychelles came back to me a decade later (with Brian Archer), but in the meantime I had been given this opportunity to work with the government of Jamaica.

WTO has always had a blasé attitude toward travel. Although we had discussed Jamaica over a period of months prior to my traveling, I was given only a few days notice about my first visit to the Caribbean, with the travel made by the cheapest means possible. This meant that instead of a direct flight from London to Kingston, I had to take a flight to Miami and then catch an Air Jamaica flight from Miami. This not only added several hours to the traveling time, but also presented me with a new challenge; I did not have the required visa for entry to the United States and was summarily arrested and confined in a small room with some Puerto Rican families for five hours in transit.

Embedded as Tourism Economist

By this time, I had seamlessly drifted across from being a macroeconomist who did the occasional impact study, to one who was primarily building economic impact models for countries that were significantly dependent upon the services sector in general and tourism in particular. My transformation was complete; I had somehow become a *tourism economist.*

Thus, in 1985 I made the decision to move from Bangor University to the University of Surrey to join Brian Archer and Steve Wanhill. This was the start of a tourism economics career that would take me to many countries around the world, including islands in the Caribbean, the South Pacific, the Indian Ocean, and the Mediterranean.

Jamaica was at an interesting stage of its economic development with three main sectors: agriculture, bauxite, and tourism (if one ignores other somewhat less legal outputs that do not naturally fit into the Standard Industrial Classification (SIC) system). By this time, I was used to working remotely in distant countries, but Jamaica was much larger than Gibraltar (geographically as well as economically), and this required some adjustment to the way in which I operated. After meeting with the government officials and agreeing what was to be achieved, I set about undertaking the research from awareness campaign, through data collection, to model construction and report delivery.

The data collection is one of the most important arts involved in constructing input–output models. It requires businesses from all sectors to provide data more confidential than the data they release to the inland revenue agencies. This requires a good sales pitch and the ability to persuade people that the researcher is trustworthy. The study in Jamaica had many memorable moments, such as the time I persuaded a group of consultants that it was safe to visit a theater located in a dangerous part of Kingston. Having persuaded my three colleagues that we would be driving in, parking outside the theater, and driving back, I remember the sheer horror as I sat there watching the end of the performance realizing that I had locked the car with the keys still in the ignition. Upon leaving the theater, we set about looking for a piece of wire or anything that might go through the small gap in the window of the car so that we could unlock it and drive back to the safety of our hotel. Soon a crowd gathered and I was feeling increasingly guilty and concerned about the welfare of my party. Fortunately, one of the crowd ran off down the street and soon returned with a boy who had the longest and thinnest arms I have ever seen on a human body; he soon had his arm in the car and unlocked the door. I pushed a $10 note into his hand, thanked everyone, and drove my party back to the hotel. They did not speak one word to me for the next three days!

On another occasion, I had planned my strategy for visiting the businesses across the island, but ended up feeling exhausted and in need of a break. So I decided to return to Kingston from Negril late one night, having been firmly told not to drive through Jamaica's heartlands at night, only to get hopelessly lost and then, after doing a circuitous route back to

Kingston, finding that my hotel had let all of its rooms to the West Indies cricket team. Tired, stressed, and hungry, I needed to find an alternative, but the hotel manager insisted on introducing me to each member of the cricket team. I was in Jamaica when the tourist arrivals exceeded 1 million for the first time, and there was champagne and merriment all around (including a very strange TV interview that I gave where the reporter thought that I was a totally different Dr. Fletcher; neither of us realized this until we got down to talking about the hospital in Kingston).

The Jamaica impact study was followed by another four projects for the government, including a labor study. The Jamaica economic impact report was widely circulated for a nonpublished document and I subsequently came across copies in Brazil, Chile, and as far away as New Zealand. This amazed me, given this was before the days when electronic documents freely circulated on the internet. Now I was firmly embedded as a tourism economist, and there was no turning back. Studies followed in the South Pacific, where I went on a tortuous 11-week visit. During this time, I was to build impact models for Western Samoa, the Solomon Islands, and the Republic of Palau. Each group of islands I visited held their own charms and presented their own challenges. My flight to Fiji (my base for the duration of the visit) saw me arrive at the UNDP self-catering flat on a Sunday, with no food, and I was due to depart to Western Samoa the following day. Landing in Western Samoa, I saw a Boeing 737 that had landed just before my flight and was covered in the blood of a herd of donkeys that a protestor to the airport expansion had driven onto the runway. No humans were hurt, but I understand that the pilot was suffering from shock.

It was in Western Samoa that I went to a dinner put on for my benefit and fell victim to an unpleasant parasite that did not agree with the antimalarial tablets I was taking in preparation for my impending trip to the Solomon Islands. Within 48 hours, I was suffering quite badly with fever and muscle spasms. A visit to the hospital resulted in me being booked on the next available flight back to Fiji so that I could be seen by the consultants at the hospital in Suva. While waiting for my flight, a colleague, Roger Doswell, had arrived to do some hospitality training and promptly slipped in the shower and suffered a rather nasty fracture to his arm. Thus, both Roger and I were transported like the walking wounded back to Fiji where we tried to explore what it was that made us travel to the other side of the world and end up in hospital. Incidentally, on that trip, I flew across the dateline on my birthday, so I guess that makes me a year younger!

Throughout the later 1980s and early 1990s, I continued undertaking economic impact studies and building input–output models for islands in the

South Pacific. I also ventured into the Indian Ocean where I built impact and forecasting models for Mauritius and, with my friend and colleague Brian Archer, the Seychelles. By now I had integrated environmental matrices into the input–output modeling and combined both with forecasting modules so that the impact models, which were now software based, provided powerful policy assistance to governments. Although my interest in capturing the environmental impacts of tourism within the same framework as the economic impacts was through a genuine belief that we needed to fully appreciate all of the impacts of tourism, like many tourists I have not always behaved in a way that was respectful to the environment. This includes whizzing around the snow-clad slopes of Vermont on a very loud and powerful snow-mobile, to the occasion when, during a visit to the islands of Vanuatu in 1990, I found some really attractive shells on the beach near Ulei and put six of them in my pocket for my children. Returning to my hotel in Port Vila, having driven all day with these shells in my pocket, I put them on my dressing table, had dinner, and retired for the night.

During the early hours of the morning, I woke to the sound of tap-dancing and, switching on the light found, to my horror, that these shells were still inhabited and the crabs were running around on the top of the dressing table. I then, to my shame, put these six crabs out into the hotel corridor, closed my door, and went back to sleep. In the morning, when going down to have breakfast, I found five of the crabs at the end of the corridor, with the sixth one at the stairwell. Full of guilt, I collected up my cast of crabs and carefully took them to the harbor, returning them to a more familiar habitat, albeit at the opposite end of the island. I have not collected any shells since then.

The greatest challenge of my academic career as a tourism economist came in the guise of the *Scottish Tourism Multiplier Study*, which was published by the Scottish Office in 1993 as three research monographs (Surrey Research Group 1993). This project involved the construction of six input–output models for a variety of geographical areas that were intended to be representative of the different economic structures found in Scotland. Thus, these included urban, island, rural, and remote rural areas. The data from these six areas were then pooled and cross-sectioned to create hybrid models that reflected the economic impacts of tourism in urban, rural, and remote rural areas, irrespective of where they were located. Between September 1991 and February 1992, I had 17 members of staff flying from Heathrow to Scotland to interview more than 1,000 businesses. The construction of the models and the writing of the reports were a daunting task and I worked through many nights and weekends to meet the project deadline.

The output of that study has formed the benchmark for tourism economic impact studies throughout the United Kingdom from that time to the present day, and the coefficients from the model are still found in some of the commercial impact models being used at subnational levels. The *Scottish Tourism Multiplier Study* was also the first time that I had developed an interactive software model for government agencies to use, with many lessons learned from that experience. To start with, FORTRAN, although the bread and butter of languages for economists, is not a user-friendly language for noneconomists. Therefore, the unfortunate officials in the Scottish Office had to work with a "black box" of a program; the most attractive element of the output of the software was the histograms made up out of asterisks. The lesson learned from this adventure into software-based models was to search for an alternative presentation format, which I found in the form of Microsoft's Visual Basics and the Excel Program.

It was good to have rejoined my Bangor colleagues at the University of Surrey; in fact, the three of us were referred to as the "Bangor Boys" by the other staff. During my time at Surrey, we developed our research capabilities, reaching further across the globe. We also took on new staff, such as John Latham and Chris Cooper, to continue the expansion of the programs and research. I have found that each colleague one works with brings a new dimension, such as that brought by John Latham. An accomplished mathematician, he worked with me to fulfill a project for Hilton Hotels. This involved developing a way of determining the likely market share of a new hotel through the use of intersecting cones. The variety continued with other projects like the expert yield system that he and I developed for the Strand Hotel in London. Interesting though these were, none of them can take the place of my passion for building impact models.

When I left Surrey in 1996 to set up the International Centre for Tourism and Hospitality Research at Bournemouth University, I took with me several of my colleagues from Surrey, including John Westlake, Fred Lawson, and Chris Cooper. Thus, I embarked on the last steps of my journey as a full-time tourism economist by creating a new center that would soon outstrip Surrey University in terms of the size of our postgraduate cohort and the research and publications that flowed from our collective endeavors. Ironically, when we moved to Bournemouth University, we were known as the "Surrey Boys." I have often wondered what one has to do to be identified as being someone at the institution where the person is currently based. The center has been a tremendous success, with well over 150 Masters students, 50 PhD students, home to two of the leading international journals in tourism (*The International Journal of Tourism Research* and *Tourism Economics*) and to a leading textbook, *Tourism Principles and Practices*, which in its first edition (now moving into its fifth) back in 1993 was created out of the lecture notes written by Steve Wanhill, David Gilbert, and me. We did so because we were not able to find a suitable text that reflected our knowledge and research interests.

CONCLUSION

In summary, the greatest skills required to be a tourism economist are those of persuasion, in the sense of persuading businesses to hand over data that they would not share with members of their own family, or persuading ministers that inbound tourism is an export and can generate more economic activity than the value of tourist spending. The earliest requests for me to build economic impact models came from ministers of tourism, who wanted to argue for a larger budget and tended to be interested only in the bottomline figures that came out of the results. Today the requests are based more on genuine needs for planning, and ministers are interested in the way in which tourism interacts with the rest of the economy and how its positive impacts can be enhanced. The most important technical challenge I faced was in transforming input–output models into software versions that could sit on the computers of directors and ministers of tourism, from my first attempts with Fortran to the most recent web-based versions.

In terms of my travels, I have probably been to more countries and seen less than most people as I clutched my briefcase on remote desert islands. I often tell people I feel like the boy who is looking into the sweet-shop window, watching the tourists enjoying themselves, as I hurry on my way to the next meeting. The travel itself has left indelible experiences, from being the only passenger on a Nauru Boeing 737 flying from Palau to Fiji when Air Nauru managed to lose my bags, to being told "Goodbye Sir! I am so sorry," on an Air India flight somewhere over the Persian Gulf.

The title that I gave to this chapter reflects a number of things, first that from my early days I had never contemplated becoming an economist, let alone one that works in academia. Second, I gradually slipped into tourism economics, rather than setting out on a path that would lead me in that direction. Finally, I am a terrible tourist. While I enjoy seeing the variety of cultures and environs that results from having the world as your "office," I do not enjoy taking holidays as they take me away from my work and I find it difficult to relax without having a computer monitor in front of my eyes.

Although my traveling and research are now limited, as I spend much of my time in meetings and carrying out management duties as director of the International Centre of Tourism and Hospitality Research and head of Bournemouth University Graduate School, I still get the same "buzz" from my economic modeling. The most recent project that I have completed is one funded by the WWF and UNEP. This research set out to construct a sustainable tourism investment model for coastal destinations. However, like many research projects, the journey is not always linear and does not always take people to the place that they envisage when they set off. The model that has been constructed benefits from three decades of building impact models and includes recognition of the difficulties we face when trying to engage the private sector in terms of data collection. At the model's core is a self-generating input–output model, an environmental matrix, and a forecasting module. Being mindful of the fact that governments (and economists) continually request data from businesses without providing anything tangible for them in return, I developed a system of rewards based on the level of engagement. Thus, to persuade the private sector to reveal the data needed to construct the impact model, the results give them an artillery of business, economic, and environmental performance indicators and benchmarks. In this way, businesses that engage with the model can drive the production more efficiently and measure their success by comparing their performance with the minimum, average, and maximum in their sector. It has been my academic ambition to complete tourism impact models by integrating the social aspects of development into the economic and environmental elements. This is the focal point of this tourism economist's current research agenda.

Chapter 4

From Transport to Tourism

Peter Forsyth
Monash University, Australia

Peter Forsyth has been professor of economics at Monash University since 1997. Most of his research has been on transport economics and especially the economics of air transport, and tourism economics. He has been a frequent speaker at the Hamburg Aviation Conference, and in 2005 he delivered the Martin Kunz Memorial Lecture. He has also done substantial research on tourism economics and policy. His research has covered measurement of the benefits of tourism, assessment of international price competitiveness of tourism industries, and taxation of tourism. Recent work has involved using computable general equilibrium models in analyzing tourism and aviation policy issues. Current research includes climate change policies and their impact on aviation, and developing models to assess the implications of climate change policies, such as the Australian Government's Emissions Trading Scheme, for the tourism industry. With Larry Dwyer and Wayne Dwyer he wrote *Tourism Economics and Policy*. Email <peter.forsyth@buseco.monash.edu.au>

INTRODUCTION

My entry into tourism economics was a matter of accident and design. My main field of interest has been the economics of transport. I had become interested in this field as an undergraduate; while at Sydney University I had

The Discovery of Tourism Economics
Tourism Social Science Series, Volume 16, 43–56

ISSN: 1571-5043/doi:10.1108/S1571-5043(2011)0000016007

done an Honours thesis on applying cost-benefit analysis to urban transport, supervised by Ted Kolsen, one of Australia's leading transport economists.

After working at Macquarie University for a couple of years, I got a scholarship to Oxford University. At that stage, Oxford was noted for, among other areas, applied welfare economics, and I was at Nuffield College, which was, and still is the best college for economics. I had intended to work in this area and transport economics. I had not worked out what my thesis would be about, when Ian (IMD) Little walked into my room and asked whether I would like to do some work explaining the rationale of peak pricing to the British Airports Authority, which owned the major airports of the United Kingdom. I accepted his challenge, and decided that this would be a good topic for my thesis. My supervisors were Denys Munby, a transport economist, and John Fleming, a general applied microeconomist. Nuffield College was an excellent place to do research, as it was home to a really strong group of young economists studying for their D.Phils (as PhDs are known in Oxford). While I was still working on my thesis, I published a paper on the "Third London Airport" controversy. This attracted attention from Peter Abelson, who was with the commission inquiring into it, and he produced a critique of the paper. From then we got to know each other, and we have been friends, and arguing with each other, ever since (more later).

As a result of this work, I became interested in the economics of aviation, and decided to work in this area. I tended to work mainly on airlines, having got the economics of airports out of my system, though I have been involved on airport work again over the last 10 years or so (and have dug out my old thesis to see what I said about a number of topics). When in Oxford, I got to know another Australian, Rob Hocking, who was working on this before he came to Oxford. He had done very interesting work on why, with two airlines, flights always left at the same time, even when there might only be one flight a day for each airline. He was interested in getting back to studying airlines, and when he came back we commenced working together. Sadly, this collaboration did not last long, since he died not long after returning from Oxford.

I worked away on the economics of airlines for a number of years. On some of this, I was joined by Christopher Findlay, who wrote a PhD thesis on Australia's international air links, and who had done work as a research assistant for Rob Hocking. Findlay went on to other areas, but not before joining me and Larry Dwyer on tourism in the late 1980s (of which more later). My first job after returning from Oxford was at the University of New South Wales in Sydney. This was a "return home" for me. I lectured and researched here till about 1984. At around about that time, Larry Dwyer returned home to the University of NSW (at that stage, I decided to leave for the Australian National University (ANU) in Canberra).

Then in around 1985, I was asked to do a study of aviation in the Pacific for the National Centre for Development Studies at the Australian National University (ANU). The editors of the book, Tom Parry and Rod Coles, asked me if there was anyone that I could recommend to do a parallel study of tourism. I managed to persuade a reluctant Larry Dwyer to become involved. At that stage, he had done no tourism economics. Initially he did not want to switch from his work on product innovation, but eventually I managed to persuade him that tourism economics was a promising area to become involved in.

Initially, I became interested in the nexus between aviation and tourism. I sketched out a paper on the interaction of the two, partly in response to an Industries Assistance Commission Report on Travel and Tourism. However, the turning point was a request from Ray Spurr, for Christopher Findlay and me, to explore the issue of direct foreign investment in Australian tourism. Spurr had been in the Diplomatic Corps, and had been Ambassador to Lebanon and Syria, and who had moved to the Department of Tourism. This was a hot issue at the time—it was becoming politically sensitive, with complaints that the Japanese investors were taking over the tourism industry (nowadays, there is very little Japanese investment in tourism). I thought it would be a good idea to work with Dwyer, who had gone on to undertake a major report on tourism in the Pacific. The work on investment was published as two reports by the director of the Bureau of Tourism Economics, Bill Faulkner (who went on to an academic job and was a key figure in the establishment of the Sustainable Tourism Cooperative Research Centre (STCRC) until his untimely death). This was a catalyst for further work, particularly to do with the impacts of investment and the benefits and costs that this investment created. From that work on, I have devoted a substantial part of my research effort to tourism economics, while still retaining my interest in and involvement in aviation and other aspects of economics.

Dramatis Personae

In telling a story, it is important to say who was involved. Larry Dwyer has been my partner on most of the research I have done on tourism economics. There have been some exceptions, such as the research on the nexus between aviation and tourism, which I have mainly done on my own, along with my research on aviation economics. However, most of my study of tourism economics proper, dating back 25 years or so, has been with him. This remains the case until now. Dwyer also does a large amount of work on his own and with other researchers. As already noted, I have done a large amount of work in other areas as well, particularly in the economics of transport (especially air transport), along with unrelated work on areas such as the economics of regulation and booming sector economics (Dutch Disease) where John Kay and I first applied the model to the British North Sea boom. (The model could very well be applied to the case of the impacts of the current mineral boom to tourism in Australia).

Over the years, I have also done considerable work with other colleagues, especially Ray Spurr. Indeed, he first started my work with Larry, when, as a senior official in the Department of Tourism, he commissioned us to do the report on "Foreign Investment in Tourism." About 15 years ago he left the public service for academia, and we began working with him as a colleague. Many of the studies that we have done have been as coauthors.

The other group of colleagues with which I have had a close relationship are the modeling team: Thiep Van Ho, Daniel Pambudi, Serajul Hoque, and Tien Duc Pham. In the last 10 years or so, we have become more reliant on modeling approaches to analyze tourism issues, and thus our team has become an integral component of our group.

MY PERSPECTIVE

The General Equilibrium Perspective

As I became interested in the economics of tourism, the problem of how to measure the benefits of tourism suggested itself as a priority. The work on foreign investment was a catalyst for this (it is useful to assess how foreign investment affects the economy, but is this investment worthwhile or beneficial?). The issue of the benefits of tourism is a fundamental one. But many have claimed that tourism, and especially foreign tourism, is good for a country, not many had been specific about why this is so. Some would identify benefits with the increase in expenditure, and others would be more specific and suggest that the impact on GDP would be the best measure.

It is clear that the issue of benefit measurement goes to the heart of policy on tourism. For example, what are the gains that a country gets from promoting tourism? If a country imposes a tax on foreign tourism, what does it gain, and lose, through reducing its flow and any reduction in economic activity that this industry could create? In terms of air transport policy, does it make sense for a country to liberalize its skies in order to increase tourism, granted that its own airlines could well suffer a loss of profits? Is it worthwhile for a country to add to tourism infrastructure given that the main gainers will be foreign tourists? To what extent can countries seek to attract events, such as the Olympic Games, and to what extent do they benefit from these? It is difficult to think of many issues in tourism policy analysis that do not call for a measurement of the benefits for tourism.

Thus, one of my priorities was to develop a theory of the measurement of tourism benefits or alterative the welfare gains from tourism. This is set out in theoretical detail in one of our first papers and it forms the basis of an extended body of work in this area (the main paper was coauthored with Larry Dwyer and published in *Annals of Tourism Research* (1993)). The basic approach is one of using applied welfare economics, in what is, to an extent, a cost-benefit framework. In this respect, it is a standard approach that has been used for many applications, such as tax theory, industrial organization, and health economics. Thus, we start with a shock to an economy, such as an increase in tourism, and then track through what affects it might have. If there are few distortions, then the effects will be small—on the other hand, distortions could be widespread. We look for the types of distortions that could be important for tourism, and indicate how they might be measured. Thus, tax distortions could be important with tourism, though distortions at the level of firms, such as monopoly, are not likely to be very important except in specific cases. As usual, there can be a problem if the economy is not fully employed; this creates a problem of how to adjust for this. Again, the standard approach is to use a shadow wage if there is not full employment. Given that additional demand for tourism infrastructure can give rise to price increases, there can also be a terms of trade effect.

Consequently, one of my objectives has been to embed the analysis of tourism policy in applied welfare economics. But another crucial objective has involved taking a general equilibrium perspective. Some issues can be handled using a partial equilibrium approach, but many cannot. For example, when promotion of tourism is considered, additional tourism will create positive impacts on the economy, but they also create negative impacts, as resources are drawn from other industries (the crowding out affect). Thus, the net effect on welfare (of additional promotion) will be reduced, and can be negative. When a tourism policy has a big effect on the labor market, and the economy is not fully employed, there is a problem of determining just how large the overall impact on employment will be. Evaluating the impacts and benefits of special events is a good example of why a general equilibrium approach is needed; these events contribute positively to economic activity but also draw resources away from other industries, and their overall impact is uncertain.

Originally my work with Larry Dwyer was at the theoretical level, though we were very much aware of the possibility of analyzing it through some model, such as a computable general equilibrium (CGE) model. We were aware of CGE approaches to the measurement of the impacts, though not the welfare aspects, of tourism (e.g., the studies of the Centre for International Economics and Adams and Parmenter). We had the intention to use such models for measuring the benefits of tourism should we have the chance. This opportunity came about through the Sustainable Tourism Cooperative Research Centre (STCRC)—a funding body that promoted tourism research.

What is now a small but coherent group started out in an *ad hoc* way. Ray Spurr was asked by the CRC to commission some work on the use of CGE models, and initially he asked John Madden (who is known for his work on the evaluation of the Sydney Olympics and other special events) to do a version of a model that had a specific sector devoted to tourism. We were able to get some funds from the STCRC to advance this work, and we were able to employ our first full-time modeler, Thiep Van Ho. We became more interested in the modeling work, and could see the possibilities for exploring many issues. The leaders of the CRC at that stage were Terry de Lacy (CEO) and Leo Jago (research director), all very keen on the project.

A digression on the STCRC is in order. The CRC was set up by the Australian government to foster the study of tourism. It was well-funded and a large number of tourism projects were supported. It was probably the best-funded research center for tourism anywhere in the world. Many of the projects it supported are now well-known. Unfortunately, after de Lacy and Jago left, the Centre was unable to gain further funding.

We were able to establish a research group, initially including Thiep Van Ho, then expanded to include Daniel Pambudi, Serajul Hoque, and Tien Duc Pham. We developed a suite of models, based on general economy wide models that are widely used in Australia, to examine tourism issues. In particular, we were interested in developing a more rigorous basis for welfare measurement in tourism, but we were also interested in analyzing a wide range of problems in tourism economists. To this end, we have studied issues such as event evaluation, impacts of crises such as SARS, assessment of the effects of climate change policies on tourism measurement of yield of different markets, and the impacts and costs and benefits of tax arrangements.

Thus, we created a small though effective group that focuses on the CGE modeling of tourism questions. Perhaps the only other comparable group would be the group founded by the late Thea Sinclair and Adam Blake at Nottingham, though individual researchers have been applying CGE approaches to tourism. Our group continues to work on a range of problems, and it has broadened its scope to include development of tourism satellite accounts (TSA) at the regional or state level. In our view, CGE approaches have a particular relevance for tourism, since the effects of this industry on an economy consist of a large number of small effects, such as tax affects, and which in aggregate amount to a significant impact on the economy. But these, because they are small, are individually difficult to measure.

One issue that I and my colleagues have had to confront has been the acceptability of results to others outside the research community, such as government and industry. Fortunately, there is a widespread acceptance of CGE models in Australia, since some of the leaders in this area, such as Peter Dixon, Phillip Adams, and John Madden are based in Australia, and key government advisors like the Productivity Commission have endorsed the approach. Indeed, one of the key selling points of using models such as this, emphasized by Ray Spurr, has been that if one wants to convince Treasury of the validity of his calculations, he needs to use rigorous models rather than models that just appeal to lobbyists. In Australia, bodies such as the Departments of Tourism have seen this, and they have been keen to use the best economic advice. This does not apply, however, to Events Corporations.

Unfinished Business

It is clear that much of my approach relies on taking a "cost-benefit" approach to policy questions, but also involves being aware of the general equilibrium aspects of many problems. I have continually emphasized the use of cost-benefit analysis for particular problems, and the use of CGE models to analyze specific issues. In the main, these techniques are regarded as quite separate techniques, to be used in quite different ways. CBA is very useful in assessing whether a major piece of infrastructure such as a cruise terminal or an airport should go ahead. But, a CGE study would be appropriate when assessing the impact of a disaster such as SARS or the impact of a promotional campaign on tourism flows. Most analysts would argue that CGE and CBA techniques are complementary but different. They are seen as giving different answers to the same question (not something which appeals to tidy minds).

However, the two techniques have been used to analyze the same type of problem, and a very good example of this comes about when we are considering the evaluation of events. In recent years, both have been used in event evaluation. With Larry Dwyer and Ray Spurr, I have contributed to the theory of event evaluation, in part prompted by our dissatisfaction with the ways in which events have been evaluated in practice. In our view, events have been assessed very poorly, and there is a pressing need to reform practices. This reform is taking place, though slowly. There is a standard methodology based on the use of input–output (IO) analysis. Typical IO-based studies of events give rise to very large impacts, partly because this technique effectively assumes that all inputs are free. In spite of this, the results of typical IO studies are described as "benefits," though careful economists do not claim this. These days, this casual, use of IO models are not recommended for most applied economic or policy analysis work. Thus, not surprisingly, protagonists of the events being evaluated are happy with the outcomes.

It was a natural step to use CGE models for event evaluation. There had been a small number of studies that had used CGE approaches in the late 1990s. At least in theoretical terms, these models address the main limitations of IO approaches, but their drawback can sometimes be one of lack of availability, though with extensive use of these models, this is becoming much less of a problem. CGE models can readily be used for event evaluation, though the nature of most events, such as their short duration and limited geographical coverage, means that care must be taken when using them. Ideally, they need to be adjusted to take account of the particular circumstances of the event.

One of the catalysts for this line of work was the STCRC, and in particular Leo Jago. He was keen to get event evaluation on to a more systematic basis, and to improve the way that events were being evaluated in Australia. He undertook to herd the cats of event economists with a view to producing an agreed approach to the problem. In the end, this aim was beyond even so persuasive a person as him, though he managed to produce, with Larry Dwyer, a very useful book on event evaluation.

While much of the use of CGE models has been uncontroversial, the same cannot be said of the use of CGE approaches in event evaluation. Researchers have developed an established conventional wisdom, and policymakers (event corporations) have received it enthusiastically. This is not surprising given that events invariably appear to be very beneficial. Thus, along with my colleagues we have become involved in debates with other researchers in Australia and elsewhere. Over time I think we have made a difference. Researchers are now becoming much more cautious in their claims, and policymakers are coming under pressure to justify their approaches.

The use of cost-benefit analysis (CBA) was also a natural one for us, though we have not actually worked with its approach to event evaluation directly ourselves. In Australia, there have been a number of studies that have adopted a CBA approach, especially those by State Auditors General. From our perspective, that is a good thing, as it lends credibility to rigorous evaluation of events and validated what we have been saying. However, even here we have found that event evaluation breeds controversy. Our team has recently been involved in a debate with Peter Abelson about the use of CGE and CBA techniques in events. He is a keen user of CBA, and has done some significant studies using this approach. However, he does not accept the use of CGE models as a basis for policy formulation. This poses the question what the role of the two different approaches is.

If both approaches are "correct," do they then give the same answer? Mostly, one or the other technique is used, and there is no problem of comparing or reconciling the results. However, in a recent study (Victorian Auditor General, 2007), both techniques were used, side by side. Thus, there were two studies both of which purported to yield the current answer. This is not a satisfactory situation. In my view, it is possible to integrate the two techniques in such a way that they will, in principle, give the same answer. One of the critical requirements is that the benefit to welfare measure is the same. Thus, the net benefit calculation of the CBA should be the same as the net benefit calculation of the CGE model. In practice, the outputs of CGE models that have been used for event evaluation have been in terms of impacts on GDP, not net welfare gain (a notable exception is that of Blake, 2005). However, it is normally a straightforward matter to include a welfare measure as part of the output of a CGE study (though, in practice, some researchers are hesitant to do this). Once this is done, the two can be compared, and ideally they should come up with the same answer. In practice, they will not; but this gives the evaluator more information and it becomes possible to diagnose why the two are different. CBA studies can be as detailed as wanted, while a CGE study will be constrained to the level of disaggregation in the model.

Climate Change and Tourism

In my work on the economics of tourism, I have not done a lot on the environmental aspects, though I have done occasional papers. I have not considered myself expert in the environmental economics of tourism per se, but I have been aware of the environmental effects of tourism. With Larry Dwyer and Harry Clarke (1995) I published a paper on the problems in using economic instruments in addressing them. However, we are able to use our models to explore various aspects of policy that includes an environmental dimension. The most important of these comes about with climate change. We have looked at the wider aspects of climate change and tourism in a study of Australian tourism, how it is affected by climate change, how it affects climate change, and what policies governments can implement to mitigate it (Forsyth et al 2007).

Again, the influence of the STCRC was crucial. This was an area of particular interest to Terry de Lacy. Toward the end of his work at the STCRC, he developed an agenda of studies that he would like to have supported. This covered a wide range of topics, including the economic aspects. Several of the projects I have become involved with stem from his agenda.

In the first of these, I have had an ongoing concern to measure the carbon intensity of tourism, for Australia and its regions. The work that our team has done forms a logical extension of our work on TSA. It is a straightforward step to combine a TSA with measure of carbon intensity of industries to develop a carbon footprint of tourism information on the carbon intensity, which is now readily available for countries such as Australia. The measure involves using an IO model to aggregate the various contributions of industries to carbon outputs. Yes, I do use IO techniques when the subject calls for them. This is useful in measuring the interindustry structure of a production process, but they are not intended for use as a model that attempts to measure the impact of changes.

As in other countries, the climate change debate has become a live one, and Australia is one of the few countries that have been considering a broad approach to reducing its carbon emissions. There have been several government reports on the issues to do with an Emissions Trading Scheme (ETS). Significantly, they use a CGE model to examine what impact an ETS would make, in terms of reduction of emissions, GDP, and employment. Australia has now adopted an emissions trading scheme as its preferred policy, to be applied to all industries except agriculture (though it has recently put this policy on hold). Thus, it was a logical step to apply a CGE approach to assess the impacts of this policy on tourism. The model that we have used is equally appropriate for an ETS or for a broad-based carbon tax, and it is consistent with the modeling for economy wide analysis. The model suggested that the impact of a small (around US$20) tax would not have a big impact on tourism, at around an additional 1%. This is not surprising, as the design of the broad-based scheme is intended to have a small impact on a wide range of industries, and so effecting a large reduction in CO_2 at low cost. It is consistent with the view that efficient climate change policies can be effective without imposing high costs on the economy.

I have also become interested in how airlines are affected by policies to reduce carbon emissions. This has implications for tourism. As it stands, international airlines are often excluded from climate change mitigation policies. Thus, both the New Zealand and Australian ETSs exclude international airlines, though they do include domestic. The most significant carbon policy likely to come into operation in the near future is the one being planned for the EU in 2012. How this will work has considerable implications for tourism. Under current plans, the airlines will gain a high proportion of their permits free of charge. Thus, it is likely that the airlines will gain, since they will be allocated rights that are scarce and valuable. However, their passengers will pay, as airlines raise the fares reflecting the costs of emissions permits. Exactly how airlines will react to this system is not certain. Will they raise prices to profit maximizing levels, passing the cost on to passengers, or will they moderate the price increases in order to gain market share? Over time, as carbon process rise, this could have a significant impact on tourism. This work is being done with my colleagues in Europe (more later).

Measuring Competitiveness

My time at ANU was enjoyable and productive, but different environments create new opportunities. My work on competitiveness was stimulated by my move from ANU to the University of New England, in Armidale NSW. This university used to have a very well-known econometrics department, and I began to work with Prasada Rao, an econometrician with expertise in index numbers.

Measuring the competitiveness of tourism is a recurring theme of my work. In competitiveness measures, there are two broad strands of research: measuring the price competitiveness and measuring more general aspects of the concept. Our work has concentrated on the first of these, though Larry Dwyer has also contributed to the second strand. We have sought to both measure and use different concepts, to see what factors determine price competitiveness (e.g., what are the roles of domestic prices, exchanges, and general goods prices in determining price competitiveness of a country). In this respect, we were among the first to use data on the purchasing power parity measures for price and exchange-rate measures. Nowadays many researchers are using them, though many still use unadjusted exchange rates as a price variable in demand studies, even this is inaccurate and unnecessary.

Our first work was in developing a general measure of the price competitiveness of tourism, which was a task for the Tourism Council of Australia, a leading tourism industry body. This work involved going to the basics, and using the OECD/World Bank databases on the detailed prices of commodities in the prices of the home countries. Thus, it was then possible to develop price indices of the bundles of goods that the tourists actually bought. As the commonly mentioned Big Mac index indicates, official exchange rates are not a reliable indication of the prices that people pay. Some countries have high prices, while other countries have low, for the same goods. What is more, exchange rates can go up and down rapidly, even though the prices that people pay, in their home country, did not change. Our work was timely, and we were able to publish it in a special issue of *Tourism Management* edited by Geoff Crouch.

From time to time, we return to our work on price competitiveness. A more recent piece of research on competitiveness has been the development of the tourism TWI. Many economists are familiar with it, which weighs different countries' exchange rates in accordance with their importance in their trade. We have applied the same idea to a tourism trade-weighted index. This weighs different countries exchange rates according to their importance in a country's inbound and outbound tourism expenditure. The countries that are important in terms of their general trade are not necessarily the same as those that are in important inbound and outbound tourism markets. The index can be used as a quick summary of how the country is faring relative to its competitor countries. We have also developed a similar index for airlines, the aviation trade-weighted index. Again the issue is the same, since the countries that are important competitors for their airlines are not always the same as those important for general trade.

Aviation and Tourism

In the late 1990s, I moved to Monash University in Melbourne. At this juncture, I developed strong contacts with European researchers on air transport, such as Hans-Martin Niemeier at Hamburg. This group also includes people from other places, such as David Gillen from University of British Columbia in Canada. I have become a regular at the Hamburg Aviation Conference and seminars organized by the German Aviation

Research Society, which despite its name, organizes workshops in countries such as the United Kingdom, the United States, and soon will reach Australia also. In 2005, I was asked to give the Martin Kunz Memorial Lecture at the Hamburg Aviation Conference, and I chose the topic of the interaction of tourism and aviation.

Aviation and tourism are obvious complements, so it is something of a surprise that there are few researchers who work on the interaction between the two. Not many work in both areas, and those who do, tend to work on separate topics, not integrating the two. There are a few exceptions, such as Anne Graham and Andreas Papatheodorou, and among the coming generation, Zheng Lei, and Neelu Seetaram, formerly my doctoral student at Monash. The economics of aviation was my pathway to tourism economics. I have been interested in a range of aspects of aviation, such as the issues of airline business, airport regulation, and environmental aspects of aviation. However, it is in the work I have done in airline regulation and its liberalization that has had the strongest link to tourism.

Along with several researchers, including David Gillen, I started work on evaluating proposals for liberalizing using a cost-benefit framework. Thus, to assess whether liberalizing of a route was desirable for a country, one could assess the various costs, such as lower airline profits, were more than or less than the various benefits, such as cheaper travel for passengers. Most of the additional costs and benefits are not as large as the effects on airline profits and traveler benefits, but few researchers even mentioned, still less evaluated, the benefits that might come about from additional tourism.

The earlier work that I did was theoretical, looking at how tourism benefits might tilt the balance between a country gaining from liberalization and losing from it. Some of this was done for an Inquiry into International Air Services (Forsyth 1991). At the same time, I did some back of envelope calculations, which suggested that for a country like Australia, tourism benefits could be around 10% of receipts. In the light of more rigorous estimates done later, these estimates were surprisingly accurate. Later on, when our group had a CGE model to work with, it became possible to develop measures of tourism benefits and explore the sensitivities of these measures to their determinants. While most liberalizations are positive for the countries undertaking them, this is not always the case. For example, for the Australia–Japan route, it is not in the interest of the former to liberalize because its airline gains a high share of the profits, but Australian travelers have a low share of the traffic.

This approach to measuring tourism benefits coming about as a result of aviation policy changes have been used in a number of contexts. It has been applied to Australian international aviation policy, and it indicates that the country gains from liberalization with most, but not all, of its markets. It can be applied to cases of 6th and 7th freedom routes, where airlines from third countries seek to fly (e.g., where Singapore Airlines sought to fly between Australia and the United States). The approach can be also used in assessing the merits of attracting airlines, such as Ryanair to regional airports. By doing so, it creates tourism benefits, but has a budgetary cost. This is a more rigorous approach than that typically used, which relies on the use of questionable multiplier effects.

Finally, an emerging application of the approach is that of estimating in terms of tourism benefits foregone the result of implementation of climate change policies. Several countries, especially the United Kingdom (the much criticized Air Passenger Duty) and now Germany, are imposing taxes in aviation, ostensibly for climate change reasons. The reduction in travel may have benefits for climate change, but how big are the costs through reduced tourism? These taxes are quite similar to a tax in Australia on outbound air travel, though this tax is not claimed to be a climate change measure (yet). I have just begun a study of the economic effects of this tax for the Australian government.

CONCLUSION

I am still very much involved in the economics of tourism and aviation. One priority is to explore further the links between tourism and immigration. Another, using our CGE modeling team, is to measure what impact tourism promotion has on the economy through tourism: is tourism promotion worthwhile given its costs? However, things do not always go according to plan. After being healthy for all my life, I had a stroke last year and I am gradually recovering from it. Fortunately, my wife Joan has been a marvelous support (even to the extent of correcting all the mistakes in this chapter).

This journey has been a research journey, not a teaching journey. So far, I have not yet taught a course in tourism economics. I have always worked in a general economics department, and for much of the time, a course on tourism economics was not offered. At Monash I have had some involvement with the tourism economics course, but most of that was taught by others, such as Neelu Seetaram. Now that I have just produced a textbook, with Larry and Wayne Dwyer, Monash has decided to delete the course. One day I may teach a tourism economics course.

Chapter 5

Confessions of a Data Junkie

Douglas C. Frechtling
George Washington University, USA

Douglas C. Frechtling is a professor of tourism studies in the Department of Tourism and Hospitality Management, School of Business of The George Washington University, Washington, DC, USA. By Providence, he founded and managed an independent, nonprofit research center for the tourism industries for 14 years. While there, he developed methods for measuring tourism volume and impact. Later, he consulted for a number of tourism clients, spending most of his time with the World Tourism Organization on standardizing tourism definitions and impact methodologies. When the George Washington University offered him a visiting professor position, he accepted and wormed his way into a tenured position through research on improving measurement of tourism and forecasting its future. After 40 years of laboring to standardize definitions and methodologies for measuring tourism and its impact, he wonders if it will take this long again to see academia, government, and industry recognize and employ these tools. Email <frechtli@gwu.edu>

INTRODUCTION

Growing up in Washington, DC, a government career seemed to be a good, safe place to spend my working life. However, I began my undergraduate stint as a preengineering major at Hamilton College in New York state,

The Discovery of Tourism Economics
Tourism Social Science Series, Volume 16, 57–72

ISSN: 1571-5043/doi:10.1108/S1571-5043(2011)0000016008

aiming to become an aeronautical engineer. Freshman calculus knocked that idea out of my head. Instead, I enjoyed freshman economics and chose to major in it.

Looking back, I believe it was the amalgam of sociology and mathematics that appealed to me. The head of the economics department was John Gambs, a proponent of the institutional school of economics. Institutionalists believe that economic studies should focus on the role of institutions in the shaping of economic outcomes and behavior. Leading lights included Thorstein Veblen, *Theory of the Leisure Class* (2005), and John Kenneth Galbraith, *The Affluent Society* (1998). Gambs' reputation and personality kept the extreme mathematical modeling forces at bay. The study of economics was more like studying history and politics than econometrics, and presented an agreeable field for me.

INTO THE WORLD

I was introduced to a Hamilton alum, Don Webster, who was working at the Joint Economic Committee (JEC) of the US Congress in the mid-1960s. The JEC was created by the Employment Act of 1946, the first national legislative commitment to economic growth and price stability. The Act required US presidents to issue annual reports on the state of the United Sates economy and what should be done to reduce unemployment and maintain price stability. The JEC was charged with reporting Congress's views on these annual reports.

Congressional rules required the JEC to reflect both the majority and minority parties in each house. Webster was the economist for the Republican members of the committee in the 1960s, called the Minority, and needed a research assistant. I got the job on the basis of graduating from Hamilton College with an economics major and being sympathetic to conservative economic policies. These included balancing the federal budget over the business cycle, reducing price inflation to near zero, keeping tax rates low, and restraining government spending.

Initially my duties were mostly clerical. But over time, I contributed sections to speeches and reports issued by the Republican members. Our major effort centered on reviewing the US president's economic report each January. This required gathering witnesses for hearings before the committee, writing questions and statements for the members, and drafting a reaction to the reports to be revised and approved by the Minority members. This was important because at that time no other Congressional committee was responsible for recommending macroeconomic policies for the United States. Our Minority views served as the major statement of Republican party positions on economic policies for ensuing years.

Don Webster, had spent 10 years as a journalist and strongly valued clear, concise writing. I learned this skill after months of trial and error, and came to value such communication as critical to professional success in economics. Moreover, he was interested in taking graduate courses at the George Washington University in the evenings. I was accepted into George Washington's doctoral program, so the two of us would motor down to the other end of Pennsylvania Avenue two nights a week for our courses. We were able to put the principles we learned in the classroom to work and to improve our arguments for sound economic policies.

One of the JEC subcommittees was devoted to economic statistics from the federal government. This struck me as superfluous as "everyone" knew that its statistics were valid. However, listening to debates and reading reports convinced me that only the devotion of hard-core statisticians and economists maintained these statistics at a high level of accuracy. To maintain this accuracy, some series must be revised to reflect more recent data and superior collection methods. Indeed, the quarterly gross domestic product estimates are still revised three times after their first release.

Don Webster left the JEC in early 1968 to work for Richard Nixon's second campaign for Presidency. His recommendation led to my being elevated to Minority Economist and serving as the chief staffer for the eight Republican members of the committee. Among other events, this position generated to my first publication, a report on a Congressional study tour examining approaches to building New Towns in Europe and Israel. I learned that members of Congress were not very interested in details, and instead of publishing my report as their own, they preferred that the JEC publish it under my name. Hence the birth of my first publication, probably read by 40 people in 40 years.

When the time came, I wrote, discussed, rewrote, and finally achieved consensus on the Minority Views regarding the *1970 Economic Report of the President* (Joint Economic Committee, U.S. Congress (1970a, 1970b). The fact that the president was the Republican R. M. Nixon made my job easier. Nevertheless, liberal members of the party made for some interesting contretemps in trying to achieve consensus on how to respond to the views of the Democratic members of the committee.

From Prescribing to Administering

That 1970 report turned out to be my swansong, as Don Webster engineered my appointment to be deputy assistant to the secretary of the US Treasury. I recall being reluctant to leave my Congressional job, but realized I could learn much more about economic policy in the Administration. My doctoral concentration was fiscal policy, so the new position fit in well with my studies at the university.

Moreover, while Congress could talk and pass legislation, the US Treasury Department was responsible for implementing economic policy in the areas of taxation, credit and interest rates, and our international balance of payments. The most exciting time in my government career was under John Connally's term as secretary. A very popular Texas governor, wounded when President Kennedy was assassinated in Dallas in November 1963, he was a charismatic and thoughtful politician who wanted to improve the business environment and the rate of economic growth of our nation. With a strong team including Paul Volcker, he convinced the White House to reduce adherence of the United States to the gold standard and institute wage and price controls to terminate the widespread inflation at the time. I believe Secretary Connally was successful for two reasons. He had a persuasive personality and could charm the wings off a fly. But he also kept the best, most recent macroeconomic data at hand to support his positions.

Connally's resignation in 1972 was unexpected and unwanted. He took an activist approach to economic policy formation, going head-to-head with administration officials and Congressional leaders to return the country to economic growth without inflation. In our weekly staff meetings, he challenged all of us to think clearly and defend long-held positions and opinions. He convinced me of the value of sound data in public policy discussions.

One curious find during my tenure as an assistant to the secretary was a report to the Treasury by economist and educator Peter Bernstein on the accuracy of US balance of payments statistics. I recall it pointing out that one of the weakest areas was the international travel and transportation account. The system providing these estimates was quite weak. It is interesting that this debate continues to this day, 50 years later.

As the Watergate scandal heated up, being a political appointee in the Treasury under a new secretary was a prescription for sleepless nights. I was completing my doctoral dissertation and wondering whether I wanted to sink into the Treasury as a career employee or join some other government agency. Fortunately, Divine Providence offered me a way out to a career I never imagined.

Change in Career

A cold call from a journalist about something called "travel and tourism" landed me an interview with president of Discover America Travel Organizations (DATO), the umbrella association covering all US industries serving travelers away from home. William Toohey was apparently impressed by my Congressional and Treasury positions, devotion to good writing and sound research, and earned doctorate in economics. He hired me to set up a nonprofit research center for the tourism industries called the US Travel Data Center (USTDC).

Toohey negotiated a matching grant from the US Travel Service in the Department of Commerce to establish the USTDC and operate it for a year. The Department required that the USTDC be an independent, nonprofit corporation, and we operated that way for 14 years. We opened our doors in January 1973 with a first-rate board of directors and a staff of two. The challenge was to develop sound research on the course and economic consequences of travel and tourism to, from, and within the United States. A bigger challenge was to obtain the funding necessary to sustain this effort.

A sidebar on jargon is necessary here. Forty years ago, and still somewhat true today, "tourism" was a limiting and questionable term in America. It referred to leisure travel, a luxury enjoyed by few and somewhat suspect in our hardworking country. On the other hand, "travel" by itself was too broad a term, appropriated by transportation researchers decades earlier to refer to all movement of persons once they left their homes and headed for any destination. By lumping together "travel" and "tourism," one could make clear he was referring to all trips away from home, both for personal and for business purposes. Never mind that the rest of the world was quite comfortable with "tourism" as the central word with a long tradition of referring to both personal and business travel.

The United States has become much more involved in the global economy over the last half-century, but the uneasiness with "tourism" is still evident: note the title of the US version of the tourism satellite account is "US Travel and Tourism Satellite Account." In this memoir, I will stick with the World Tourism Organization's widely endorsed approach to defining the activities we are interested in and refer to "tourism" as the activity of traveling away from one's own usual environment and returning, and "visitor" as the person who engages in this activity.

In search of valid data on tourism spending and its impact, I visited the University of Colorado at Boulder to meet Charles Goeldner in fall 1972. He was widely recognized as the leading tourism researcher in the country. His

Journal of Travel Research was the only respected peer-reviewed journal devoted to tourism in North America. His Bureau of Business Research at the University turned out bibliographies and data compendia for the Travel and Tourism Research Association (TTRA) that were the only source of annual statistical information on tourism in the country. He maintained the largest collection of tourism books and studies in the Americas and perhaps the world.

The meeting was propitious in a number of ways. Goeldner shared my interest in improving the quality and expanding the range of data on tourism in the United States. He agreed to serve on the USTDC board and faithfully did so for more than 30 years. He convinced me to join the board of directors of TTRA and eventually serve as president and chairman. Further, he encouraged me to learn the art of alpine skiing through sojourns at Aspen, Vail, Copper Mountain, and Winter Park, all in Colorado. We spent a great deal of time together and I still treasure his friendship and support.

My meeting with Goeldner confirmed the anecdotal evidence that there were a number of different estimates of national tourist spending making the rounds, and some appeared grossly distorted. Fortunately, DATO had lobbied successfully for a National Travel Survey (NTS) in 1972 to be conducted by the US Bureau of the Census as part of the quinquennial Economic Censuses program. The NTS obtained detailed data by mail through a national probability sample on trips taken to places 75 miles or more away from home and return, except for commuting to work. Estimates were reported on trips to places 100 miles or more away from home to account for possible underreporting of shorter distance trips qualifying for this survey. The survey data were expanded to a total of 237 million person-trips for the year.

A Birthing of Tourism Statistics

In 1969, Don Church, an official of the US Bureau of the Census, assessed the difficulty of obtaining valid estimates of spending of tourists through household surveys after they had returned home. He proposed a cost-factor model to estimate US resident domestic spending on travel away from home. Well-designed household surveys could gather reliable data on each trip taken in a quarter, who traveled on them, where they spent their nights, their accommodations, their transport mode, and other trip activities. Industry sources would provide the costs per unit of these activities: cost per night of commercial accommodations in a state, cost per mile of air travel and like variables that were derived from accounts rather than survey respondent recall.

My first task as director of the USTDC was to design and implement a cost-factor model joining the 1972 NTS data on tourism activity levels (miles traveled by air, nights spent in hotels/motels by state, etc.) with the costs per unit derived from industry and government sources to estimate traveler spending.

After some delays precipitated by the immensity of the NTEM programing challenge (incorporating more than 1,800 equations and detailing each of the 50 states and the District of Columbia), the *National Travel Expenditure Study* was released (Frechtling 1974). It was the first national report on estimated tourism expenditures in the United States and each of its states based on an economic model. Many state tourism offices received it with gratitude. A few that had hired consultants, universities, or other state government agencies to develop earlier estimates generally felt the USTDC numbers were too conservative. That was fine with me. We intentionally chose conservative cost factors and, by the nature of the activity data, excluded foreign tourist spending in the states.

Another initiative I undertook was an inventory of data available from various government agencies, consultancies, and publishers on long-distance travel and the industries that serviced it at the national and state levels. *The Travel Data Locator Index* (US Travel Data Center 1973, 1974a, 1974b, 1978) seems quaint in this age of the World Wide Web and search engines, but in 1973, there was no way of locating available data except through the collective memories of experts.

As I recall, the first index covered about 60 data series that I had located by talking to such experts, reading widely and pestering staff in federal agencies that might have something to do with tourism statistics. The series were indexed by subject, geographic area, and frequency. Each was listed as a publication by an organization, complete with name, street address, and telephone number. The second edition published in 1978 was expanded to 104 series in 102 publications from 28 organizations. There was no warranty as to quality, but at least the current state of tourism statistics in America was evident in one publication.

This situation was pretty dismal. The available data were virtually all supply side statistics: number of airline passengers, hotel rooms sold, motor coach miles driven, intercity vehicle miles driven, number of visitors to National Parks, and the like. Aside from the passenger data that our government required airlines to report, there were no origin–destination volumes. Annual consumer spending on travel "out of town" was available with a long lag, but nothing on business or convention traveler spending. While we might surmise that visits to parks and recreation areas were leisure trips, there was no way to obtain the proportion constituting tourism. In short, there were very few up-to-date statistics on American tourism patterns, expenditures, or economic impact.

When the Arab countries announced an embargo on petroleum shipments to the Western world in October 1973, there was very little objective, national-to-regional information on the nonairline portion of tourism. Legislation was introduced in Congress to restrict dwindling petroleum product supplies to "essential" sectors of the economy, and these did not include tourism. Some members of Congress proposed gasoline rationing as a solution without any consideration of its devastating effects on tourism. We put together a loose coalition of researchers to and cobbled together a report on the size of the tourism industry and its place in the national economy to bolster our side of the debate. Fortunately, the embargo was lifted in March 1974, but only after doing incalculable harm to American tourism activities and the businesses that support it. This was a wake-up call for better tourism data if there ever was one.

From Expenditures to Impact

Of course, tourist spending reveals little beyond the likely distribution of tourism's economic impact among states and industries. In 1974, the US Department of the Interior engaged the USTDC to produce a Travel Economic Impact Model (TEIM) that would provide annual estimates of the employment, payroll income, and federal, state and local tax revenue generated by tourist spending at state and county levels (Frechtling 1975). The Department needed these estimates to project the impact of a potential oil spill in the Baltimore Canyon off the middle Atlantic coast. Our model produced the baseline estimates for the Department's required environmental impact statement. Interestingly, although the oil companies received approval to begin drilling, evidence of oil deposits justifying major drilling investments never materialized.

Nevertheless, the USTDC began to publish estimates of tourist spending and the resulting employment, income and tax revenue in each of the states and the District of Columbia in 1977. This has continued annually to this day. In 1985, under contract to the US Department of Commerce, the USTDC began a series of annual estimates of foreign tourist spending and its economic impact for each state based on its continuing "In-flight Survey of International Air Travelers."

These estimates required a great deal of base data. Our state and city stakeholders wanted them as soon after the calendar year as possible. But the underlying statistics were subject to revision as time went by. To ignore these revisions is bad research practice. Yet the howls generated by such changes defied description. We were accused of generating estimates that "didn't stand still!" But we settled into the practice of revising the previous year's impact estimates for the states when the results for a new year were published. But when the TEIM went through a major recalibration in 1989, we were reminded how much people disliked change.

Challenges of Tourism Surveys

Such annual estimates of tourism's economic impact require annual surveys of US resident tourism activity. The Census Bureau was responsible for conducting such a national survey once every five years at most. In 1973, a contract was signed with Home Testing Institute to conduct monthly mail surveys of households in its panel database by a questionnaire based on the 1972 NTS instrument (United States Bureau of the Census 1973). This data collection effort continued through 1974 and 1975.

The results were quite disappointing. The number of trips reported per household was substantially higher than the Census Bureau found for 1972. Further, the annual estimates for a number of states gyrated wildly. We surmised that this panel was composed of people who were far more active travelers than the overall US population for nearly every demographic category. This may well be a design effect of surveying people who have agreed in advance to participate in consumer surveys and are rewarded for doing so. We tried a mail survey through a probability sample of US households in 1976. The response rate from mailing to nearly 6,000 households throughout the year was only 56%.

So in 1979, we switched to a monthly telephone survey of households selected through stratified sampling of 1,700 US households each month through RL Associates of Princeton, New Jersey. Response rates topped 60%, but the reporting was much faster than the mail surveys. The variability of the estimates settled down and we secured reasonably valid monthly national data on travel away from home. These estimates appeared to track well with sporadic data series from other sources, and served as the foundation for annual estimates of the economic impact of tourism. One important lesson we learned from these efforts is that it is harder to produce an objective, consistent, coherent monthly series measuring a phenomenon like tourism than it is to turn out one-off studies.

Meanwhile, the Census Bureau was planning for the 1977 NTS. I prepared a list of improvements that should be made to the 1972 effort and presented them to the TTRA board of directors. After discussion and revision, I presented these to the US Senate subcommittee on Foreign Commerce and Tourism in 1976. These improvements centered on ensuring reliable estimates of person-trips were available for each of the 50 states and the District of Columbia. A number of them were implemented in the 1977 NTS.

While considerably expanded from the 1972 effort in terms of sample size and topics covered, the 1977 NTS demonstrated a major weakness of the federal economic censuses. While covering the tourism activities of US residents in 1977, the results were not released until October 1979. By then, the country was suffering from another disruption in petroleum supplies from the Middle East. Patterns evident nearly two years earlier were not very relevant in an environment of limited gasoline supplies and soaring prices. This sad insensitivity to timely reporting was repeated when the Census Bureau next (and last) conducted a survey of tourism activity. The 1995 survey, while exemplary in methodology and coverage, was not released until November two years later.

Trying to Raise the Bar

During my term as president of the TTRA, I addressed the 1979 national conference on "What's wrong with travel research?" I noted there were a host of analytical techniques used in tourism research, but that they were applied indiscriminately without following the rules that guaranteed their validity. Little attention was paid to the quality of data analyzed. Studies published in the growing number of journals appeared to have few practical applications. There was no generally accepted body of knowledge about tourism behavior and its consequences. As a result of these failures, few in industry or government make use of research results published in journals or pay any attention to them at all.

Finally, I lauded the efforts by Brent Ritchie at the University of Calgary and Chuck Goeldner to edit a comprehensive handbook of tourism research as the state-of-the-art guide to research findings and practices. The first edition of *Travel, Tourism and Hospitality Research: A Handbook for Managers and Researchers* was finally published in 1987, with an improved edition in 1994. To this day, I am surprised at how little these landmark efforts have been cited in journal-published tourism research. It appears that tourism researchers have an aversion to growing our combined intelligence about tourism and its consequences. Reinventing the wheel is more popular than helping improve a lasting vehicle.

The word, "analysis," comes from a Greek word, "analusis", meaning to break up into elements. When academics and others analyze data or history or behavior, they are examining the constituent parts of a phenomenon in detail in order to draw conclusions. Books, particularly textbooks, on the other hand, are integrating: they join parts together to make a coherent whole. Students and others should be able to go to the textbooks on tourism economics to determine the state of this field of study. This is precisely what is done in universities and research centers. But those publishing the analytical articles in the myriad journals in this field pay scant attention to what has already been codified. As a result, I still see tourism research articles published as if nothing has progressed since 1979. This is clearly evident in the history of definitions and classifications in tourism.

Foundations of Sound Tourism Research

From my beginnings in this field, I have believed our country could not have valid data on tourism without agreeing on definitions of the main variables. I recommended a set of definitions to the 1975 TTRA Conference. These received little traction that I could observe. However, these and other studies I authored came to the attention of Enzo Paci, chief of the Department of Statistics, Economic Analysis and Market Research of the World Tourism Organization (UNWTO). After I left the USTDC, he engaged me in 1988 as UNWTO "Expert" in a long-term project to obtain international agreement on definitions and classifications for tourism and a new methodology for quantifying the direct economic impact of tourism in nations called "tourism satellite account." I continued in this capacity until shortly after his untimely death in 1998.

Enzo Paci was a visionary with a knack for getting things done. With the support of the Canadian government, UNWTO conducted a weeklong "International Conference on Travel and Tourism Statistics" in Ottawa in early 1991. This was the first worldwide conference to reach agreement on improving the world's tourism statistics since seminal definitions of international tourism were approved by countries gathered in Rome in 1963.

I presented a paper at the Conference entitled, "A Proposed Work Program for Tourism Marketing and Economic Statistics" (1991). I enumerated seven fundamental principles of a rational approach to collection and use of statistics on tourism markets and economic impact. These introduced and supported what I called the "Prime Tourism Economic Objective"—to increase tourism's net contribution to the economic welfare of the residents of a community, state or province, country or group of countries. I argued that it was the net economic benefits of hosting tourists that governments at all levels seek. This requires measuring both the gross economic benefits of tourism and the gross economic costs. The former are well known and have been enumerated above.

Economic costs, however, are seldom estimated. They include all monetary expenditures by all levels of government related to hosting tourists. Examples are variable expenses, such as border control and customs activities, fixed costs that are initially determined by tourist volumes (such as infrastructure maintenance and security services), and public investment expenditures required to service tourists (new roads, air terminals, information centers). While the literature on measuring and analyzing the economic benefits of tourism to an area has grown voluminous, there has been little published on measuring the economic costs (Frechtling 1994a, 1994b, 1994c). This is an area that still deserves study by governments that wish to allocate their scarce budget resources wisely.

Statistical Dreaming

Led by Enzo Paci, several of us UNWTO experts traveled the world promoting the standard definitions and classifications of tourism activities. In 1992, I told the annual conference of the TTRA that I had a dream of a better world of international tourism statistics. This brave new world would be characterized by certain realities:

1. Data on international tourist flows by country are current and available from UNWTO in useful detail.
2. The 184 countries currently reporting to UNWTO all provide monthly data on tourist departures and related expenditures with no more than a four-month lag.
3. Academic researchers publish articles without a confusion of definitions and collection methodologies and all employ data from the UNWTO in their analyses to the exclusion of alternative sources.

I would argue that through the efforts of UNWTO, dream elements one and two above have come true in the ensuing decades. However, there has been little progress in getting academic and other researchers to employ the standard definitions, classifications, and methodology codified by UNWTO and approved by the United Nations Statistical Commission in 1994.

After this watershed UNWTO international conference, I wrote manuals for UNWTO on collection and generating tourist statistics, conducting surveys, and forecasting demand (Frechtling 1995a, 1995b). It is unclear what impact these had on the tourism data collection and analysis activities of individual countries. I prepared a special report on the US tourism statistical system for Statistics Canada and the US Travel and Tourism Administration in 1995. My investigation found the US "system" of tourism statistics comprised seven distinct data collection programs, plus statistics form Canadian and Mexican authorities. The US portion failed to observe most of the new UNWTO definitions and classifications. One of the most frustrating obstacles to interpreting data from these programs was failure to agree on how far someone must travel away from home to be considered a tourist. These varied from "out of town" to 50–60 miles to crossing an international border.

A New Tool for Impact Measurement

Fortunately, by this time, the UNWTO supported by OECD, Eurostat, the Canadian government, and the national statistical agencies in a number of countries, was making substantial progress toward agreeing on the framework for the tourism satellite account (TSA). Authorized for national income accounts in 1993, the TSA would conceptually cover all productive activities serving tourists, was connected to the main national economic accounts and followed similar accounting rules, and was an account requiring observations or counts of economic variables. After hundreds of hours of meetings and thousands of pages of discussion, the "Conceptual Framework for the Tourism Satellite Account" was approved by the principle economic and statistical bodies of the world in 2008. This effort necessarily required changes in the World Tourism Organization's standard definitions and classifications, which were also approved in 2008 (UNWTO 2008). Finally, the world had a comprehensive and coherent way to enumerate the direct economic contributions of tourists to national economies and standard terminology to facilitate communication regarding these efforts (Frechtling 2006).

Of course, having standards and seeing them applied widely are worlds apart. The US Travel and Tourism Satellite Account produces excellent quarterly updates on the economic contribution of tourism in this country. One would think that this would serve as the national benchmark and methodological source for tourism impact studies at regional levels. But instead of adopting the terminologies and accounting procedures specified by UNWTO and its statistical agency colleagues, consultancies, universities, and others have appropriated the term, "tourism satellite account," to title studies that have nothing to do with either tourism or accounts.

This has raised considerable concerns at UNWTO. At its March 2010 meeting in Madrid, the organization noted, "Such activities threaten the credibility of the TSA as a sound, comprehensive method of measuring the direct contribution of tourism to national economies." I enumerated six reports by consultancies and academics in the United States in two years that were called "tourism satellite accounts" but were, in fact, little more than standard economic impact studies for states.

This is an ironic development. After years of laboring in the UNWTO vineyards for rational definitions and valid methodologies, our efforts were so successful that unscrupulous or uninformed research organizations have borrowed and applied the TSA name to their own research products for sale. UNWTO has made considerable progress in halting the assaults on its TSA brand by international organizations. But the battle has shifted to domestic venues less vulnerable to UNWTO exposure. Efforts to enlist US government assistance in discouraging such deception are ongoing but fruitless so far.

Sound Research Programs are Vulnerable

Indeed, another important lesson I have learned in practicing tourism economics is the tendency for successful research methods and programs to be vulnerable to appropriation by others. After 14 years of building the credibility of the USTDC as an independent, well-financed, and credible center for gathering, analyzing, and publishing sound research on tourism to, from, and within the United States, its board of trustees agreed to merge the USTDC with the Travel Industry Association (TIA). The argument advanced was that TIA needed the research resources and reputation of the USTDC to assure TIA's future success in advancing the interests of the tourism industry in the country.

This occurred in 1986. A year later, I left to lead a new hotel marketing company devoted to assisting independently owned luxury hotels to compete against the chains. My extremely able lieutenant at the USTDC, Suzanne Cook, was appointed Senior Vice President of Research to head up the enhanced TIA research entity. But in 2000, the name of the USTDC disappeared from use. Since then, TIA, now US Travel Association, has reduced the size and programs of its research department.

In 14 years, dozens of tourism research officials and executives and scores of state tourism directors achieved something unique in the world: a nonprofit center devoted to creating sound tourism research and to its broad dissemination, supported by industry dues and grants, and aggressively serving the needs of it stakeholders. It is difficult for me to view its termination as anything less than a tragedy.

NEW OPPORTUNITIES

My venture into hotel marketing did not prove successful. So I did what any self-respecting professional researcher does upon losing his job: I went into consulting. After serving two years in this wilderness, I joined Don Hawkins and his colleagues at The George Washington University in teaching and administering the first Masters degree in tourism administration in North America. Through God's grace, I have risen through the ranks to full professor and chair of the Department of Tourism and Hospitality Management in the School of Business. It is extremely rewarding to conduct sound research and then present the results for discussion in the classroom. Best of all, I get to teach the tenets of valid and reliable research to future generations of tourism managers.

Much more work remains, to raise tourism economic research to the levels of other branches of economic study. There is still too much futile research published on the economic impact of tourism. Fortunately, the tourism satellite account campaign has raised the bar for national studies (Frechtling 2010). But industry and local research is still sorely lacking in the domains of validity and ethics.

A research study is valid if it actually measures what it purports to quantify. There is no research technique so widely and badly used in our field as the probability sample survey. Reviewing the methodologies of hundreds of studies is a frustrating project. In some cases, it is clear the methodology is flawed and the results cannot represent a defined larger population. But in a majority of the cases, a reader cannot tell whether the methodology leads to valid results, because it is so sparsely presented. The American Association for Public Opinion Research and other respected associations have published codes of ethics for the conduct of probability sample surveys. The foundation of these codes is transparency for verification. Even our best journals fall far short of presenting these methodologies in a transparent manner. How can a field of study even consider calling itself science without this foundation?

The 19th century Danish philosopher Søren Kierkegaard famously said, "Life is to be understood backwards, but it is lived forwards." If I had known what a struggle pushing the rock of sound tourism economic data up the mount would be, I sometimes wonder if I would have begun. I have seen progress in improving the quality and expanding the range of tourism economic research. The world has a set of standard definitions and classifications approved by the highest levels of international statistics. But these appear only in a minority of studies to now. We know how to conduct sound surveys projectable to larger populations to assist in measuring tourist spending, but this is seldom evident in published research. We know that the heart of scientific advance is verifiability yet techniques like computable general equilibrium models are as obscure as any occult ceremony. When the data underlying our economic estimates change, then our estimates based upon them must change as well. We need the courage to make these revisions and explain them to our stakeholders.

There is cause for hope in the United States. The Travel Promotion Act signed by President Obama in March 2010 makes $200 million or more available for promoting international travel to the United States. Built into this legislation is the requirement that the effectiveness of the program in increasing jobs and income be continually evaluated. This will require substantial improvements in the current programs measuring inbound tourism and tourist spending. Such prospects gladden a data junky's heart.

Chapter 6

Convolutions and Happenstance

William (Bill) Gartner
University of Minnesota, USA

William (Bill) Gartner is a professor of applied economics at the University of Minnesota. He currently lives in Stillwater, Minnesota with his old but faithful dog Cinder. When he is not in Minnesota, he can be found in various parts of the world enjoying the work that comes with travel and the camaraderie of friends. His career has been marked by work on all the continents except Antarctica. Although known for destination image research more than anything else, development economics work has been the most enjoyable as it involves cultural understanding integrated with economic tools to get the job done. Bill was for eight years the director of the Tourism Center at the University of Minnesota. He has served as honorary dean of the Faculty of International Economics at the Macau University of Science and Technology, and holds several visiting professorships at European universities. Bill is a fellow of the International Academy for the Study of Tourism serving four years as the academy's secretary, two as vice president, and was then elected president for two terms (four years). Email <wcg@umn.edu>

INTRODUCTION

In sixth grade, the rector of our school wrote to my parents on my report card "Look at all these ups and downs. He will never amount to much." My mother saved that report card and I have it today as a reminder of all those

The Discovery of Tourism Economics
Tourism Social Science Series, Volume 16, 73–88

ISSN: 1571-5043/doi:10.1108/S1571-5043(2011)0000016009

who never look beyond the most obvious. It reminds me to search for what is hidden and not clear to those who are only interested in scratching the surface. The rector's criticism also provided me with an incentive to prove him wrong. So even though he was a class A jerk, I am grateful for his unintended assistance to my career.

I entered university student life without a real clue as to what I wanted to do with the rest of my life. I remember filling out a career survey and completing the question as to what you would like to be doing in 15 years with the answer "retire." About the only things I was passionate about at the time were outdoor activities, primarily hunting, and fishing. But university life was exciting and fun. I really did not want to graduate. During the summer breaks, I had to work to earn enough money to pay for my education. My parents worked hard to raise five children and they sacrificed to send us to a private primary school, but while very supportive of their children receiving a college education, they did not have any money to fund this. So I worked on a road construction crew for a couple of summers and with a sewage line construction company for a couple more. This job was enough to convince me to stay in school, do well, and find some other ways to make a living.

I graduated from Michigan State University with a degree in resource development. What do you do with a degree in resource development? No one seemed to be able to answer that question. But the classes were interesting and I did well enough to receive inquiries about pursuing an MS degree from Washington State University and the University of Delaware. I thought Washington State University would be ideal as it is surrounded by some of the best and hunting terrain in the United States. You could tell where my mind was at. Delaware was less interesting to me; I would pick up their application, fill out a few lines, and put it away again. Finally, I sent it off to them with the form completed in three different colors of ink. After graduating with my BS, I went to work in sewage line construction once again. I heard from Washington State University that I was accepted, but they did not have an assistantship for me right away. I was welcome to enroll and see if I could pick up some work while there. I decided that I would find a job where I was and think about graduate school the following year. Having made that decision, I quit my sewage line construction work and headed to the Sawtooth Mountains in Montana to do some backpacking and high mountain fishing. After a week in the mountains, I came back to civilization and checked in with my parents. They told me that a professor from the University of Delaware had called and there was an assistantship waiting for me if I could be there in two days for the start of classes.

For those not familiar with US geography, this was a four-day trip that I managed to make in two, including a stop in Detroit to pick up some clothes. I arrived at the University of Delaware in time and began my MS studies. One of the reasons I had been complacent about filling out the University of Delaware application is that I knew nothing about the place, except it was on the East Coast where plenty of people lived. I found the university and the little town of Newark to be what I needed to dispel prejudices I had kept about Easterners and their way of life. The professors in the Agricultural Economics Department were top notch and I received a great education with plenty of work experience. It was also the beginning of my foray into the realm of economics. Although I had taken the necessary microeconomics courses for my BS degree, they did not excite me. But at the University of Delaware I was learning about commodity markets, resource economic issues, and recreation economics. My MS thesis was a benefit-cost analysis of the state's master plans for its parks. When reading the master plans, I was wondering why a multimillion dollar swimming pool was planned for a park that was on a lake. Now I had the tools to critically analyze all the suggested park "improvements." Days and days of hand calculations, using only the first-generation calculators, allowed me to argue from an economics perspective, using travel cost methodology, that adopting the master plan would result in a waste of public money. There simply were not enough users to justify the expense. Today there is no swimming pool at that park, but it probably had more to do with the actual cost rather than my critical analysis. Still it was that exercise that opened my eyes to what economic analysis could do. I was beginning to get hooked.

TOURISM RESEARCH

I was still thinking about recreation or resource economics when I enrolled at Michigan State University to pursue my PhD. Tourism was not really on the radar screen at that time. There were a few academics, among them John Hunt and Clare Gunn, who had embraced tourism studies and were pioneers in the field, but I had never heard about them or their work when I started my studies at Michigan State University. Upon completing my studies and while finishing my dissertation, I was hired on a one-year contract by the Department of Parks and Recreation Resources at Michigan State University to teach a couple of courses. At the time, I was finishing up my dissertation which dealt with the influence of natural resource attributes on property values in an area of Michigan that was primarily devoted to seasonal home development. I found this economic analysis to be exciting as I was finding out a few things that turned around my perceptions of what would make land more valuable. My dissertation was nearly completed at about the same time that my one-year contract was set to end. But in a stroke of luck, I was invited to a lunch to meet with some representatives from the Waterways Division of Michigan state government. They had been under pressure to review their funding model which was used to support county sheriff offices that provided water safety services, including training, policing, and search and rescue. Before lunch was over, we had agreed on a research project, which I would lead, to determine just how much state support each county's sheriff office should receive for this service. It was one of the largest grants that the department had ever received and I was only a temporary employee.

It was during this research project that I developed one of the traits I use extensively today. When conducting any type of analysis that deals with resources or personnel who manage resources, I make it a point to conduct a great deal of fieldwork to not only meet the people in charge but also accompany them while they do their work. For the marine safety project, this meant going on a search for drowning victims or to rescue stranded passengers on a disabled boat in Lake Huron. We almost did not come back from that one. I was also a passenger on a sheriff's boat when the sailboats entered Mackinac Bay after finishing a grueling race from Port Huron on the Lake Huron side. It was a sight to see the sailboats round the corner with their spinnakers deployed. There were other benefits from doing the fieldwork. One night in Michigan's Upper Peninsula, I was stopped for speeding, as I was in a hurry to get to my hotel. I think there was a football game I wanted to watch. After taking my license to check on my criminal status, the deputy came back with only a message from his boss. He told me to take it easy. His boss was the sheriff I had met with earlier in the day. It helps to be a bringer of potential monetary resources. I finished the project by developing an extensive econometric model that was accepted for use by the state and county sheriff offices for future funding of marine safety work. Again I was impressed with the economic tools that could be used to solve many different issues.

My work at Michigan State University was winding down when an announcement crossed my desk that the Travel and Tourism Research Association was going to meet in Las Vegas. I brought it to one of the professors in the department and said that we should attend and start getting involved in tourism, as much of the research we were doing had a tourism bent to it. He agreed and I was excited to be going to Vegas until I was told that he was going and I was staying put. Still I had a feeling that I would be doing more tourism work in the future.

The future arrived within the year as I took a position as director of the Institute of Outdoor Recreation and Tourism at Utah State University. The institute had been started by John Hunt and he had just left to take a position at George Washington University. This was my first meeting with John who I have collaborated with on image papers since. The institute was a soft money shop. A major reason I was chosen to be its new director was the research contract I had brought in at Michigan State University for marine safety research. Hunt had established a long running relationship with the Utah Travel Council to conduct annual work for them on the tourist trade, including those traveling in cars, by plane, and, later under my direction, by motor coaches. My first meeting with the Utah Travel Council director did not go as expected. I was excited about conducting some economic analysis, but was told it was time to revisit Hunt's earlier work on Utah's image. I was a bit perplexed, as I began seeing myself as an economist. When told that this was their top priority and they were willing to provide all the funding we required, I reminded myself that we needed the money to keep the institute viable. That is how I began to conduct destination image research; it is also the research with which my name is most often associated. Necessity was the operative word and I became a destination image researcher, something that has followed me to this day.

Where to from Here?

Running a soft money shop is like managing your own small business. Chasing after any and all contracts that seem like they fit into your field became the norm. Although we did some basic economic impact analysis, mostly spending patterns, at the institute, we did not perform any real econometric modeling as the contracts received were mostly for practical marketing purposes. We also did not have a tourism program at Utah State University. I taught the only tourism course at the university and there were no graduate students interested in pursuing this line of inquiry. Time to move on.

I moved to the University of Wisconsin (UW)-Stout in 1986 and took a position as director of the MS program in hospitality and tourism. This was an opportunity to work with students on tourism-related research. Although the university was primarily a teaching institution, it did allow for contract research. There were two things that happened at this institution that would define my career as one that focused more on development economics than other forms of economics. One of those opportunities arrived via a phone call from an organization named MUCIA (Midwestern Universities Consortium for International Activities). It represented the Big Ten universities as a form of a consulting company going after, primarily, contracts and grants from the United States Agency for International Development (USAID). One of the principals at the consortium, Jim Riordan, felt that MUCIA should be pursuing tourism as a development strategy.

Although USAID was not that interested in funding tourism development projects, he felt there were other companies or organizations that would. He contacted me about developing a marketing strategy for MUCIA for international tourism projects. Ironically, although the UUW-Madison, as a member of the Big Ten, was also a member of MUCIA, the other system campuses (apart from UW-Milwaukee) were not considered its members. All other Big Ten universities included their system campuses as MUCIA members, but UW-Madison always had a bit of a status issue when it came to the system campuses. Nonetheless, I worked with MUCIA to set up the tourism marketing portion of their portfolio and actually did some preliminary work for them in Yugoslavia in 1989, along with Alistair Morrison. The focus of our work was to develop a tourism program at the University of Maribor in the soon-to-become independent state of Slovenia. Nothing much came from this effort except I made some new friends who I still visit today. Further, I have a bottle of homemade Slivovitz given to me by a card carrying communist, which he was sure to let me know. Maybe he thought I was an agent of the government but no matter, the Slivovitz was great!

The next MUCIA project was the one that would turn me into a development economist, but first I must mention the other thing that greatly helped me develop my career. It was an opportunity to work with one of the faculty members at UW-Stout, Jafar Jafari. His office was across the hall from mine and we would engage in frequent debates, play poker with some other colleagues, baccarat at the bar, and, over time, became close friends. His friendship and support continue to this day. Although I was not thrilled with the quality of the faculty at UW-Stout, Jafari was definitely the exception. I remember the day he showed me the first issue of *Annals of Tourism Research*. He had the entire collection in his office. The first issue was produced in the department using mimeograph machines. It was a thin volume and there was no way anyone looking at it would figure it to become the world's leading tourism journal. But there is one thing I learned from him. If the end product is important enough, the amount of time spent making it the best of its kind is irrelevant. His tourism library was second to none. It was better than what could be found at UW-Stout or for that matter the much larger and more prestigious institutions of UW-Madison or the University of Minnesota. He graciously allowed me free use of his journals, books, and other educational resources. When I eventually published my book on *Tourism Development*, most of which was completed during my time at UW-Stout, it was due in large part to the use of Jafar's library and the wisdom that came from discussing issues with him. I will always look back at my move to UW-Stout as one of the most strategic of my career, but there was no way of knowing at that time it would turn out to be such an opportunity.

Now back to MUCIA. Jim Riordan called one day and said that they had just finished visiting with a contingent of Ghanaians and that he was organizing a three-week trip to write a proposal for a development project in Ghana. Would I like to be part of the group? I did not hesitate. I joined with Barb Koth who at that time was representing the University of Minnesota which was a bona fide member of MUCIA. Barb worked at the University of Minnesota Tourism Center, a place I would become familiar with in a few years. Barb and I tried to leave Minnesota in the spring of 1987, but our flights were changed due to severe weather. Instead of flying into and through London on our way to Accra (one of the quirks about USAID work is that you must leave the United States on an American flag carrier or one of its code share partners), we were re-routed through Frankfurt. Unfortunately our luggage went to London. We arrived a day late and without any luggage into the tropical climate of Accra.

Almost upon arrival, we attended a reception at the ambassador's residence to welcome and allow us to meet some of our Ghanaian colleagues. I mentioned to one of the embassy staff that I did not have any other clothes apart from what I was wearing; she said that she would try and round some up and I should stop by and pick them up the next day. At that time, Ghana was an economic disaster just recovering from years of isolation from the West. Breakfast consisted of beans and bread and there were no Western clothes stores to be found. The next day I was presented with a pair of nylon sweat pants, which were hell to wear in the tropical weather, and a Minnie Mouse tee shirt. I went to my meeting with the minister of education wearing that shirt. Once he found out why I was dressed so inappropriately, we shared a good laugh. The next day we did manage to find a batik business run by a Ghanaian woman working out of her backyard. No pants but I was able to wear a nice locally produced and colorful batik shirt to future meetings.

We spent three weeks in Ghana working with colleagues from the Smithsonian Institution, Conservation International, and the International Council on Monuments and Sites. Our proposal, quite voluminous and detailed, was sent to USAID and we returned home to pick up our lives. Months and months went by and we heard nothing. One day I received a call that the proposal was funded to the tune of approximately $5.4 million. I was also told that since UW-Stout was not officially a member of MUCIA, the tourism part of the contract was going to the Tourism Center at the University of Minnesota. I initially thought my time had been wasted until the Tourism Center hired me as a consultant to help implement the contract. That was great. I was able to work on the project and I was paid for it. We began our work in 1988.

I soon realized that working in Ghana was unlike any other place I had ever worked. My colleagues were great, but things did not happen as I had expected. We set meetings for 8:00 am Greenwich Mean Time (GMT) and no one would show. I initially thought that because they used GMT things would happen as expected. After a few meetings where our colleagues never showed, I asked what was going on. One of my Ghanaian colleagues informed me that GMT meant Ghana Maybe Time. But I learned to cope and I also learned that development work takes a special mindset. In terms of economics, it includes the sociocultural and environmental dimensions. Nothing is done based on economics alone. To be successful requires attention to the culture in which the development work is being conducted and to the environment where it is all taking place. Ghana, for me, was the best training ground I could have ever have had with respect to organizing my thoughts and approach to development.

In the second year of the project, the University of Minnesota was looking for a new director of their Tourism Center and I was approached about becoming a candidate. I knew the staff fairly well, having worked with some of them; besides, it was getting to the point at UW-Stout where the narrow mindset was taking its toll. Apart from Jafar Jafari, there were very few faculty in our department that understood the research process and even fewer that understood anything about development. It was time for me to move on. I joined the University of Minnesota as director of the Tourism Center, with tenure in the Department of Applied Economics in 1993. This new position came along at the same time that I was informed of my election into the International Academy for the Study of Tourism. It was a good year.

The Grass was Greener (or in this case Maroon and Gold)

The position at the University of Minnesota was an opportunity that comes along rarely in one's career. Although the university had some faculty engaged in tourism research for many years, it had no formal program. The

Tourism Center under the first director, John Sem, had already established itself by producing high-quality programs. Many academics would have known about it for its rural tourism handbook and accompanying videos. It was a nice platform to build upon. One major advantage that made the director's position appealing was the creation of the Carlson Chair. Curtis Carlson, founder of Carlson Companies, had provided a generous gift to the business school at the University of Minnesota. That business school now carries his name. Carlson Companies was heavily invested in tourism businesses, with some of their more prominent divisions being Radisson Hotels and Carlson/Wagonlit travel agencies. In the process of donating over $30 million to the university, a sum of $250,000 was dedicated in the form of a challenge grant directly to the Tourism Center. The agreed grant requirements called for an additional $250,000 to be donated by other firms and individuals. Once this goal had been reached, the university would provide $500,000 from its Permanent University Fund. It was envisioned that a total of $1 million would become the principal for the Foundation. I arrived when most of the legwork had already been completed and only had to spend a little time chasing the few remaining dollars.

The Foundation is in place today and is capitalized at well over $1 million. A percentage of the earnings is made available for Tourism Center programs each year and the principal is never touched. The use of the earnings was under complete control of the director. This was a major reason I was excited about this new opportunity as it almost guaranteed we would be able to develop new programs. It was also a time that the university was fairly flush with seed money for new projects. Shortly after I was hired, the head of extension, which was the parent home for the center, asked me to think of one or more new programs that we could develop. He informed me that over $300,000 would be available for new program development. After talking with the staff, it was decided that a customer service program would be our first priority. The money was provided and Cynthia Messer assumed control of this program's development. It has been a staple for the center since and it has evolved, under her direction, into more than just a customer service program for tourism businesses.

Another program that existed when I took over as director, Festival and Event Management, was in decline. With an infusion of funds and under the direction of Kent Gustafson, it has become a very strong program and was the first center program to have an online presence. In addition to our extension programs, we also decided to develop a research program. For those unfamiliar with the land grant university system in the United States, it basically is a system that has three primary interests (teaching, research, extension).

Teaching and research, similar to other universities that are not part of the land grant system, are what one expects them to be. Extension is a program area that provides education to nontraditional audiences, such as homeowners, farmers, small businesses, etc. The Tourism Center, as mentioned, was part of extension, but we felt that for us to do a better job information, from focused research, was what we needed to complement our existing programs. It was a long process to develop the research program.

We began to develop the program by soliciting input from every tourism-related organization in the state. Center staff crisscrossed the state to be present whenever one of the targeted groups held a membership meeting. We were added to the agenda and we asked a simple question "tell us what causes you the most problems with conducting your business." Answers ranged from government regulations to the more common need for marketing information. After the association meetings that took over six months to complete, we compiled over 100 different problems which we turned into research problem statements. The next step was to meet with representatives from each of the associations and present them with the problem statements. We briefly discussed each problem statement, which had been organized into categories such as transportation, marketing, economics, and the like. Association representatives then went through rounds of selection where the lowest scoring problem statements were eliminated. The most relevant remained and one, conducting visitor profile analysis, remained as the top priority. We also listed the other problem statements, in order of priority, for each category.

The next step consisted of raising awareness of the research problems that needed to be addressed. We hired a lobbyist to make our case before the legislature. We knew this was a long shot at best, but it would keep the issues from going away. Although I could have used the Carlson Foundation money to hire the lobbyist, it was decided to seek funding from individuals and tourism-related organizations for this effort. In this way, we could argue that the issues were so relevant that people were using their own funds to support the cause. In fact, two of the contributors wrote personal checks from their own account for this purpose. The legislative session ended with no money being allocated for the Tourism Center's research program, but the awareness and the need were elevated to a higher level. Shortly after the legislative session ended, the Minnesota State Office of Tourism Director provided enough seed money for us to complete five community visitor profiles. In addition, some of the other research issues related to transportation were funded by the Minnesota Department of Transportation (MNDOT). When I met with the head of research for MNDOT, it was only with the intent of making him aware of the issues and the support for the research from statewide tourism associations. He had been looking for an opportunity to connect more with tourism interests, and before leaving his office I had a commitment to fund over $300,000 in transportation-related tourism research. The center now had a bona fide research program and it continues to conduct tourism research even today.

One other major project that I took over as director was the ongoing project in Ghana. As a consultant for this project while at the UW-Stout, I was involved with the development decisions we had been making. Now it became my responsibility to make those decisions and implement them. The only change was that I was no longer being paid as a consultant, but instead did this work as part of my appointment. The loss of consulting money was offset by the excitement that came with implementing some of my ideas which were developed in full consultation with our Ghanaian staff. The Ghana project was major work. I traveled to Ghana three to four times a year and spent two to three weeks there on each trip. This work provided the basis for my continuing involvement in tourism development and the contacts I developed along the way would lead to more work in other countries (Peru, Israel). Not all of the ideas we implemented in Ghana were successful, but those that worked have helped develop a strong base for tourism in Ghana's Central Region.

As previously mentioned, the Tourism Center was one of the four subcontractors on this project. It was my job to train Ghanaian staff and private sector operators (such as tour operators) to take advantage of the development work that was being accomplished. My team developed a strategy of building first a domestic tourism base and adding the international aspect to the infrastructure that was being created. Our ideas were met with a great deal of skepticism. How could you develop a domestic tourism base when the country was so poor was an often heard caution. Yet we knew that building an international base first was almost impossible. At the time, a trip to Ghana was very expensive. Very few international airlines served Ghana and their prices were high due to lack of competition, extraordinarily high fees imposed for using airspace by countries that the planes flew over, and the high levels of business travel that are common for developing countries receiving aid from international donors.

Given the economic constraints, a big increase in international leisure travel, especially since the country had few developed tourism attractions during this time, did not seem possible. Instead we focused on the international community that had a high presence in Accra, the country's capital. Even in poor countries, there would be people with money; the expatriate community was not large but definitely not poor. Thus began our effort to target those already in the country (domestic tourism). Our most successful venture was to develop a tourist road map. There were no useful road maps in existence at the time. The one that was available did not identify the condition of the roads, which for the most part were in poor shape, and did not list any attractions along the way. I contracted with a geography professor at the University of Cape Coast to draw a map of the road system and any attractions in the region. The finished product was a work of art. Icons of pineapples (designating roadside fruit and vegetable stands) were located on the map; Posuban shrines, which are fanciful militia headquarters and unique to the region in which they are found, were identified and located on the map. Icons of people in swimsuits playing volleyball on the beach were used to designate public beaches free of riptides. Kakum National Park, a product of the overall project, was featured prominently. One of the remaining issues before we could digitize and prepare a tourist road map was to drive each of the roads, first to determine if they existed as no one was sure that they all did, and second rank the condition of the road.

The end product identified, through color, the condition of each road, expected speed that could be maintained on the road, and type of vehicle needed to use the road (such as four-wheeled drive, sedan, and bus). We then digitized the final map and printed them for free distribution. We also added some elements to it that would aid and encourage tourists to spend more time in the region. We provided a list of six must things to do or see while in the region and identified where travelers could stop for food and refreshments. The latter might not seem like a big thing, but since the bars and restaurants were often only identified by a blue/white-striped fence, it was not obvious what type of service was being offered. The maps were a hit. In fact one stop I made at a government tourist information center revealed no maps or brochures (we also printed these as another marketing tool) were available. This seemed strange as I had been assured that this information center had recently received a large shipment of both items. When I asked the clerk as to what had happened to them, she assured me that they are all safely stored in the office. When I asked why, the answer was that people were stopping in and taking them without paying! One thing I learned in Ghana is never assume someone knows what you want done. More training followed.

The success of the map was evident in the number of expatriates, living in Accra, who were now taking time on the weekend to visit the central region, two hours away by motor vehicle. Some of the comments we heard were that now they were aware of central region attractions and knew how to reach them. One of the criticisms we received was that the maps were not printed on plastic paper and the heat and humidity of the climate tended to destroy them faster the more they were used. In a way, this one was one of the best compliments we could have received. Our maps were being used! We also saw other signs of development progress. New hotels were being built in the central region.

One of the major accomplishments of the project was the design and construction of a canopy walkway in Kakum National Park. This effort was undertaken by Conservation International, one of the subcontractors. In a near tropical rainforest, which describes Kakum, the bush is so dense that it is almost impossible to see wildlife at ground level. There are forest elephants in Kakum National Park, but getting close enough to see them is difficult and dangerous as it would put a person too close to these large animals. In my time in Ghana, I heard the elephants and saw fresh droppings, but I never saw the beasts. The idea was to abandon walking on trails and looking for ground animals and instead take people up to the tops of the trees where numerous monkey species, parrots, other forest birds, countless butterflies, and interesting flora, including orchids and ferns, could be observed clearly and in close proximity. There are only a handful of these canopy walkways found around the world and Ghana has the only one found on the continent of Africa. Before the canopy walkway was officially opened, we began to market the experience to social groups based in Accra. It became a status symbol to visit the walkway and many social groups organized trips to the central region for this experience. It was another form of domestic tourism which provided the backbone for tourism development in the region.

Given the nature of the work in Ghana, I became acutely aware that economic reasoning alone would not ensure project success. The complex and rich sociocultural system had to be not only considered, but included as an integral part of project implementation. How people made decisions was critical to the success of our venture. I spent a lot of time learning as much of the culture as I could in order to achieve a higher success rate with our various activities. All development success must take into account not only economic outputs but those arising from the sociocultural and environmental spheres as well.

Ghana was a great experience and I could write another chapter with stories from time spent there, but suffice it to say it has been the learning environment for the international work I have done since. From a scholarship perspective, though, it only resulted in a few publications. Still the experience more than offsets the time commitment and lack of scholarly output.

Life after Power

After eight years of being Tourism Center director, it was obvious to me that I needed a change of scenery. I was dealing with the third extension director since coming to the University of Minnesota. He was in a budget-cutting mood and he neither appreciated nor understood what the center had accomplished. I was ending a five-year appointment as director and it was assumed that I would accept another five-year appointment, but there were troubling signs. University budgets were being slashed. I would have had to take a staff of eight full-time equivalents and pare it to three. Three is what I began with and I did not have the desire to go back to the point of beginning. I decided to exercise the clause in my contract that allowed me to join the Department of Applied Economics as a full professor. The change was not easy. I had to give up control of the Carlson Foundation, among other things, which had been used for extension programming and research. I had to develop an independent research program, although I continued to work on center projects. But, within a year, the adjustment was made and I was involved with other exciting projects.

With my administrative work behind me, I was able to concentrate on building a research program. More visitor profile work was completed, but some of the most satisfying work has been in the area of economic impact. I have completed work for the Minnesota Department of Natural Resources on the economic impact of coldwater angling (trout and salmon) and with the Minnesota Grape Growers Association on the economic impact of grape growing and wineries in the state. Given my approach of finding out as much as I can about the subject, primarily through the use of personal interviews and site visits, these two studies have been as much fun as any I have experienced. I was also able to develop a web-based economic impact calculator for all small- and medium-size airports in Minnesota. This was fun because of the challenge it posed—how to develop a simple-to-use instrument that can calculate the economic impact of any small- or medium-size airport. It has been developed and is operational.

Since being elected to the International Academy for the Study of Tourism in 1993, I served four years as the academy's secretary, two as vice president, and was then elected president for two terms (four years). Involvement with the academy was challenging as it was still a very young organization and required a great deal of structure. But it was also extremely rewarding as now I was able to meet some of the people whose scholarship was instrumental to my research foundation. People like Erik Cohen, Dick Butler, Geoff Wall, Valene Smith, Steve Wanhill, Stephen Witt, Brent

Ritchie, Graham Dann, Boris Vuconic, and hosts of others were together in one place every two years. It was a great opportunity to continue learning and at the same getting to know some of them as friends. It also allowed me to meet people who were willing to host our biennial meeting. Nevenka Cavlek at the University of Zagreb, Croatia became a good friend after our first meeting to arrange the 1999 Academy Conference. She has also organized the International Tourism and Hospitality Academy at Sea. Along with my crazy friend and fellow academy member, Julio Aramberri, I have been an instructor in her program since its inception. In a similar manner, the folks at the Institute of Tourism Studies in Macau, who hosted our 2001 conference, became friends and it also led to a decade worth of work in Macau culminating in being named the honorary dean of the Faculty of International Economics at the Macau University of Science and Technology. My time in Southeast Asia has also given me the opportunity to develop a great relationship with one of the finest hospitality and tourism schools in the world located at Hong Kong Polytechnic University. Kaye Chon, Haiyan Song, and the other faculty of the school are world class and I have been blessed to be a part of what they do.

My work has also taken me more and more in recent years to Europe. I have had great times working with friends such as Raija Komppula at Eastern Finland University, and holding visiting professorships in the Faculty of Economics at the University of Ljubljana working with Tanja Mihalič and at the Faculty of Tourism at the Munich University of Applied Sciences working with Thomas Bausch and Theo Eberhard, among others.

CONCLUSION

Probably in this book, the reader will see that there are many ways to develop a career in tourism economics. I would not categorize mine as typical, but I doubt there is a typical career. I have been lucky to be presented with interesting challenges, and being opportunistic by nature my career has been one of fortunate circumstances. Some of the luckiest events have been people I have met along the way. Many of those personalities have been mentioned already, but others deserve to be included, for example, people like Chuck Goeldner, who I count not only as a friend but someone who took the time to provide needed and valuable guidance. He did not have to reach out to me, but I am very glad he did. This is a hallmark of the tourism academics I have met along the way. People who take the time to mentor and guide those who they think can make a contribution. The current editor of the *Journal of Travel Research*, Rick Perdue, was such a prolific publisher of quality papers that I looked to him as someone to emulate. He and I have become good friends over the years. There are many others, and I will think of some of them who should be mentioned here after this chapter has gone to press. They are no less important; if there is a lesson to be learned from this, it is to welcome criticism and help wherever you find it. It all works out for the best in the end.

In closing, there is one other characteristic of my life that I feel has allowed me to succeed. I do not work as hard as some of my colleagues, because there are some things in life, unrelated to academics, that bring a sense of recharge and purpose to my life. For those who know me, they know where to find me in the fall of the year. In case I ever go missing, look in either North or South Dakota for a man with a black dog both too foolish to come out of the rain or snow as long as there are ducks and pheasants flying. I let my work go, some may say suffer, during this time of year, because there are some things more important than figuring out the elasticity of visa regulations. Enjoying life and all it has to offer brings rewards both in the academic realm as well as in the personal domain of self-actualization. It has been a great career and life so far and with October just around the corner, as I write this final sentence, I see no reason to suspect things will change.

Chapter 7

Tourism Economics at the Margin: The Perspective of a Utility Outfielder

Thomas J. Iverson
University of Guam, USA

Thomas J. Iverson is professor of economics, chair of the business administration division, and executive director of the sustainable development institute, at the University of Guam. He has taught management information systems and the full complement of economics courses at the university, since he arrived in 1988. Prior to that, he served eight years in the Graduate Center of Kentucky State University, teaching in the Master of Public Administration program. In Guam, working closely with the Guam Visitors Bureau, he helped to redesign their visitor exit surveys and produce a very rich data set of visitors to Guam, as well as a new design for the resident attitude surveys. Recently he produced an economic impact study for one of the largest ocean preserves on the planet, the Mariana Trench Marine National Monument. He is a registered consultant with the Global Development Network and with the Asian Development Bank. His research interests include sustainability, forecasting, resident attitude surveys, and natural resource valuation. He has published articles, book reviews, and notes in most of the major tourism journals. Email <tiverson@uguam.uog.edu>

The Discovery of Tourism Economics
Tourism Social Science Series, Volume 16, 89–99

ISSN: 1571-5043/doi:10.1108/S1571-5043(2011)0000016010

INTRODUCTION

When offered the wonderful opportunity to contribute to this volume, my ego was so pleased that some time passed before my economic reasoning began to raise questions. What market value is there in the musing of dinosaurs? While cathartic for those of us writing, why would our stories be of interest to a general audience? My initial idea was to address my chapter to university students, but the new generation does not read anything as long as a book chapter. Ultimately I am hoping that more mature students and those embarking on a career in tourism research may find value in my simple story.

Without a clear template, my first draft began at the stimulating but often confusing stage of choosing a major and an academic path in the early university years. Having the opportunity to see early drafts of other contributors, I noticed that many began their stories with the influence of their parents and childhood experiences, so I will begin from there as well.

Our family was initially on the path to becoming the traditional and exemplary "average family of four" with mom staying at home with her domestic duties and dad working as an engineer at Honeywell. This changed, in ways that I did not appreciate for many years, when dad decided to abandon his career path for a job as an education director for our church. My brother and I were too young to understand the financial sacrifice that this entailed, and we thought it was quite natural to have a huge garden, to freeze and preserve food for the winter, and to have French toast for supper as a "treat." While I was embarrassed to wear homemade clothes to school, and to ride my mom's old bicycle, my parents conducted their business in typical Norwegian-American fashion—they simply did not discuss their problems with us.

Instead, they filled our lives with wonderful experiences: canoe trips into the wilderness, with blueberry pie in reflector ovens; camping trips to state parks, with evening campfire talks by the local naturalist or park ranger; and the dreaded weeding of the garden, later rewarded by the bountiful harvest. What an odd memory to recall gorging on fresh peas or raspberries! I did not realize that my chores, things like breaking the ice in the rabbits' water bowls in winter, collecting eggs, and so forth, were passing on a tradition of self-sufficiency and sustainable living that was natural to my parents' generation, but was quickly lost in mine.

Even our idyllic setting was not sustainable due to external forces of development. Our beautiful meandering creek, where I would ice skate in the winter and catch snapping turtles in the summer, was dredged into an ugly straight drainage ditch for a major housing development. With my parents' dream fading, and perhaps due to financial pressure, we sold our home and moved into the city where I learned to smoke cigarettes, play pinball, listen to the Beatles, and act out the modern life of a juvenile delinquent.

The subsequent years held little of importance and can be mercifully skipped, but deeply implanted in my psyche from my childhood experiences were a profound love of nature and a healthy distrust of developers and their ability to manipulate government. These were totally submerged during my high school years, where I essentially slept through the whole experience, but were perhaps reawakened in the stimulating environment of the Vietnam War and the "Sixties."

I was aghast at the idea that the government could force me to go to war and kill people, and can still recall the surreal experience of watching our lottery numbers scroll over the TV screen, randomly triaging my cohort into those who would serve (unless they had connections), the gray area of those who might be called, and those of us with high numbers who were free to continue with our lives. University education was not a deferment for me but an expectation, as education, for Norwegian-Americans, is somewhere between God and family. We reached a cordial compromise where I was able to get far away from home, but attending a Lutheran university that had all the appearances of our homogeneous Scandinavian culture, albeit in Texas. I had no idea at the time that the low student–teacher ratio at this private school was the best thing for someone like me, so it was simple luck that I fell into an environment with caring, dedicated professors.

RESEARCH

Like many tourism researchers, my academic journey was one of various twists and turns. Few of us began our careers thinking "I will specialize in tourism research." Likewise, economics was a sideways move for me, as I was initially a math major. Noting my frustration with proofs and the unreal, my math professor recommended that I check out economics. Sure enough, *x*'s and *y*'s were replaced with the more real *price* and *quantity*. I did poorly in my first exam, but that was enough motivation to figure out the logic of economics; I was hooked.

I often wonder how many of us are permanently influenced by excellent teachers. Attending a small private school, many of my economics courses were taught by an engaging and brilliant professor who was a "disciple" of Ray Marshall, the eminent labor economist at the University of Texas (UT). I was drawn to the pragmatism of Marshall, particularly the targeted approach to alleviating poverty through training and work education. I had a simple goal of following in his footsteps, to the extent possible, and was happy to earn a teaching fellowship at UT. This was at the end of the era of the "Texas Institutional School" and I embraced the intellectual roots of institutionalism, planted by Thorstein Veblen and John Commons, as articulated by the senior faculty at UT.

As I formed my dissertation committee under Marshall's leadership, my almost complete plan was rudely interrupted when President Jimmy Carter selected Marshall to be his secretary of labor. Thus began the pattern that would eventually lead to my interest in tourism: learning to adapt to the unexpected. Perhaps it is trite, but we can often remind our students that when one door closes another often appears. For me it was the desire to support myself while reforming my dissertation committee, and I found meaningful work experience with the City of Austin as a "Manpower Planner." This practical experience, particularly my duties as an intergovernmental liaison, provided valuable insights into the workings of the public sector. I also enjoyed a stint as a project coordinator for the Austin Area Urban League, where I learned quite a bit about the practical difficulties of implementing employment and training programs.

Finishing my PhD in 1980, I could not foresee that the career path I had chosen (developing and evaluating employment and training programs) would become a dead end under the Reagan Administration, as these federally funded programs experienced major budget cuts. I had accepted a position in the Graduate Center of Kentucky State University, where I ambitiously planned a track in the Master of Public Administration program, specializing in labor relations, collective bargaining, and employment and training. It soon became clear that it was time to adapt again, as we could not, in good conscience, train managers for programs that were rapidly shrinking.

Cross-Training

This was the beginning of the microcomputer boom and there was a real need for organizational change, particularly in mainframe-oriented environments. I cross-trained in management information systems (MIS) and developed and taught a track, consisting of several courses, in that subject area.

I had strayed from my original career path, but enjoyed the new challenges of learning organizational theory, management psychology, and the related disciplines of our Master of Public Administration program.

I was fascinated with the important bodies of theory that we had not been exposed to in our economics education, and the mutual ignorance across the fields of psychology, economics, and information systems. I found that the techniques of systems theory meshed very well with institutional economics, as the structure of institutionalism (identifying actors, within an environment, under working rules) could be examined with systems analysis. More importantly, no problem is too complex when it can be disassembled with systems theory, and economic problems can occasionally be daunting. The inclusion of MIS into the business undergraduate curriculum was initially prodded by the microcomputer revolution, but I found that MIS techniques were essential to breaking down the disciplinary turfs that so often obfuscated problem solving in the real world.

I was able to draw on my intergovernmental work experience when teaching MIS to our graduate students (many were state employees, as we were located in the state capital). Through theses and professional projects, I learned many of the practical realities of program implementation and the economics of the public sector. The most exciting developments at this time appeared to be outside the realm of economics, as popular publications like Megatrends and Theory Z were broadening our perspectives and questioning conventional wisdom.

So, feeling like there was something more "out there," I accepted a three-year contract at the University of Guam, thinking it would be a temporary fling on a tropical island. Twenty-two years later, still at the same institution, I can reflect on a career that has been greatly enriched by my contacts and colleagues in the sphere of international tourism, an area that I embraced primarily because it was the sole driver of Guam's economy. My contribution to the discipline has been slight, small works on the periphery, but the insights along the way may help to document the rich and open character of tourism research in general.

Tourism Studies

Eschewing precise definition, I will simply compare the study of tourism with the discipline of economics from my personal view. While both are relatively new fields of study, economics has become hardened into rigid schools of thought and entrenched opinions. My first forays into the tourism associations, particularly Travel and Tourism Research Association conferences, were so refreshingly hospitable that I knew I could be happier in the tourism world. Perhaps a couple of anecdotes could help to illustrate this.

I recall attending a conference where I came a little early and noticed that Doug Pearce had registered. I had recently read a paper of his, and took the opportunity to call him to see if he was available for dinner. Though we had never met, he graciously accepted, explaining that he had dinner plans already, but I was welcome to join him. Having done so, I greeted his dinner companion and, in my typical focused way, began to question Doug about his paper. Satisfying myself with the specifics, I turned to his companion, who had been introduced to me as Richard Butler, and I asked him "so what kind of work do you do?"

This was my introduction to the magnanimous nature of our academy, as Butler did not skip a beat but patiently explained the concept of the lifecycle of a tourism destination. With a dismissive—"Oh! Kind of like a product lifecycle in marketing, huh?"—I brought the discussion back to Pearce's paper and my own work, some minor contingent evaluation study of a proposed marine observation business. It was only much later that I realized that, in showing no shock or amusement in my ignorance of one of the classic tourism themes and being totally oblivious to the fact that I was dining with a tourism icon, these colleagues were warm-hearted individuals who understood that there is no single path to tourism research and that many of us may be blind to the important discoveries outside our base disciplines.

Not having learned my lesson, I repeated my gaffe soon after, when I met Clifford Geertz at a conference in Indonesia. I understood that he was a dignitary at the meeting, but I had no idea of the nature of his work and immediately asked him what his area of research entailed. Years later, when I had become aware of the contribution of Geertz, particularly to the study of Bali, I shared a paper that I had written about Balinese taboos with Hilly Geertz to get her feedback, and we ended up having a delightful dinner where she gently critiqued my naive anthropological view. She also graciously committed to spending an afternoon with our students in a field school setting in Bali, a wonderful free-form Q&A session in a relaxed homestay setting. She was honored the day before for her 50 years of intellectual contributions to understanding Indonesian culture.

Realizing that I was not well grounded in tourism classics and methods, I pursued projects that I was comfortable with, mostly quantitative analyses. With limited resources, it is a little daunting to embark on research on a small tropical island, so I developed time series models of tourism arrivals and conducted studies on natural resource valuation—projects that could be accomplished with secondary data or minor survey research. I was less comfortable in areas such as market segmentation and more sophisticated forecasting models, so I sought help externally. This was only possible due to a chance meeting that essentially jump-started my "career" in tourism economics.

While at a TTRA conference, and in a casual conversation with Pauline Sheldon and Jafar Jafari, they mentioned that they were starting a discussion group called TRINET. As I was familiar with LISTSERV technology and had conducted research on microcomputer networking, I was an enthusiastic early member. Gone were the awkward communication windows of using the phone to communicate with stateside colleagues who were 14 time zones away. There was immediate access to colleagues in New Zealand and Australia, many of whom were working through issues of Asian tourism growth and capacity issues similar to those we faced on Guam. More importantly, I could collaborate with colleagues, adding credibility and valuable review to my work. Joe Ismail contributed his modeling expertise to my forecasting project; Connie Mok graciously worked through a market segmentation study with me. I met her for the first time, in person, some years after we had published our paper in *Tourism Management* (Mok and Iverson 2000). James Mak has been like a colleague next door, as I ask him questions periodically and we discuss tourism economics; but I have yet to sit down to a dinner with him and say thank you.

In this manner, it was possible for a person of low distinction, working in what is primarily a "teaching institution," to establish a minor reputation in the field of tourism research. Without TRINET this would have been incredibly daunting, the kind of thing that workaholics (Martin Oppermann comes to mind, and others I will not mention who are still with us) might accomplish, but not me.

Someday the archives of TRINET will be mined by an inquisitive graduate student and our gaffes will be revealed, but in spite of the learning curve we went through, there was always an attempt to maintain a level of professionalism and at least a modicum of respect. I joined other lists, relative to my interests in economics and culture, but they were either boring or quickly fell into tirades and personal attacks. TRINET, instead, took on the character of the founders, Sheldon and Jafari: cordial, committed, professional, and compassionate. Within that framework, and particularly for those of us at the margins, TRINET has served as a lifeline to tourism research and education, an open door into the inner sanctum.

Through these relationships I have had the confidence to continue to expand my horizons, and to improve the relationships between tourism research and economic development on Guam. Our tourist exit surveys have produced very consistent and high-quality data sets. We were able to implement a series of resident attitude surveys, fine-tuning them with the assistance of John Ap. Mike Robinson's work on cultural tourism gave me a framework to pursue studies in heritage and culture within the economies of Bali and Guam.

This may lead to different views of what a 'career' should encompass. I have enjoyed being a generalist and exploring both quantitative and qualitative methods in interdisciplinary studies. A visiting economist, though, remarked on my description of my career "Oh, you are like a utility outfielder." For the baseball challenged, this means a person who sits on the bench and is able to substitute for any of the three positions in the outfield (left, center, and right field). The dismissive comment did not offend, because I feel that many economists overspecialize, remaining in little niches throughout their careers. I have not made the first team, in that sense, but I have enjoyed the continuous learning that is required when tackling new economic problems. Even the utility outfielder feels like part of the team sometimes.

My view, developed through my cross-training in public administration, MIS, and later in tourism, is that the world's problems are interdisciplinary. My collaboration with anthropologists, archaeologists, and sociologists, among others, has taught me some degree of patience and to try to be open to new ideas. Yet this can be very frustrating, as we are taught to highly value our disciplinary methods and discoveries. When I hear or read extended postmodern discussions, I have a tendency to interrupt "Have you read Veblen?" Likewise when jargon becomes the centerpiece of a thesis, I want to write in my editorial review "Have you read George Orwell's essay on writing?" While I go back to John Urry's classic often, to refresh my own gaze, I am typically excited to gain a new insight while simultaneously wishing that Orwell's advice had been taken to make this important work clear and concise. Worse yet is the attempt of junior faculty to mimic the prose of the more obtuse works, with the false perception that the tangled jargon is actually understood by the average reader. Again, as a reviewer, I write "this probably makes sense to you, but perhaps only to you; try to read this as a novice."

Part of the frustration of interdisciplinary work is the realization that there are many perspectives that one might take toward economic and social problems, and one would like to avoid being trapped in a limiting method. Institutional economics provides insight into the choices that are made by the various actors within their environments, and systems analysis makes it possible to decompose even complex problems and situations. Yet this approach, which I find so rewarding, has been relegated to a backwater of the economics profession.

New approaches, utilizing more of the psychology of the actor's choices, may provide a better launching pad for new economic paradigms. The work of Robert Frank is particularly appealing for those of us trying to inspire the new generation. As a teacher, I have enjoyed using his approach of posing everyday life questions that have answers grounded in basic economics, including the importance of traditions. Extensions of this work into culture might be a path that aspiring young scholars could take to reinvigorate tourism economics.

It is postulated here that greater discussion of method would be productive for our little niche of tourism economics. Too often we argue about the appropriate definitions of tourist demand or supply, or which model most appropriately measures "the" economic impact of a decision. Input–output models are routinely applied as if they produce "answers," in spite of our awareness of their limitations. Rarely do we discuss the ultimate objective of our work, how to move from analysis to postulating or planning future systems.

What societal objective should be established in such cases? This mystery was solved, for me, when I began to study the concept of sustainability. But while sustainable development has an immediate appeal (like ecotourism) to our sensibility, it must be defined, and this may occupy us for some time. In my case I use a simple definition of leaving the world a better place for our children, but this does not address the issues of capital substitution and the fine points that we must continue to articulate and study. It is a starting point though, isn't it? If we continuously ask if a policy or practice is sustainable, we are at least asking the right question. Eventually we will move away from asking the wrong questions and using obsolete models.

For example, consider the emphasis, in forecasting tourism demand, on *arrivals* and/or *expenditures* as dependent variables. One of my life goals, as yet unrealized, was to formulate a sustainable theory of tourism promotion based on tourism *yield*. Simple examples from the island of Bali can illustrate the concept of tourism yield.

One tourist area, Nusa Dua, was created as an enclave of five-star hotels for several reasons. The area is close to the airport, comprised scenic but marginal land, and the inhabitants were barely able to produce subsistence livelihoods. There was also some concern that tourism growth would alter the balance of the culture in Bali, in areas where tourism was already established, and the idea of an enclave would somewhat isolate this effect. The result is a collection of beautifully designed hotels with every amenity, but very little of the cultural interaction that made Bali famous. Reliance on imported products and workers means that there is substantial leakage from the local economy and thus a relatively low multiplier effect for the spending. The local inhabitants of Nusa Dua have gained very little from the high-spending tourists who stay in the enclave, and residents periodically revolt by demanding jobs or blocking the roads to the area in protest. In contrast, the low-end tourists, including backpackers, typically stay in smaller "homestay" accommodations in the villages, with a high proportion of their more meager spending staying in the local community. Relations between tourists and locals are generally much more positive in these areas.

CONCLUSION

As economists, we need to develop and provide better models that represent not just the pecuniary yield of the tourist segments, but also incorporate the environmental and social impact of these groups. Without this knowledge, without these models, we see decisionmakers following the typical approach of trying to maximize arrivals or expenditures, without regard to leakages or differential multipliers. National tourism organizations and consultants often extol the merits of the luxury segment, quoting the high spending of Japanese tourists, for example. Tourism ministers will target "quality" tourists, without the realization that their marketing efforts may produce a zero-sum result since the other national tourism organizations are doing the same thing.

This is a challenge that I would like to throw out to the younger generation of tourism economists. Stop trying to emulate the work that has been done and think outside the box. At a recent tourism economics conference in Chiang Mai, I was disheartened to hear the response of a young graduate student when queried about the method used in her paper. She replied that they copied the method used in an article in *Tourism Management* (case closed, no further discussion). It was interesting to see that, even though the study problem demanded a different method, a wrongly applied technique from a paper published in a major journal was sufficient to quell the criticism.

When frustrated like this, I try to remind myself of the compassion of my favorite colleagues and mentors. We are reaching out with tourism programs into many regions of the world where English is a second language, yet we are requiring our students to read classic tourism literature and pressurizing them to publish in the major journals, in English. We might devote more efforts to translating important works. After all, I learned much about interpersonal relationships from "The Little Prince," which lost little in its translation. We also could follow up on an idea of Kaye Chon, to find the innovative works, the "jewels" written in other languages and translate them into English and other languages, so that our literature has a broader domain.

Soon this type of argument will seem incredibly obsolescent, as books and journals fade into the background. The younger generation appears to disdain reading; instead, we must get their attention with a video, a game, or an experience, a PowerPoint structure supplemented with attention-getting visuals to compete with TV and the web. My students use a free web-based e-book with automated labs and quizzes, with options to purchase audio mp3s of the text, flashcards to study, and pdf downloads of individual chapters.

Those of us who love books, who love to read, and who enjoy the written word will become gradually irrelevant. I do not write this in despair, just in recognition of the changes that I see. Barring some sort of Luddite backlash, the world will become increasingly technologically dependent, with people focused not so much on the big screen TV (3D notwithstanding), but on the Star-Trek-like handheld pads through which their life will flow, at least conceptually. Hopefully we will create the space in between, and teach our students to see their true purpose, within that space, in which the issues that really matter can arise.

Chapter 8

From Steamboat to Tourism Economics

James Mak
University of Hawaii at Manoa, USA

James Mak is professor emeritus of economics at the University of Hawaii at Manoa and a fellow with the University of Hawaii Economic Research Organization. He came to Hawaii in 1970 after receiving a PhD in economics from Purdue University. His teaching and research interests focus on tourism policy analysis from an economics perspective. In addition to his latest tourism book, *Developing a Dream Destination, Tourism and Tourism Policy Planning in Hawaii* (2008), he previously published *Tourism and the Economy: Understanding the Economics of Tourism* (2004). He has served on the editorial board of the *Journal of Travel Research* and still sits on the editorial board of the University of Hawaii Press. He derives great pleasure from using economics to unravel the mysteries of tourism. Email <jmak@hawaii.edu>

INTRODUCTION

I wonder how many of the contributors to this *The Discovery of Tourism Economics* volume were formally trained and began their careers as tourism economists? I imagine not many. Even at my own institution—the University of Hawaii at Manoa—which currently has eight PhD economists

The Discovery of Tourism Economics
Tourism Social Science Series, Volume 16, 101–116

ISSN: 1571-5043/doi:10.1108/S1571-5043(2011)0000016011

who devote a significant amount of their time in research and/or teaching in tourism, most drawn to tourism from other fields in economics. The American Economic Association does not recognize tourism as a distinct field; hence, besides being scholars of tourism, I and others, who are not in the School of Travel Industry Management, are engaged in diverse academic pursuits.

I arrived at the University of Hawaii in the fall of 1970 after obtaining a PhD degree in economics from Purdue University, Indiana. I was hired to teach in a hot field at the time—cliometrics, which applies economic theory and quantitative analysis to the study of history. Among US economic historians, I am still best known for the research and coauthored book (Haites, Mak and Walton 1975) on the economics of Mississippi River steamboats before the Civil War. I never would have guessed in graduate school that what began as a first-year research paper in a required one-year economic history class at Purdue University would become standard reference on the antebellum "transportation revolution" in American economic history textbooks. My stated plan in graduate school applications was to study economic development and international trade. Having grown up in China and Japan, I was especially interested in the development experiences of emerging countries in Asia. To paraphrase a famous line from a poem by Robert Burns, the best-laid plans of mice and men often go awry.

The year 1970 was also a major election year in Hawaii with federal, state, and local political offices up for grabs. The gubernatorial campaign was especially heated. The Republican candidate, Circuit Court Judge Samuel King, mounted a vigorous campaign against the incumbent Democratic Governor John Burns who refused to publicly debate his opponent on the issues, having famously said, "any damn fool can take stands." Judge King's daughter, then in college on the East Coast, took a leave from her studies to return to Hawaii to help her father's campaign. While home, she visited with the chairman of my department and asked if he could help her find a professor who might be willing to direct a readings course for her on Hawaii's economy. The chair asked me and I agreed, even though I had stepped off a plane from Chicago just a few weeks ago and knew very little about Hawaii's economy. She and I would learn together. Judge King did not win the gubernatorial election; years later I would appear before him (now a US district court judge) as an expert witness in an antitrust case involving allegations of illegal pricing in the Honolulu tour bus industry.

Putting together the readings course was surprisingly enjoyable, as it took me off-campus to survey available resource materials on the local economy, and it also gave me the opportunity to meet quite a few people in town who were very knowledgeable about America's 50th and newest state. Aloha! Welcome to Hawaii. "Ol' Man River" might just as well be on the moon.

After the semester was over, I thought to myself, if Judge King's daughter was interested in learning more about Hawaii's economy, surely there must be many more like her among our own student body. Why not develop an undergraduate course and add it to the department's regular course offerings? I did. Happily, on one of my visits to the Bank of Hawaii research library in search of teaching materials, I met my future wife who was a librarian there. (I asked her where I might find a good place to eat lunch downtown, and her boss suggested that she take me to the bank's cafeteria.) Prophetically, Econ 311—Hawaii's Economy—was a big hit among our undergraduate students. Indeed, while cleaning out my office for retirement from the university last fall, I found a term paper in my files submitted by one of the first students in that course; it was written by the current (in 2010) president of the Hawaii State senate and a successful candidate for a Congressional seat. I sent it to her and she responded with a thank-you note and recalled how much she enjoyed the class. As important as tourism had become to Hawaii's economy, a significant part of the course naturally focused on the economics of tourism in Hawaii. The university's other upper division campuses in Hilo on the Big Island and at West Oahu would later offer their own versions of the course. It would take me another 30 years to develop a separate course on tourism economics.

In 1972, Robert Ebel (colleague and former classmate in graduate school and now lifelong friend) and I began writing an every-other week column on Hawaii's economy for Honolulu's morning newspaper. None of our other colleagues would accuse us of pretending to be Milton Friedman or Paul Samuelson (both Nobel laureates), whose weekly op-ed pieces were featured in the *Newsweek* magazine, but many local readers found our economic way of thinking about Hawaii's issues novel, and at times, even provocative. In one column on tourism, we suggested that a hotel room tax (Hawaii did not have one then) would not seriously hurt the tourism industry and would be preferable to raising the state's broad-based general excise tax. In another, we explained that putting a moratorium on new hotel construction on the Big Island until average annual occupancy rates reached 80% as hoteliers and environmentalists wanted would not achieve long-term "quality" tourism growth for Hawaii. Surprisingly, not one person ever called or left a threatening message on our voice mail. (Years later I did receive such a message when I suggested that a US$5 per person admission fee at the Hanauma Bay Nature Preserve should be levied on both residents and tourists if the purpose of the fee was to generate revenues and reduce attendance at the preserve.) Perhaps we were just being ignored. The *Honolulu Advertiser* paid us a flattering sum of $30 per column. It was not a lot of money even in 1972–73 considering the number of hours it took to write a single column. I once calculated that we were not making the equivalent of the state's minimum wage. Each column took so long to write because economists, generally, are notoriously inept at explaining their ideas to laymen. Over time, we did become better at writing for noneconomists, a skill that would become very valuable in our careers. Many of the best columns were revised and packaged in a thin paperback in 1974 that was used in the state's community colleges. The newspaper columns ended in 1974 when Bob Ebel and I both accepted visiting appointments at Purdue for a semester and he decided not to return to Hawaii and instead embarked on a very successful career in the nation's capitol. He has been the biggest supporter and promoter of my tourism research ever since. For me, a comic book on the economic history of Hawaii would follow in 1978. Much later, a textbook on Hawaii's economy would be published by the State Department of Education in 1989 and used in the public schools. Both were products of collaboration with two friends from the University's Center for Economic Education who greatly stimulated my interest in promoting economic literacy among the state's K-12 teachers and students. For three years in the mid-1980s, I served as the volunteer executive director of the Hawaii Council on Economic Education.

TOURISM RESEARCH

In just a few short years after my arrival in the islands, my involvement in the community multiplied. During the first global energy crisis of 1973, and at the request of the Hawaii Legislature, I was on loan to the legislature for one session to help lawmakers investigate the oil companies doing business in Hawaii. Lawmakers wanted to know if the long lines at the gas pumps were the result of a conspiracy among the oil companies to withhold gasoline supplies. We found no conspiracy. Soon afterwards, I was invited by the Hawaii Visitors Bureau (HVB) to be a member of its Research Committee. That invitation launched my career as a tourism economist. However, I was not the first faculty member in my department to do research on the economics of tourism; my colleague Moheb Ghali was already doing excellent work developing and testing regional economic models that incorporated tourism as a distinct sector. His models of Hawaii's economy enabled him to perform interesting simulations on the effects of alternative tourism policies on the economy. In one article (1976), he noted that while tourism contributed to the state's economic growth, it also contributed to the instability of growth. Hawaii's economy has become more volatile with tourism. My own research will have a more "micro" flavor.

The HVB Connection

Hawaii has had a tourism bureau since 1903. The first one was named the Hawaii Promotion Committee; the name was changed to the Hawaii Tourist Bureau in 1919, and finally to the Hawaii Visitors Bureau in 1945. As an organization whose primary mission was to promote tourist arrival to Hawaii, its research mission—or more accurately, data collection and generation—was often overlooked. The Hawaii Promotion Committee began collecting tourism statistics around 1911 and it and its successor organizations strived constantly to improve them. Beginning in 1950, the HVB formed a Research Committee "to direct the collection, dissemination, and improvement of visitor statistics." The Research Committee met regularly (several times) each year; its members, except for the director and deputy director of HVB's research department, served *pro bono* and were drawn from the industry, state and county government agencies, and academia. Over the years, Hawaii's tourism statistics were widely regarded to be among the best in the world. Being an island destination, where every person arriving had to come either on a ship or plane, definitely made it easier to keep track of numbers. A few cynics contended that Hawaii's statistics were the best because everybody else's was so bad.

During the many years that I served on the Research Committee, helping to review its data and refine its collection methodologies, I came to regard highly the quality of HVB's statistics. They were also very comprehensive. Through its three survey programs—the basic data, the tourist expenditure, and the satisfaction—the Bureau collected information on arrival numbers, trip duration, repeat visitation, daily spending, satisfaction, tourist origin and personal characteristics, and the like. Survey instruments were occasionally revised to reflect changes in the tourism market place. Processed data were made widely available and were free through the public library. Over time, HVB's data became more important to the state than to the Bureau; in 1997, state lawmakers transferred the research program to the State Department of Business, Economic Development and Tourism, when the Hawaii Tourism Authority was created.

To an applied economist like myself, HVB was a treasure trove of potential tourism research data. In the 1970s, few academic economists (anywhere) were engaged in tourism research. Evelyn Richardson, the director of the Research Department at the HVB, kindly allowed me to access the raw survey data for research purposes while keeping confidential the most sensitive personal information. How could I give up such an opportunity? Steamboat economics or tourism economics, it was still economics, and the tourism data were right at my door. Tourism was beginning to explode around the world, yet it was little understood by policymakers and shunned by academics. I jumped at the opportunity. So did some of my graduate students who used the HVB data to write their PhD dissertations.

The first paper using this data was published in *Journal of Travel Research* in 1977 and compared tourist daily expenditures using data from two separate data collection programs. HVB's expenditure program asked a sample of tourists to record their purchases in a diary each day during their stay; the satisfaction program sent questionnaires to selected samples 30 days after their visit and asked them to recall the amount they spent while vacationing in Hawaii. Econometric analyses of the two sets of responses found that the recall method tended to underreport their spending. A subsequent paper (Mak and Moncur 1980a) analyzed their decision to use travel agents to make trip arrangements; another (Mak and Moncur 1980b) examined destination choice and length of stay in each destination when traveling to multiple destinations. A 1987 article coauthored with Pauline Sheldon (from her PhD dissertation) determined the likelihood of a tourist purchasing a prepaid package tour (as opposed to traveling independently). The last two would become topics of separate chapters in my book, *Tourism and the Economy: Understanding the Economics of Tourism* (2004).

The three articles demonstrated that consumers behaved in a manner consistent with individual utility maximization. Whether or not they were aware, they were using cost-benefit analysis to make choices when they travel. The implications for the tourism industry are substantial. High-speed computers and the Internet will eventually reduce demand for travel agents and change their traditional roles. As more people gain travel experience, they will demand less inclusive prepaid package tours and opt instead to go independently or purchase stripped-down package tours. If a destination wants tourists to stay longer, it must develop more attractions. While these views were hardly news to economists, it was still important to demonstrate that economics can improve our understanding of tourist behavior and contribute to better tourism business management and the design of policies.

The State of Tourism Economics: The Early Years

In my initial review of the state of the art in tourism economics research in the 1970s, I found the landscape quite barren. A hot topic was tourism multipliers, which put forth the notion that money spent on tourism trickles down throughout the economy as the initial expenditure triggers subsequent rounds of spending and respending, creating more income and jobs. Tourism seemed to be a good candidate to put many developing countries on the path to economic growth. It could do the same for local communities as well. The idea was so fetching that the World Bank had (but no longer) a department of tourism in its Washington DC offices. (I even made a recruiting visit as a potential job candidate.) Soon, an army of people was calculating and applying tourism multipliers and touting the potential economic benefits of tourism, festivals, sporting events, convention centers, and so on. I was guilty of doing some of that myself. Some studies were pretty shoddy, and even quality work was too often misunderstood and misused. I actually heard from one person in the tourism industry who opined that a dollar spent by a tourist generated six dollars of income in Hawaii (a more accurate figure was less than one dollar, including the multiplier effects). Beginning with Brian Archer's (1977) seminal work, the flow of research on tourism multipliers or impact analysis continues unabated. Only a few tourism scholars were questioning whether tourism's social costs might exceed its social benefits.

In my literature search, I was impressed by a few studies that later were to influence my own research. Although they were published in obscure places, they are still worth reading today. One of them was Mitchell's (1970) article titled "The Value of Tourism in East Africa" published in the *Eastern Africa Economic Review*. I found it particularly appealing because, as economists, we always regard tourism's real impact on the economy as the difference between the actual state of the economy and the hypothetical state (i.e., its counterfactual) if there were no tourism. Mitchell explained that resources employed in tourism have alternative uses, and if there were no tourism, these resources would be employed in other economic activities. Thus, he wrote, "If all resources are priced at their opportunity cost, the net value of tourism will consist of (1) indirect taxes [commodity taxes] on goods purchased by tourists, *plus* (2) receipts to government for services provided, *less* (3) the cost to government of providing the services used by tourists and promoting tourism" (pp. 4–5). That would provide the minimum estimate of the net value of tourism. Of course, some employed resources may have zero or very low opportunity costs; for example, the economy may have very high rates of unemployment and hence all or part of the income of the workers currently working in this industry is a net gain from tourism. The bottom line is that its net value to the economy is much less than what is usually stated in conventional impact analyses. What I found most insightful about Mitchell's article was how important tourist taxes play in the net value calculation.

Another article that drew my interest was Gray's "Towards an Economic Analysis of Tourism Policy," published in *Social and Economic Studies* in 1974. He noted that since every destination has unique attributes, economic rents are created and these rents should be extracted (taxed away) for the benefit of the residents of the destination. ("Economic rent" or simply "rent" is income derived by the owner of a scarce resource above and beyond what is necessary to induce the owner to offer it for use.)

It is unfortunate that Gray is not among the group of contributors to this *Discovery* volume. An economist at Rutgers University with a specialty in international trade, he began to study tourism because it was a natural extension from trade in goods to trade in services. He was the first to type tourism either as "sunlust travel" or "wanderlust travel." His categorization was an oversimplification to be sure, but I found it useful because destinations like Hawaii and other tropical places that offer "sunlust" travel face many competitors with similar tourism products, and over time their market power quickly becomes eroded as the number of similar destinations continues to increase. This has tremendous implications for policymakers. His article (1982), "The Contributions of Economics to Tourism" in *Annals of Tourism Research* was the first major essay to identify the economic concepts and tools—economic rent, public goods, market segmentation, demand sensitivities, and cost-benefit analysis—needed to understand tourism. Much of my own work in tourism has applied the concepts and tools that he identified.

Finally a consultant report written by Princeton University economics professor William Baumol (Mathematica, 1970) compared the amount of money spent by the state government to provide services to tourists and the industry, taking into account direct and indirect revenues and costs to the public treasury. I found the study illuminating for several reasons. First, it showed that tourists who spent more money per day generated higher revenue–cost ratios than those who spent the most amount of money during their trip. Thus, from the standpoint of the public treasury, it was better to attract upscale, big spending tourists even if they stayed fewer days than budget-minded ones who stayed longer. (In those days, not many people thought much about the fact that big spenders also tend to use more of a destination's resources and generate more waste and thus leave a bigger environmental footprint.) Attracting upscale tourists is the current strategy of the Hawaii Tourism Authority. Second, arrivals to Hawaii generated more revenues to the state treasury than the money spent on them. I have always been surprised that not more destinations have tried to ascertain if tourists paid their own way as far as the pubic treasury is concerned. Third, Baumol warned that costs to service tourists tend to rise faster than revenues generated from them, hence it was important to update the study from time to time.

I was commissioned by the State Department of Planning and Economic Development to do a follow-up study in 1978 with additional analyses on the Neighbor Island counties (*State Tourism Study: Public Revenue-Cost Analysis*). There has not been another one done since. Many have cited Baumol's report as reason for not levying a hotel room tax in Hawaii since tourists already covered the cost of public services they consumed. Baumol, however, emphatically pointed out that his study "cannot lead to the conclusion that a tourist tax is either desirable or undesirable." Paying for public services used by tourists is not the only reason to tax tourists.

By now it should be obvious that my interest mainly lies in using the analytical prowess of economics to evaluate tourism policy, particularly tax policy. Among the hodge-podge of tourism research projects that I have worked on in my career, the topic that has attracted the most attention has been taxation. When the US Advisory Commission on Intergovernmental Relations (1994), the editors of *Encyclopedia of Taxation and Tax Policy* (Max 2005), and Dwyer and Forsyth (2006) ask you to write papers on the taxation of travel and tourism, it is probably fair to conclude that you know something about it. Fortunately for me, it is a topic of interest to both economists and tourism scholars and practitioners.

Taxing Tourism

No subject in tourism generates more heat than taxation. Unfortunately, discussion on its merits often generates more heat than light. Very little has been based on solid empirical analysis. Over the years, I have tried to provide some of that analysis.

It is still widely believed that destination politicians find it easy to tax tourists because they are transients and do not vote. The proliferation of tourist taxes around the world since the 1980s gave credence to that perception, but that perception is not entirely correct. Even if tourists are unable to vote against the enactment of taxes imposed on them, the local business owners who serve them can, and they often form well-funded, politically powerful interest groups to defeat or delay efforts to tax tourists and the industry. For example, the US timeshare sector has been extremely successful in defeating attempts by state and local governments to levy taxes on timeshare occupancy (Kwak and Mak 2009). The US timeshare industry now enjoys a sizable tax advantage over the traditional lodging (hotel) sector. In 2010, the cruise ship industry successfully lobbied Alaska's governor and the state legislature to cut the $46 head tax on cruise ship passengers after the tax was enacted by a citizen ballot initiative in 2006 (Jainchill 2010a). A spokesperson for online travel agencies that are engaged in legal fights against US local governments who want them to pay hotel room taxes on the retail rather than the wholesale prices of the rooms rented, recently stated that "Taxes raise prices. As a matter of principal, generally we think taxes on tourism are a bad idea" (Baran 2010). The group is now lobbying Congress to pass national legislation to prohibit such taxes.

Not everyone believes taxes on tourism are always a bad idea. In some localities, the lodging industry has enthusiastically supported the imposition of hotel room taxes to pay for tourism promotion and the construction and operation of convention centers. For a number of years, the US tourism industry has lobbied hard to persuade Congress to pass the Travel Promotion Act that would levy a head tax on tourists from visa-waiver countries to fund promotion of foreign travel to the United States. President Barack Obama signed the bill into law in March 2010. Sometimes taxing tourism is an idea that even the industry can embrace enthusiastically.

Ultimately, in formulating tourism policy, the well-being of destination residents is paramount. In *Tourism and the Economy* (2004), I explained that there are four reasons why destinations tax tourism:

1. It diversifies their sources of tax revenue. Because demand for tourism is sensitive to economic growth, including tourist taxes in the local revenue structure contributes to the system's revenue elasticity.
2. Taxing tourism is one way for destinations to get back what they spend to provide public services to tourists. Economists call it tax exporting.
3. Taxes can correct for market failure. When prices set in private markets result in either too little or too much of some activity, taxes are a way to set the prices right to encourage the right amount of the activity. Environmental taxes are one example. Another example of market failure is the inability of the tourism industry through collective efforts to raise the desired amount of money to pay for destination promotion. Because destination promotion is a public good, the incentive is for everyone to

try to free ride on someone else. Taxing tourism is one way to ensure the desired amount is raised equitably.

4. And the most controversial, it extracts economic rent. A former mayor of Honolulu put it in another way (Keir 1973:A1): "No one quarrels with the right and logic of government to demand royalties such as for oil in Alaska. A hotel room occupancy tax is no more than a request for royalties from entrepreneurs and businessmen who are mining our natural resources—our beautiful climate, our sun and surf, our flora and fauna ... Even if tourists are paying a 'fair share of expenses' there is nothing wrong in charging the tourist who enjoy the cream of our resources a little bit more for that privilege." Many countries impose entry or departure taxes to extract rent from tourism.

The hotel room occupancy (or bed) tax is currently the most widely employed tourist tax around the world. Hawaii's statewide transient occupancy tax was enacted in 1986, and it took years of debate before it was passed. When I was searching for empirical literature on hotel room taxes in the mid-1970s, I found nothing. I was commissioned to write one for the interim tourism advisory council which was established by legislation in 1976 to help draft the state's first tourism plan. The industry and some labor groups opposed such a study, but the advisory council felt that there was sufficient legislative and public interest to go ahead. The paper, coauthored with my undergraduate student, Edward Nishimura, concluded that there might be few room nights lost if the state were to enact a modest hotel room tax and that such a tax can generate additional tax revenues to the state but at a small cost in lost private income. Chuck Goeldner, then editor of *Journal of Travel Research*, later asked me to let him publish it in the journal (1979) even though it had already been published in another journal. In 2000, it was reprinted in Clem Tisdell's *Economics of Tourism* volume in Edward Elgar's *International Library of Critical Writings in Economics* series. But the paper had no immediate policy impact as the completed tourism plan (1980) did not include a recommendation to levy a hotel room tax.

Two of my colleagues and I prepared another hotel room tax study commissioned by the State's Tax Review Commission in 1984 using different data and more sophisticated methodology. A revised version of that paper was later published in *National Tax Journal* (1985) and was also reprinted in Tisdell's volume. The paper came to the same conclusion as the earlier one that a modest hotel room tax would not harm the industry and would be preferable to a broad-based tax such as raising the state's general excise tax. The burden of a broad-based tax would fall more heavily on residents than on tourists. I would like to think that the study helped the legislature to finally pass a hotel room tax (5%) in 1986. But there were other circumstances involved; the state was looking for money to greatly increase funding for tourism promotion and to pay for a "world class" convention center. After the tax was enacted, a follow-up study was done to ascertain what actually happened (1992); it turned out the tax had no negative impact on the industry whatsoever as the entire tax was (forward) shifted to tourists. In my latest book, *Developing a Dream Destination, Tourism and Tourism Policy Planning in Hawaii* (2008), I concluded that enactment of the hotel room tax was good for Hawaii and for the industry. Hawaii's county governments, which bore the heavier share of the burden of providing public services to tourists but could not levy their own hotel occupancy or sales taxes to pay for them, received a share of the hotel tax revenue. Previously, they had to beg the legislature for appropriations. The industry achieved what it wanted most, more money for tourism promotion and a $350 million convention center. Of course, tax rates had to be raised in 1994 and again in 1997 to pay for those items, but compared to tax burdens in other major destinations around the world, Hawaii was still not a high-tax destination.

After closing the chapter on hotel room taxes, I turned my attention to other tax and finance issues in tourism. These include recent studies of timeshare occupancy taxes in the United States and Hawaii, Alaska's head tax on cruise ship passengers, using the local property tax in different ways to appropriate gains from tourism, the effectiveness of using tax incentives to encourage hotel renovation and investment to rejuvenate an aging destination (Waikiki), the merits of charging admission fees at unique tourist attractions (Hanauma Bay Nature Preserve) to generate revenues to pay for maintenance and to ration attendance, and development exactions in tourism. I believe that there still are a lot of opportunities to study the appropriate role of government in a tourism-dependent economy.

Tourism in Asia and the Pacific

Over the years, I never lost interest in Asia. It helped that I was living in Hawaii and working at the University of Hawaii, which has a strong interest in Asia and the Pacific. I spent the summer of 1995 as a visiting professor at Kobe University, Japan (right after the Great Hanshin earthquake); the campus was located not much more than a 15-minute walk from the house I lived in when I was a child. Following my visit, another visiting faculty from Carnegie Mellon University and two of our colleagues at Kobe University edited a book of short, accessible essays (and cartoons) explaining the mysteries of everyday economic life in Japan from an economics perspective. Among other things, why are there no personal checking accounts in Japan? Why is gift-giving so popular? Why are vending machines so prevalent? Much to our delight, *Japan, Why it Works, Why it doesn't* (1998) has been adopted by quite a few Asian and Japanese studies programs in American colleges and universities.

My first foray into Asia-Pacific tourism research was a jointly authored article with a friend from the University of British Columbia, Ken White, who, among other things, has also written about Antarctic tourism. The paper, titled "Comparative Tourism Development in Asia and the Pacific," was earlier presented at conferences in Honolulu and Cairns and subsequently published in *Journal of Travel Research* in 1992. While it was not methodologically a sophisticated paper, we analyzed outbound travel at a time when there was little scholarly work done on outbound tourism. National outbound statistics were scarce and, when available, often of poor quality. Japan was an exception. For obvious reasons, countries were (and remain) more interested in inbound travel, which brought in foreign exchange, than outbound, which expended foreign exchange. When it comes to trade in tourism services, apparently it is better to receive than to give. Statistics indicated that inbound tourism was growing faster in Asia and the Pacific than any other region in the world. While income was (and is) the most important determinant of outbound travel, our research discovered that another important reason for the rise in Asia-Pacific tourism was the liberalization of outbound pleasure travel adopted by a few major Asian countries, especially Japan. We noted the differential effects of currency restrictions and quantity restrictions (outright ban) on travel; outright bans are more restrictive than currency restrictions. The study highlighted the importance of national barriers in the flow of international tourists.

Since the 1980s, China has been liberalizing outbound travel by allowing its citizens to visit preferred countries under its Approved Destination Status program. In a forthcoming article (Arita et al 2011), my colleagues and I find that while countries receiving Approved Destination Status reap a bonanza in mainland Chinese visitor arrivals, the Chinese version of selective travel liberalization both stimulates overall travel from China and diverts travel to newly designated countries from all other countries, including those which have received earlier preferential designation. How a country chooses to liberalize travel matters. In the case of China, the study suggests that as more countries are designated as approved destinations, there is less obvious reason for China to keep the program.

Comparing outbound travel among countries requires new measurements and terminologies. In *Tourism and the Economy* (2004), I coined the term "travel propensity," which is calculated as the ratio of total number of departures to population (thus, its value can exceed 1; a few countries have 1). A country may send large numbers of tourists abroad, but it may also have a huge population resulting in a low travel propensity. In our 1992 study, we found that, among countries in Asia and the Pacific, Japan sent the largest number of tourists abroad in 1987 (6.8 million departures) but it had a lower travel propensity than Singapore (0.7 million departures), New Zealand (0.6 million departures), Australia (1.6 million departures), Hong Kong (1.4 million departures), and Malaysia (2.1 million departures).

The concept of travel propensity can be applied to any population subgroup in a country or region as well as to whole countries. My colleagues and I used it in our study of the impact of population aging on future Japanese travel abroad (Mak, Carlile and Dai 2005; Sakai, Brown and Mak 2000). While the articles were well regarded by tourism scholars—the 2000 paper received the 2001 Best Article Award in the *Journal of Travel Research*—I have been puzzled by the lukewarm interest in this issue by the travel industry. With population aging rapidly in the developed countries (and even in China), I had hoped that the travel industry would have taken preemptive steps to study the potential effects of this coming mega social change and begin developing strategies and products in anticipation of future changes in demand. The effects of demographic change on travel are already visible in Japan.

I have also been keenly interested in the liberalization of the passenger transport sector around the world and its beneficial impact on travel and tourism. US domestic airline deregulation began in 1978 and has now spread to other parts of the world, reducing the cost of travel to consumers and stimulating travel and tourism. I remember describing the spread of airline deregulation from the United States to Japan, Australia, and Europe at a workshop on Japan's "New Economy" in the 21st century, and one of the participants made an astute comment that the trend was inevitable because, where there is head-to-head competition, the inefficient regulated national airlines could not compete against the more efficient deregulated private airlines. Privatization and deregulation were foreseeable outcomes of globalization, and those countries that drag their feet will have to live with long-term subsidies that could become politically unacceptable at home. Along with the proliferation of "open skies" agreements that strike at the heart of protectionism in international aviation, air transport liberalization has played a significant role in the democratization of travel. Economists have long preached that government regulations that protect incumbent businesses from competition generally lead to less service, higher prices, and lower quality.

In two recent articles (Mak, Sheehey and Toriki 2010; Blair and Mak 2008), I suggested that the 124-year-old US Passenger Vessel Services Act, a cabotage law that prohibits foreign-registered cruise ships from carrying passengers between US ports unless they also stop at a foreign port, has outlived its usefulness and should be repealed. I am pleased to learn that the Greek Parliament has just repealed a similar law on non-EU registered cruise ships operating in Greece (Jainchill 2010b). Brazil had done the same via a constitutional amendment in 1995 (Nweze 2006:101).

In stark contrast, my colleagues and I found (Blair, Mak and Bonham 2007) that when the US Department of Transportation (DOT) granted antitrust immunity to two dominant Hawaiian inter-island air carriers—Aloha and Hawaiian Airlines—to allow them to collaborate to set (i.e., cut) total seat capacity on major inter-island routes after the terrorist attacks of 9/11 sharply reduced demand for tourist travel, air fares spiked upward despite assurance by the two airlines in their application to the DOT that fares would not rise. Moreover, fares continued to rise for some time after the expiration of the cooperation agreement between the two airlines. Tacit collusion apparently replaced overt collusion. The moral of the story is that competition is good for consumers and antitrust immunity protects sellers often at the expense of the public interest. Indeed, the value of competition is one of the enduring messages of my steamboat book.

CONCLUSION

"Aloha," when used as a greeting in Hawaii, means "hello" and "goodbye." On December 31, 2009, I officially "retired" from the University of Hawaii. Forty years have quickly slipped by during which a large part of my career was devoted to teaching, research, and being personal witness to the rise of a new field in tourism—the economics of travel and tourism. I am delighted to have been at the starting line. It has been a fun ride, more so since I had the privilege of working collaboratively with so many colleagues and friends. Except for the two tourism books mentioned here, most of my published articles owed much to their help and collaboration. To them I extend my sincere appreciation. *Mahalo nui loa.*

In closing this reminiscence, I am reminded of the uplifting farewell written by one of my favorite newspaper columnists, Ellen Goodman, who also "retired" this year; she wrote, "I will let myself go. And go for it." I too may be letting go, but don't count me out quite yet. My current project is an essay reinterpreting Richard Butler's tourism area life cycle from an economics perspective. Like academic careers, tourism destinations may rise and fall. The article argues that the optimum tourism development policy is not one whereby Big Brother (the government) intervenes to save tourism at whatever cost, but one that examines tourism not in isolation but as part of a larger economy.

I strongly believe that the future of our field is brighter today than when I started because tourism has become a more important global phenomenon, with *caveats*. I see two main challenges that also present opportunities. First, we need to work harder to get tourism economics into the classroom at our universities. The state of tourism economics education, especially at US universities, is deplorable. Last year I conducted an informal survey of over 2,000 subscribers to the University of Hawaii School of Travel Industry Management TRINET list serve on course offerings in tourism economics at their school. Not one respondent from the United States, including my own university, reported that tourism economics is a required course for their tourism majors either at the undergraduate or graduate level. Responses were more encouraging from European, Australian, New Zealand, and a few Asian subscribers. Obviously, many schools still believe that tourism economics education is not really that important even if tourism is important to their national and local economies. The field will not be taken seriously until we change that attitude. Some TRINET respondents noted that their programs have had difficulty finding qualified teaching faculty. Admittedly, it is more difficult to teach an entire course than it is to write an occasional article on a narrow subject in tourism economics. It has been said that necessity is the mother of invention; if tourism programs were to require their students to take tourism economics, faculty would become more readily found. Demand will create its own supply.

Second, research on tourism economics should not become so esoteric that it becomes a club activity only to be shared among a few tourism economics scholars who are able to read them. Our job is to use economics also to uncover the mysteries of tourism to inform noneconomists—managers, policymakers, and the general public. Failing that, we will become irrelevant. I can go on at length about research opportunities, but I see many more "low-hanging fruits" out there than when I first began my career as a tourism economist. The opportunities are limitless.

Chapter 9

My Journey through the Worlds of Tourism

Tanja Mihalič
University of Ljubljana, Slovenia

Tanja Mihalič is a professor at the Faculty of Economics, University of Ljubljana (Slovenia). Her education in economics, business administration, and environmental policy was obtained at the universities of Ljubljana, Indiana (USA) and St. Gallen (Switzerland). She started in the field of classical tourism economics and moved to environmental economics and management in tourism. She collaborates with many national and international tourism organizations, and is a member of AIEST and Tourism Sustainability Group of the European Commission. Her voluntary and professional involvement in a real world of ecolabeling and sustainable tourism management has played an important role in her work. She is a head of Institute for Tourism and some tourism masters degrees that include the European joint Erasmus Mundus European Master Tourism Management (EMTM). Email <tanja.mihalic@ef.uni-lj.si>

INTRODUCTION

This chapter is about tourism and economics and my journey through both of them. It is about my passage through the three different worlds of academic research, tourism business practices, and the teaching of the economics of tourism.

The Discovery of Tourism Economics
Tourism Social Science Series, Volume 16, 117–130

ISSN: 1571-5043/doi:10.1108/S1571-5043(2011)0000016012

I was born in Slovenia, the northern part of former Yugoslavia, on the sunny side of the Alps that separated the Central European market-oriented capitalistic countries from the socialist economy of my country. I completed my education at the Faculty of Economics at the University of Ljubljana (FELU) in a country with a sociopolitical system of self-management based on social ownership where private property, market forces, and the service industry of tourism were not valued. During the years of my education, exchange rates for the Yugoslav currency dinar made international travel expensive and journeys were limited to bordering countries Italy (renaissance, jeans, and shoes), Austria (coffee, chocolate, and skiing), and other Yugoslav republics, mainly along the Adriatic coast (beaches and romantic sunsets).

I graduated in international economics believing in a new economic order that would be based on fair and equitable economic and social principles, and thus close the gap between developed and developing nations. I thought my work would be connected to international trade. My first real job experience came from a big import–export company. Unfortunately, my duties were limited to paperwork and my experience of foreign places was restricted to typing names of countries on export invoices. I then took a job with a large corporation where I was responsible for controlling and planning the financial flow of its subcompanies, including large hotels and one tour operator. I learned how expensive investment in tourism superstructure can be and that international development aid had two sides. On the one hand, hotel ownership was a nightmare because hotels were built with money from the World Bank and international loans at a time when the dinar was losing its value in relation to the dollar. On the other hand, hotels were a blessing because they were a source of cash and foreign exchange for the head company. From a financial perspective, the tour operator was no problem at all.

The FELU offered me the position of a research assistant, and although I was reluctant to leave the company, I chose an academic career above a corporate one. Despite the fact that I did not experience much in the way of tourism during my studies, I choose the area of tourism as my academic field. I was convinced of my choice by Janez Planina (1927–2003). He began in 1961 to lecture on the economics of tourism and in 1985 still had a vision of developing the field at FELU and of the economic and social tourism potential for Slovene and the world economy and society.

When I entered tourism research, I read the pioneering tourism work by Hunziker and Krapf (1942), *The Outline of General Tourism Science*. This book was an attempt by Swiss scholars to develop a general theory of tourism. The work was economic based and significantly influenced the tourism economics doctrine in Slovenia. It became clear to me that tourism cannot be perceived by economic instrumentation only and that tourism is not a single discipline or theory, but a multidisciplinary platform of knowledge. Nevertheless, from my viewpoint as a researcher of economics, it is not the multidisciplinarity but the duality of economics and noneconomics in tourism that is relevant. Tourism is studied by either noneconomic scientists or economists who draw from their specific backgrounds and focus on their specific discipline.

To gain an understanding of all aspects of tourism, I took a tourist guide exam and began to work in this field in order to understand tourist activity from this point of view. Simultaneously, I visited restaurants, hotels, and agencies to become familiar with the management in tourism companies. My first undertaking was to discover how restaurants calculate their costs and how they create a market price for a cup of coffee. This simple project was quite challenging for a beginner. Then pricing methods for food, accommodation, and travel packages followed. The first full research project in which I took part was forecasting tourism demand in the Yugoslav Republics, including Slovenia. It was discomforting to discover that holidays in Slovenia were for some European tourists an inferior commodity, but the coefficients of elasticity were statistically significant. The work culminated in a monograph published in Slovenia. At that time, there was no call for international publications at FELU and in Slovenian academia as a whole. The system that encourages academics to publish according to impact factor criteria has only affected the Slovenian region in the past decade.

While gathering research, I also began practical lectures on the subject of tourism. My classes set a foundation by clarifying basic characteristics of the field and definitions of tourism. The United Nations World Tourism Organization (UNWTO) was helpful in this regard. St. Gallen University also had a helpful definition of tourism, stating that "Tourism is the integrity of relationships and phenomena which stem from the traveling of people, in which this traveling doesn't incur permanent residency." Or more poetically, "Tourism is the realization of a desire for traveling which dwells within each of us" (Planina 1961:9).

JOURNEY THROUGH TOURISM STUDIES

My desire to travel through the world of tourism studies had begun at that point and it has lasted a quarter of a century so far. In the beginning, my studies were led by Janez Planina, a geographer and economist and one of the first professors of tourism in Slovenia and in Yugoslavia. A remarkable man and mentor, he had studied under one of the legendary founders of tourism research, Kurt Krapf at the University of Bern in Switzerland. Krapf had a significant impact on tourism studies both at FELU and in the Central European region. When I joined academia in 1985, the focus was still largely commercially and economically tinted; tourism was seen as a source of foreign currency and a benefit to the national economy. In addition to this balance of payments motive, interest was turned to the tourism multiplier. The ability of tourism to multiply its economic effects was widely studied in order to find arguments in favor of expensive investments at the beginning of tourism development. Other popular topics included theoretical discussions of the impact of tourism on development, employment, and the valorization of natural resources, and the study of tourism rent.

Tourism economics has been continuously present as a study program at FELU, and its content has always been clear and unambiguousness: tourist supply and demand, market and price structuring, the economic impacts of tourism, and tourism policy. Macroeconomic and developmental economic issues were influential in the 1960s and 1970s. The criticism of the potential of tourism to contribute to economic growth (and wider development) at the regional or country level was not yet coded into the discussion, although it was already a topic in the wider tourism academic community abroad.

Janez Planina (1963), the author of *Tourism Economics* (published only in the Slovene language), suggests that tourism economics is not a general name for a general theory about tourism, but is a field of study that observes and explores the economic causes and effects of tourism. Economics interprets tourism from two angles: first from an economic perspective looking at the national economy, and then from a business perspective looking at tourism companies. In the time of Planina's book, the environmental problems of tourism were not understood or discussed, and environmental economics of tourism was not part of the discussion. Because of Planina's attachment to the Marxist doctrine, a large part of the book was devoted to the study of tourism rent from location and from its attractiveness, predominantly natural.

I began my journey into tourism studies at a time when there was still no Internet and no globalization. After World War II, when Yugoslavia was founded, domestic tourism was prevalent and foreign tourism had only just began, and only the noneconomic impacts of tourism were being studied. Traveling was seen as a means of promoting peace in the world, increasing understanding and brotherhood among Yugoslav nations and nationalities, a means of recreation for the laborforce, and a means for improving the state of health and expanding the cultural horizons of the population. The economic impacts were secondary considerations. Later, with the development of international tourism, the sociopolitical environment of tourism changed. The deficit in the balance of payments in Yugoslavia, and the related need to increase the inflow of foreign currency, forced top political figures to acknowledge the foreign currency potential of attracting foreign tourism. Thus, the economic dimension of tourism was finally recognized more than 20 years after Switzerland and nearly 30 years after neighboring Austria. Later, other economic impacts of tourism were recognized, and tourism research activities developed. The foreign exchange and employment impacts were two particular areas that were emphasized in political circles, along with a lesser emphasis on tourism's ability to contribute to the economic development of less-developed regions. However, economic policies during the 1970s and 1980s were supporting the development of traditional industries and not tourism, which remained only a declared priority. At the end of the 1980s, social and political changes suddenly left the tourism industry entirely subject to the forces of the market. In 1991, when Slovenia separated from Yugoslavia and became an independent, capitalistic, and democratic country, the development of tourism became an interesting subject, and in the society the attractiveness and its image also increased. However, the World Economic Forum (WEF) concluded in 2009 that governmental prioritization of tourism development in Slovenia, which is crucial for successful policy and development, was still quite low. In line with that, till today this academic study still has not reached the image of the more traditional disciplines, although tourism as a research and consultancy field is attracting many academics from other disciplines.

These were the conditions under which my journey began into the academic world of tourism at FELU in Ljubljana, Slovenia. Not until the fall of socialism in Europe and the advance of globalization was the university able to intensify efforts in internationalization of our study programes. I, however, succeeded in spreading my international wings a bit sooner.

Scientific curiosity, and the desire to verify what I found to be the general economic legacy at FELU, drove me to study part of my Masters degree abroad. A scholarship enabled me to spend a semester at Indiana University in the United States and gain new knowledge by studying for a master of business administration (MBA). While there, I became aware of the digital divide as I entered a world of personal computers and quantitative methods. I prepared calculations for my masters degree in which I researched the role of production factors of labor and capital with the help of Cobb Douglas's production function in case of Slovene tourism industry. At that time, it was my top subject, but I never returned to it again. I wanted to pursue environmental economics and tourism.

Cobb Douglas was only an emergency exit for me. I had wanted to study tourism from an environmental angle for my MBA, but because I could not find literature or mentors, I had to postpone the topic to a later time. The topic remained a challenge when I came to pursuing my doctorate, but I had decided to study economics, the environment, and tourism. I had to find my sources abroad. Through the library exchange, I found an article by Claude Kaspar (1973), a professor at the University of St. Gallen, which was entitled "Tourism Ecology: New Dimension of Tourism Science." In the article, Kaspar defined tourism ecology as the science of the relationship between tourism and the environment. These were the beginnings of a discussion that later culminated in the sustainable tourism development concept. It was difficult to maneuver between the "undeveloped" terminology as I sailed among Slovene, German, and English articles. I was caught by expressions such as environment and natural environment, surroundings, milieu, space, and ecology, when I shaped my doctorate model. In that period, the discussion of environmental impacts was largely limited to the natural environment, and even today tourism literature often uses the term "environment" as a synonym for natural environment.

I summed up Kaspar's idea of tourism ecology as the science of the relationship between tourism and its environment, this "ecological environment" I defined in a broader sense as not only natural, but also social and cultural. The only source on which I could rely at that time was the World Bank which stated that the term "environment" "refers not only to the naturally occurring milieu ... but also extends to the sociocultural milieu which man has created ..." The term "ecology," which is usually used in reference to the biological sciences "is used to refer to the relationship between organisms and their environment, including, most especially, the man-environment relationship" (1975:5–6). It became clear to me that tourism ecology had an economic dimension; tourism was not only seen as an economic phenomenon, but also had an ecological dimension (natural, cultural, and social). There was also a third dimension: the sociopolitical dimension. This dimension refers to environmental awareness and pressures toward ecological behavior, and includes political opportunities to create and implement ecological policy. The identification of these three basic elements of tourism ecology formed a triangle model that is still relatively advanced and relevant today because it includes the areas of political science, political economy, and political ecology. Current models of sustainable development and the indicator models based upon them have confirmed that the implementation of ecological policy is not possible if there is not a sociopolitical dimension built into the model.

After reading Kaspar's article, I chose to study at the University of St. Gallen, and in 1991 I planned to leave for a semester of doctoral study in Switzerland. As my husband was working on an international project for a Swiss company at the time, moving from a dinar-based Yugoslavia to a Swiss franc-based Switzerland would not be an economic problem for us. Unfortunately, when Slovenia proclaimed its independence in June 1991, the Yugoslav army closed the borders and we were not able to leave the country. During the 10 days of war that followed, I spent some of my time in a shelter as Yugoslav aircrafts flew overhead at supersonic speeds breaking the sound barrier above my home city of Ljubljana. I finally arrived in Switzerland in August of 1991 and my classes started in September. I remember a professor of environmental economics telling us that people are good by nature and that their behavior is fundamentally good. Thus, environmental problems will be solved on ethical grounds: people simply need to gather information and understanding about the environmental impacts of their behaviors. Coming from a war, it took me some time to see the possibility of this approach. I felt that the freedom to discuss ethical behavior might start after certain conditions, particularly material, are met. In 1991, Switzerland had a per capita income of US$ 35,000, in Slovenia it was five times lower, and in Yugoslavia (including Slovenia) it was 10 times lower (UNSD 1990). Not surprisingly, the debate on environmental ethics in Yugoslavia was nonexistent. There was much more potential to solve environmental problems in neoclassical market-based economics, where one could charge for the use or consumption of environmental resources.

At the time, the head of the Tourism and Transport Institute at the University of St. Gallen was Claude Kaspar, Hunziker's successor. After completing my doctoral semester at this institution, I stayed on as a doctoral student of Kaspar's and worked for a half a year on a project, to transfer tourism knowledge from Switzerland and Austria to Eastern European countries. Because I took over several tasks at the institute, the work on my doctorate was slow, and I recall my anxiety every time a new work was published in the field of tourism and ecology, environment, or place. With the help of the institute's library, I obtained new material as soon as possible and read it immediately to see if an author had beaten me to the punch, and made my research obsolete. Luckily, the articles dealt with the ecological issue primarily from the sociological point of view. The economic issues were present to a somewhat greater degree in Austrian professional literature on tourism; however, it did not deal with complex economic and ecological and environmental theory.

During my doctoral studies, I came across the idea of environmental economics and also discovered the occurrence of environmental damage theories. I was particularly influenced by Swiss welfare economist Bruno Frey's (1985) work, *Environmental Economics.* A great deal of his thinking found its place into my research work. According to him, environmental damage can be explained by three sets of theories: system, growth, and behavioral. Environmental damage occurs because the existing socio-economic centrally planned or market system does not work because of the growth of the world population and economy and because of the improper environmental behavior resulting from the absence of environmental ethics and knowledge. It is possible to apply theories to the field of tourism and from these applications derive economic and administrative instruments for removing and reducing environmental damage. In his works, Frey extends the horizons of economics beyond standard neoclassical ones by including insights from other disciplines, including political science. This probably caused the birth of the sociopolitical dimension as an element of an ecologically friendlier tourism development in my model.

The above-mentioned model was published in *Environmental Economics in Tourism* (Mihalič and Kaspar 1996). Christian Laesser, then assistant at the institute, translated my awkwardly written German text into an academic style, and for that I am grateful to him and am still in his debt. The book was published in German language and *Annals of Tourism Research* reviewed the book, writing,

> within the field of sustainable tourism research, it is fair to say that up to now a comprehensive treatment of economic theory and derived policy issues has been missed. In this sense, the author's contribution represents a step forward towards the maturation of a still young field of tourism research. (Hjallager 1997).

I no longer had to worry that someone else would publish my ideas before me, but the book was published only in German (and later Slovene), and did not reach the Anglo-Saxon academic circles. However, a partial summary of this work was later published in *Ecotourism Policy*, edited by Fennell and Dowling (2002).

During my stay in Switzerland in the 1990s, the Tourism and Transport Institute at the University of St. Gallen celebrated 50 years of teaching and researching tourism. An international meeting for German speakers took place to discuss the relationship between science and practice. At FELU, the tourism multiplier and the idealized positive national economic impacts of tourism was still influential. The debate advanced in *Tourism: Blessing or Blight* (Young 1973), was just starting to penetrate. The Swiss approach, however, was both practical and business-orientated. Although there was not yet any talk about destination management at that period, it was later developed in the form of corporate functions by Thomas Bieger, Kaspar's successor. The institute studied economic impacts at the full circle destination level. However, there was not any concrete research or models in the field of environmental economics and tourism, neither in Switzerland nor in the world community. During that period, most discussions about environmental issues were held in noneconomic science circles.

In 2002, I spent part of my first sabbatical at the University of Surrey as a visiting researcher, and prepared some English texts based upon FELU doctrines of tourism economics. The classification of the economic impacts of tourism were summarized as follows: on the balance of payments, on general economic development through the multiplier effect, on regional economic development, on inflation and deflation; on employment, and on the valuation of environmental goods and their positive and negative connections to overall economic development. The text was edited by Sharpley and Telfer (2002) for their book *Tourism and development: Concepts and issues.*

During my time in Switzerland, I was invited to join the Association Internationale d'Experts Scientifiques du Tourisme (AIEST). Although Slovenia had replaced the weak Yugoslav dinar for the Slovenian tolar, the exchange rate was still against me. The membership fee for AIEST would have been more than half of my FELU's socialist salary in 1991. But economic change in Slovenia after independence was taking place at an enormous speed, and I joined the organization in 1992. At a conference in Paris (1992), I met many of my international tourism colleagues for the first time. The conference discussed the topic of the "Freedom of traveling," which was a good topic for me because it referenced one of the themes of my doctoral research. According to the environmental growth theory applied to tourism, it was easy to see that tourism demand was growing fast and with it environmental damage and consumption of environmental resources. In addition, environmental systems theory suggests that traveling cannot be perceived as a free commodity. If so, traveling would mean the free consumption of the environment. It raises the question of the equity of this consumption when only a relatively few people can freely travel, with most from wealthier countries (even though all people possess the same right—if not ability to exercise that right—to travel and consume resources). Inspired by the work of Boulding (1985), who suggested birth certificates as an economic instrument to regulate the world's biggest problem (population), I developed the tourist certificate. Although the models for the implementation of environmental pollution certificates already existed at that time, and even though models existed for the implementation of certificates for the use of space for tourism purposes, the tourist certificate was a prominent novelty. It was met with interest only in narrow circles, but I still believe that this is one of the best potential economic instruments for wider environmental issues in tourism. The certificate could help control tourism growth, seasonality, and other environmental impacts, as well as wider developmental problems that are addressed by sustainability, including world poverty and equity. The implementation of tradable tourist certificates would mean financial compensation would be available for not traveling, and this would bring money into less-developed countries to stimulate future development programs, promote a new international economic order, and provide a way for tourism to contribute to closing the gap between rich and poor countries.

Through membership in AIEST, I was present at the congress in Bariloche, Argentina (1993) when Richie and Crouch presented a model of tourism competitiveness (Ritchie and Crouch 1993). On the basis of this model, I published an article in *Tourism Management* (Mihalic 2000), which defines environmental destination management as a factor of competitiveness. The article introduced a systematic division between environmental management on environmental impacts (EI) and on environmental quality (EQ). Both aspects are interrelated. The cost-saving aspect of environmental impacts management is an incentive for managers, while environmental concern is what is appreciated by potential tourists. As a factor of destination competitiveness from the standpoint of potential tourists, the EQ of a destination is important and influences destination choice more than EI. However, from the standpoint of a destination manager, EQ is more complex and expensive to manage than EI.

In 1999, the AIEST congress was in Slovenia. The focus of the congress was economic-orientated: "Tourism as a Strategic Development Factor for Places." For Slovenia, as a new destination, the theme of tourism competitiveness was still quite present and we were influenced by De Keyser and Vanhove's (1994) model of competitiveness. Years later, the Integrated Competitiveness Model by Dwyer and Kim (2003) was also calculated into Slovenia's thinking. Although older studies of competitiveness based on the Yugoslav legacy of tourism economics had acknowledged the significance of natural resources, the focus was on traditional economic benefits and costs. Not until the change in thinking after 1991 was the competitive significance of natural, cultural, and social resources put to the forefront of sustainable tourism development.

After my time in Switzerland, I collaborated with many other universities, but I never found such a strong presence in the field of tourism economics as I had at the universities in the ex Yugoslav republics. In 2009, I came closest to an institutional economic discussion of tourism when I spent a part of my second sabbatical at the University of the Balearic Islands, Spain. I was impressed by their master in environmental economics program, where I gave lectures about competitiveness and tourist confidence indices (TCI). I had become interested in TCI survey and brought it to Slovenia as a result of a collaboration between FELU and UNWTO after 2000 and my role in the UNWTO Education Council. In comparison to traditional demand forecasting methods of tourism economics, confidence indices have many strengths. At present, UNWTO calculates and publishes TCI for world tourism and for world regions, but Slovenia is the only country that has applied the same methodology at the country level. TCI proved itself during the global financial and economic crisis of 2007–10, as it helped Slovenian tourism industry to forecast tourism demand in uncertain economic conditions. During my stay at the University of Balearic Islands, I was also invited to join the International Association for Tourism Economics, and this will certainly lead me to new places in the near future.

JOURNEY THROUGH THE EXTERNAL WORLD OF TOURISM

So far, a large part of my academic research work was dedicated to ecological or environmental awareness and ecolabeling in tourism. However, I was also gathering knowledge outside academic circles in this area. In large part, this knowledge emerged from the tourism industry and in collaboration with international environmental organizations and consultants. The story of this development begins, however, at the beginning of my tourism career. At the start of my career, I read widely on the field of tourism. Discussions about mass tourism and the works of Jost Krippendorf, particularly *Holidaymakers* (1984), had an impact on me. Even though the book was written for a general audience, it provided me with elements for a different kind of thinking about tourism outside mainstream thinking in tourism practice. Thinking about alternative tourism, soft tourism, responsible tourism, and other types that wanted to surpass the negative impacts of mass tourism kept me busy for quite a while. Some of my thinking was presented in Buhalis and Costa's (2006) book in a chapter on nature-based products, ecotourism, and adventure tourism.

In Slovenia, the first time we publicly spoke of nonmass tourism was at a conference at the end of the 1980s. At a round-table discussion, there were tourism executives from the Slovene airline (which was then ordering large airbuses to increase its business volume), as well as travel organizers, and hotel managers who counted on tourism in big numbers. At that meeting, my thinking about moving away from mass tourism was unanimously rejected. In 1992, I gave a lecture on eco-labeling at the Alpe Adria tourism fair in Ljubljana. Many (including some who had been at the previous roundtable) listened carefully, but did not support the discussion about the significance of the EQ of Slovene beach destinations. Tourism employees never even heard of Blue Flag Program for placing flags on beaches to indicate the quality of the water and environment. After the lecture, some participants even suggested that EQ thinking would harm Slovene tourism. Water quality had been strictly confidential during that period of socialism, and results were accessible only by the office of President of the Republic. Yet, on a global market, water quality had already started to influence tourism demand.

After independence in 1991, Slovenia opened its borders to environmental consultants and knowledge began to pour in. This new environmentally friendly climate enabled me to contribute to a strategy for tourism development in 1993. It was first time that sustainable development would be considered. At the time, it was more declarative than actionable, but this was progress, and it was the beginning of ongoing collaboration with the public sector in the area of tourism development strategies. The government became interested in the EQ of tourist destinations in order to improve the competitiveness of Slovene tourism. A request landed on my desk by the minister in charge of tourism to help bring in the Blue Flag Program for beaches and thus reopen the discussion about water quality.

Environmental behavioral theory and ecolabeling had matured and began to come into practice, even though more in the public than in the private sector. For years, I had been trying to bring in the Blue Flag Program, which is an international symbol for clean and ecologically run beaches and marinas. It had been difficult to do, because for a long time there was not any understanding by business of its importance. I had also worked to gain national acceptance into the Foundation for Environmental Education (FEE), which runs the Blue Flag Program. It had not been easy because Slovenia was a new country, a country where a war had taken place in the recent past and there was an ongoing war in its vicinity (in the Balkans). Nevertheless, along with some colleagues and environmental and tourism enthusiasts, we succeeded in founding a nongovernmental organization in 1995 that became a part of the FEE international organization. That same year, we received our first Blue Flag marina and a year later our first Blue Flag beach. I became president of the national FEE organization and remained the head for 12 years. Great thanks go to the sacrificing and dedicated colleagues who made great shifts toward more environmentally friendly tourism in a time when this was not even talked about in the public and private sector. In academic circles, however, the discussion was vibrant, and I published quite a few book chapters, conference proceedings, and papers during the same period.

Through my work in nongovernmental environmental organizations and eco-labeling, I joined the executive board of FEE and was named to the Tourism Sustainability Group and the Tourism Advisory Committee of the European Commission where, since 2002, I have been working on the sustainable development of tourism, more active European and Slovene tourism policies, and the sustainable and economic image of tourism. In 2007, this work materialized in a community document, *Action for More Sustainable European Tourism* (TSG 2007). It was one that helped to map the field for a new European tourism policy.

JOURNEY THROUGH THE EDUCATIONAL WORLD OF TOURISM

The pedagogical mission was the one that I was really most interested in when I decided to turn my back on a corporate business career and return to FELU. I gave lectures on a number of tourism subjects touching on business and economics at my home university and at universities abroad. The subject of tourism economics has always been a priority in our program. Even today, it is a fundamental subject to which all students have to listen to when deciding to pursue tourism major. The content still follows the legacy and views of Planina, but is continuously updated. From the mid-1990s, the field of environmental economics in tourism was also discussed, and it soon became a trademark of FELU tourism studies.

After 1991, great efforts were put into the internationalization of our studies, and the effort resulted in the UNWTO "Tourism Education Quality" accreditation and increased cooperation with the Education and Science Council of the organization. Internet and Internet networks, such as *Tourist Research Information Network* (TRINET) have also helped to bring the academic and scholarly community together. In 2008, we started a masters program in English, the European master in tourism management in cooperation with the University of Girona and the University of Southern Denmark. Only those who have tried to create a joint program among such different European countries will understand how much time, effort, and innovativeness all three universities needed to start the program. It won the prestigious quality Erasmus Mundus brand from the European Commission in 2009, and we have kept the subject of tourism economics at the forefront. The program also contains strongly represented content from the field of environmental economics in tourism and is shaped around new tourism education values, with sustainability as one.

CONCLUSION OR FUTURE JOURNEYS

During the time of my journeys through the worlds of tourism, the economic discussion of tourism has spread (Stabler et al 2010). Today, the tourism researcher is only a small element in a universe of multidisciplinary, system thinking, or holistic approaches. Within the multidisciplinary circles of emerging knowledge, economics has become just one of the disciplines that contributes to the understanding of the world of tourism. The boundaries undergo constant change and expansion and are sometimes blurred. New economic branches and their way of thinking are now entering tourism studies. My journey began with an understanding of well-defined boundaries of micro- and macroeconomics, expanded into the field of international, development, and welfare tourism economics in the 1980s, and today focuses on environmental economics or more holistic, ecological, and institutional economics. The research field that I mapped in the tourism ecology field (Mihalič and Kaspar 1996) has been broadly extended. New authors try to define new approaches to tourism-related problems and talk about economics of climate change, economics of biodiversity, or sustainability economics, and even "sustainomics" or travel ecology. I have been through many economic theories, branches, fields, and quasi-fields as my world has changed, but how much this researcher can advance in a lifetime remains a question that only the future will answer.

Chapter 10

A Serendipitous Journey: From Mathematics to Policy via Economics

Pauline J. Sheldon
University of Hawaii, USA

Pauline J. Sheldon, a native of England, came to Hawai'i, USA in the late 1970s and earned a doctoral degree from the University of Hawaii's Economics Department in 1983. She was a faculty member in tourism for 27 years at the School of Travel Industry Management at the same institution until her retirement in August 2010. She has authored over 70 works in various aspects of tourism including 2 books entitled *Tourism Information Systems* and *Wellness Tourism: Mind, Body, Spirit, Place*. She has served on the editorial boards of 10 of the refereed tourism journals and has been instrumental in building the BEST Education Network, TRINET, and the Tourism Education Futures Institute (TEFI). Her academic journey has passed through mathematics, business, information systems, economics, and sustainability. Her interest in creating a better world through tourism and tourism education overlaps with her interest in the growth of human consciousness and planetary awakening. Email <psheldon@hawaii.edu>

INTRODUCTION

Tourism as a field of study lends itself to multi-, inter-, and cross-disciplinary research. These approaches have characterized my research and as such my

The Discovery of Tourism Economics
Tourism Social Science Series, Volume 16, 131–146

ISSN: 1571-5043/doi:10.1108/S1571-5043(2011)0000016013

academic journey is unlike most in this book. My academic life began with the study of mathematics, moved to business and information systems, then to economics, and later to sustainable tourism policy. Economic thought has sometimes been in the foreground of my research and sometimes in the background, but it has always provided insight and understanding to the problems I chose to investigate. This chapter describes the web of people, institutions, and events that led to a life that I never could have planned. In hindsight, I notice how it has been ushered along by the inspiration of others and by serendipitous events. This chapter begins with my early impressions of tourism and moves through my varied research directions and contributions, and the networks and people that have inspired me.

Early Impressions of Tourism

I have always lived in tourism destinations. I began life in a small village near Crewe and Chester in the United Kingdom. Crewe is one of the hubs of the British rail system and Chester is a popular destination for its connection to Roman times, its Cathedral, its Tudor architecture, and its cheese. Our family moved to the North Wales coast for my last two years of high school where mathematics and physics were my main areas of study. North Wales is a quintessential tourism destination with its Snowdonia mountain range, Conwy Castle, the Victorian resort of Llandudno, and the caravan parks and strip development in Rhyl. Tourism affected our lives in good and bad ways; we were always glad when the congestion subsided after September 1 and life returned to "normal."

Two other early experiences with tourism impacted my future career. First, my parents decided that my three siblings and I should become more worldly and independent by experiencing life in other countries through twinning programs. Every summer each of was twinned with a child in a different European country for the first part of each summer. Then eight youngsters descended on our home in Cheshire for a very chaotic second part of the summer where we learned to appreciate other cultures, sometimes find tolerance and harmony in diversity, sometimes fight, and usually to be flexible. These were some of the most meaningful experiences growing up and they influenced my life profoundly. They fostered independence and a love for other cultures and languages; and on later reflection, a love for that kind of travel.

The second experience occurred in 1972 before I left to study mathematics at Southampton University. I took a summer job as a barmaid at Butlin's Holiday camp in Pwhelli, Wales. These camps specialized in inexpensive vacations for British working class families, with all meals and entertainment on site. The accommodation was in sparse cabins and life was regimented by Red Coat guides. It was a loud and alcohol-infused environment. As I pulled pints in the Blinking Owl bar and observed the events and people around me, I decided I would never work in that kind of environment again.

I mention these two experiences as they created a subconscious inner dialog about the pros and cons of tourism before I turned 20. I did not realize that I would revisit them later in my career. I graduated with my mathematics degree in 1972. Being aware that teaching was a likely career, I did a postgraduate certificate in education at Exeter University. Upon graduation in 1974, I took a job teaching mathematics and physics in a comprehensive school in Stone, Staffordshire. It was a difficult school with many challenges. During a vacation, I escaped to a meditation retreat in Switzerland where I met the man who I would later marry (William Remus). He took a job as an assistant professor in the College of Business at the University of Hawai'i, USA. I soon followed and we have been based in Hawai'i ever since.

The contrast from England to Hawai'i was immense. My first drive along Waikiki's beachfront and its massive tourism development both enthralled and shocked me. Here in the middle of the Pacific was the world-famous, glittering mile which I was now making home. There were plenty of tourism phenomena to observe, be curious about, and, even though I did not know it yet, to research. Wanting to diversify my career from teaching mathematics, I enrolled in an MBA program where two events influenced my future career. First, I had an economics professor (Jack Klauser) who inspired and challenged me to master economic thought. I found the subject enjoyable and challenging and refreshingly practical, after the abstraction of mathematics. Second, I read George Young's (1973) *Tourism: Blessing or Blight*, which contained many of the topics of my preuniversity thoughts about tourism. These two events coalesced my desire to learn how to apply economic analysis to study this phenomenon that had surrounded me most of my life and was again in Hawai'i.

ENTER ECONOMICS

After completing the MBA, I enrolled in a doctoral program in economics at the University of Hawai'i to begin my study of tourism economics in earnest. My program included all the core economic theory, a focus on international economics, and also a minor in information systems management in the College of Business, a field that was about to influence tourism dramatically. James Mak was my PhD advisor and the major influence during my doctoral studies. He had written prolifically on tourism and his work impressed me for its relevance and its rigor. He and other economists at University of Hawai'i Economics Department (Larry Miller, Sumner LaCroix, James Moncur, and Walter Miklius) were influential as I worked through the various stages of the PhD program, completing it in 1983.

Hawai'i is one of the best places to study tourism economics—not only because of these professors, but also because tourism is responsible for about a third of its gross state product. Further, the state tourism agency, Hawai'i Visitors Bureau (which later became Hawai'i Visitors and Convention Bureau), had excellent historic data on tourism. Under the directorship of Evelyn Richardson, numerous data sets were rigorously kept. The historic data on tourism arrivals and expenditures, as well as tourist satisfaction and behavior, were excellent and available to PhD students for their studies. Jim Mak suggested that I use Hawai'i Visitors Bureau data to analyze why tourists chose to travel on package tours and not independently as a dissertation topic. At that time, the majority of east-bound tourists arrived as part of a package, whereas most west-bound groups traveled independently. The study analyzed the different types of tour packages and the demand for and the supply of tour packages. To understand the demand for package tours, we used logit models and data from Hawai'i Visitors Bureau expenditure survey. On the supply side, we used commodity bundling theory (Adams and Yellen 1978) and industry structure concepts to gain insight into why travel intermediaries packaged their products. The study predicted that tour packages would become either highly specialized tours where economic rents were paid for the knowledge of the operator or unique tours, or high-volume, low-cost tours for budget-conscious tourists. In 1987, the dissertation won the Travel and Tourism Research Association (TTRA) William Keeling Dissertation Prize and subsequently generated two articles: the supply-side analysis was published in *Annals of Tourism Research* (Sheldon 1986) and the demand-side analysis was published in *Journal of Travel Research* (Sheldon and Mak 1987).

While writing the dissertation, I also worked as a graduate research assistant in the School of Travel Industry Management (TIM) on the same campus. The dean of the school, Chuck Gee, became another important mentor providing many opportunities for a challenging career in the TIM School. He was very connected to the travel industry in Hawai'i and was eager to encourage his faculty to become involved with various committees and associations where they could learn and share their expertise with decisionmakers. I worked on a number of Hawai'i-related projects with him and learned a lot about tourism decisionmaking in the state.

After completion of the PhD in 1984, I took a joint position as assistant professor at the TIM teaching tourism courses, and also at the College of Business teaching statistics and quantitative methods. This joint position quickly converted to a 100% assistant professorship at TIM—and I was home. Its early Dean Edward Barnett had uniquely positioned the school to include all aspects of tourism industry management, including transportation, hospitality, and tourism management. Working with colleagues from different backgrounds such as Juanita Liu (regional geography), Dexter Choy (economics), Fredrick Collison (transportation), and Morton Fox (foodservice), in addition Dean Chuck Gee (Dean) provided endless opportunities for interdisciplinary research.

Turgut Var visited the school and impacted my career progression significantly. He encouraged me to work on linear programming and other quantitative applications to tourism problems. We later published a paper on tourism forecasting (Sheldon and Var 1985). This paper examined the state of the art of tourism forecasting, and evaluated the various qualitative and quantitative techniques. I published more papers on tourism forecasting, examining the methodological differences between forecasting expenditures and arrivals (Sheldon 1990, 1993a). Other visitors to the school, including Brian Farrell from Canada and Doug Pearce from New Zealand, brought with them new insights and research opportunities. The joint support from the Economics Department, the TIM School, and the destination itself, prepared me well for an academic career in tourism.

Putting Down Roots and Branching Out

Hawai'i and TIM provided a very fertile ground in which to become a successful tourism academic. In the early 1980s, Hawai'i tourism was booming and approaching the mature part of its lifecycle. Despite success based on its unique environment and rich cultural heritage, there were many unresolved issues that needed research. The tourism infrastructure was starting to show the signs of age; there was a lack of authentic cultural experiences for tourists particularly in Waikiki, a product that catered mostly to the mass market, and the native population who were feeling disenfranchised from tourism. Much work was needed to move the destination forward in an era when new destinations were constantly emerging. TIM faculty and other academics on campus were often tapped for advice and input to the various policy bodies in the state. We worked with the industry's main tourism agencies such as the Hawai'i Visitors and Convention Board, its Research Committee, its Data Processing Committee, and later the Hawai'i Tourism Authority. In 1990, I was involved with the founding of a new Hawai'i chapter of TTRA, bringing together key industry and academics to discuss main issues affecting the state.

Perhaps the most satisfying of these projects for me was the 2002 "Governor's State Task Force on Sustainable Tourism." This Task Force brought together about 20 different stakeholders from all Hawai'ian islands and all sectors of the community. Its charge was to define a sustainable future for Hawai'i tourism and the path to achieve it. After two years of intense work and consensus building, we generated a very thorough report on destination sustainability, including a monitoring process of indicators and responsible agencies. The study's implementation was delayed as the state's political leadership changed, but many of its recommendations were included in the Hawai'i State Strategic Plan 2005–2015 (www.hawaiitourismauthority.com) that still guides tourism development today.

One pressing issue in Hawai'i at the time was resident perceptions of tourism. The native population and other residents were not responding well to the increasing numbers of tourists and the subsequent development. Juanita Liu, Turgut Var, and I worked on studies to investigate the nature of residents' perceptions of tourism development in Hawai'i. The studies included economic, environmental, and cultural issues and were successful in providing policy insights. Later, I replicated the study in North Wales where residents' displeasure for tourism was due to second-home owners, crowding, and congestion. Another paper, using three data sets (Turkey, Hawai'i, and North Wales), examined cross-cultural differences in residents' sentiment by focusing on attitudes to environmental preservation (Liu et al 1987). Other related studies that I worked on were an examination of professionalism and employment in Hawai'i, a study of Waikiki as a mass destination, another investigating the Chinese inbound market to Hawai'i, and research with Morton Fox examining the impact of food service on Hawai'i's success as a destination.

Chuck Gee was our dean for almost 30 years, during which time he built an excellent school with significant influence, particularly in the Asia-Pacific region. When he retired in 2000, the faculty elected me as the interim dean to follow in his footsteps—a daunting task but one that opened me to many new experiences. In particular, the policy-level meetings I attended during this time intrigued me. Meetings of the Pacific Asia Travel Association (PATA) and United Nations World Tourism Organization educated me about policymaking and how the real issues of tourism development were being addressed. Pure economic analysis did not seem to have much sway in these discussions. This was at first discouraging, but brought an appreciation for the complexities that tourism policymakers must deal with. During this time, my interest in tourism policy issues at a global level grew; issues such as risk and disaster management, knowledge management, destination governance, and environmental and cultural impacts were a few on which I worked. After three and a half years as interim dean, my desire to return to faculty life grew stronger. Six months later a new dean was hired and I happily returned to my faculty position.

In the 1980s and 1990s, TIM played a key role in tourism development in Asia—particularly in China that was just starting to open up to tourism. Chuck Gee was revered as an academic leader in China and other parts of Asia, and the school faculty had many opportunities to contribute to his work in tourism development in Asia. My first visit to Asia was with Gee and Liu to offer seminars to tourism officials in Beijing, Xian, and Guilin in 1987. Seeing the different stages of the country's economy, its politics, and its potential as yet untapped, was fascinating. Other trips followed in other parts of Asia. Later, teaching seminars to Chinese managers and students and introducing the ideas of a free market economy created interesting responses from the students.

Students from all parts of the Asia-Pacific region, often holding senior positions in their country's government, came to study in TIM, often as students in the Executive Development Institute in Tourism (EDIT) an intensive summer program cosponsored by PATA. Teaching in this and similar programs and listening to the participants' experiences taught me about the complexities different destinations were facing in their tourism policy development. In particular, I recall a student from Bhutan talking about his country's plans for tourism in the 1980s. Seeing today how its unique policy approach with the protection of the environment and culture as paramount as part of its Gross National Happiness Index is inspiring.

I have returned to Asia many times to work on projects. In 2004, an ecotourism project with the World Bank in an area close to Chongqing revealed more about how tourism policy was made in China. The project to develop ecotourism around a large lake suffering from intense pollution and nearby factories belching smoke caused the success of the project to be minimal. In the same year, I visited the University of Hokkaido, Japan to work with information technology researchers on tourism projects and to help in founding Japan's national Tourism Information Technology Association. Visits to Malaysia, Singapore, Korea, Taiwan, Indonesia, and India to teach, do research, or speak at conferences were an important balance to my European experience and upbringing and helped me to get a more global perspective of tourism development.

As mentioned earlier, my research path is not one of a traditional economist. My initial research stayed true to my economic training, and focused on understanding tourists and tourism flows through demand modeling and economic forecasting research. In addition to the package tour phenomenon, I also studied the demand for incentive travel and later wellness travel. Studies of tourism expenditure methodologies also followed. But as described above, my focus on the discipline alone weakened as tourism issues in Hawai'i and around the world emerged. I did not follow a linear trajectory of research, but instead allowed the serendipity of circumstances to propel my research journey forward into different areas while keeping my economic training always at the ready.

Information Technology Research

An important and timely research branch began with my interest in information systems management. In 1992, technology was beginning to radically change tourism. Airlines and hotels were investing heavily in computer technology for reservations and operational functions. Distribution channels were dramatically affecting travel agents and other intermediaries who were in fear as the Internet grew and disintermediation of the travel distribution channels occurred. Other types of tourism firms (restaurants, car rentals, attractions) were finding significant cost savings and increased efficiencies brought by computer systems and data networks.

The TIM School needed courses in this increasingly important subject, so I developed a new tourism information systems curriculum, and designed and equipped a computer lab for the students' use. This endeavor required my full-time energy and attention and naturally pulled me away from economics. I was now deep into the understanding of various technologies, such as global distribution systems, property management systems, and point-of-sale systems, and writing proposals to vendors of these systems to equip our lab. We acquired the Sabre system in our lab, which was an awkward, command-driven system requiring myself and transportation colleagues Fred Collison and Kevin Boberg to attend training sessions in Dallas Fort Worth. TIM was one of the first such schools to add this subject to the curriculum.

As the influence of technology on tourism grew, so did my interest in teaching and researching this fast-growing field. I was teaching both undergraduate and graduate IT tourism courses and supervising some PhD students in the Business School who were writing on IT (often with a tourism application). No tourism IT books existed at the time, so I decided to write one. It needed comprehensive coverage of all tourism sectors, such as transportation, tourism, and hospitality, to match the core philosophy of our school (Sheldon 1999). I also wrote an internationally standardized tourism IT curriculum for UNWTO, one of many that Eduardo Fayos-Sola, head of human resources for UNWTO, commissioned to bring quality control to tourism education materials for their member countries. Delivering the course in person in Madrid to groups of students from UNWTO member countries proved enjoyable and challenging, mostly because the technical competence of the students varied so much.

The adoption of technology continued to influence different travel industry sectors dramatically, and the high-tech/high-touch juxtaposition was a topic of much research at the time. My interest in IT research moved quickly from private to public sector applications. I spent my first sabbatical leave in 1994 traveling through Europe, visiting destinations and national or regional tourism offices to understand the IT issues they faced. This resulted in an article in *Annals of Tourism Research* on destination information systems and was the first to address this destination perspective of technology application (Sheldon 1993b). I have subsequently written on IT and knowledge management to handle crises in destinations, on the use of IT to enhance sustainability in a destination, and on mobile technology applications to destinations. A chapter I wrote in Larry Dwyer and Peter Forsyth's *The International Handbook on the Economics of Tourism*, entitled "The Economics of Tourism Information Technology," was an opportunity to marry my two main research areas to date, and analyze the impacts of tourism information technology from an economist's viewpoint (Sheldon 2005).

In the 1990s, I becamc involved with the various initiatives that were developing the field of tourism information systems. One was ENTER: The International Conference on Information Technology and Travel and Tourism, another the International Federation of Information Technology and Tourism (IFITT), and finally *Journal of Information Technology and Tourism* (JITT) which I served as US editor for a while. I recall an Austrian dinner in the middle of winter in the Goeldner Adler Hotel in Innsbruck during an early ENTER conference where Hannes Werthner, Jafar Jafari, and a few others discussed the need for more consolidation of this growing field. The concept of IFITT and JITT were birthed at that dinner. I still serve on various scientific committees and editorial boards related to those associations and follow the development of the field by colleagues such as Dan Fesenmaier, Charly Woeber, Andy Frew, Anna Pollock, and Dimitrios Buhalis. Without a doubt, there is more work to do on the emerging technologies, Internet marketing, website design, mobile technologies, social media, and networking. Information technology continues to structurally change tourism.

A simple IT-related contribution that emerged from my IT path is the Tourism Research Education Network (TRINET), which started in 1998. TRINET now connects almost 2,000 tourism researchers all over the world and facilitates information transfer and dialog on tourism research and education. Before TRINET, such connectivity within the field of tourism scholars was piecemeal, and living on an island it was even harder to connect. At the TTRA conference in Honolulu in 1988, I shared my idea for a tourism network with Jafar Jafari. Such networks were emerging in other disciplines and had proven effective. With Jafari's encouragement and his help in promoting it to colleagues around the world, we launched TRINET to a small test group. After making some decisions about who should be on the list, and whether message traffic should be regulated or not, we opened it up for subscriptions. After over 20 years, it still uses the simple listserv technology where messages drop directly into the subscribers' email box. Suggestions have been made over the years to use a more technologically sophisticated platform for TRINET, and for our 20th anniversary in 2008, Dimitrios Buhalis launched TRINET on Facebook. The original listserv, however, remains the preferred mode. Message traffic on TRINET can be categorized into debates on current issues in tourism scholarship, conference announcements, book review requests, and identification of colleagues working on certain research topics. This initiative gives me a sense of pride, knowing how many meaningful connections have been made between tourism scholars as a result of messages posted on TRINET, and the contribution it has made to tourism research. It has been supported by the School of Travel Industry Management at the University of Hawai'i, *Annals of Tourism Research*, Cognizant Communications Publishers, and other generous donors.

Tourism Education

As I continued on the academic track, the uniqueness of tourism as a field of study, the special considerations of tourism faculty careers, and the publish-or-perish environment for tourism academics took my interest. The multidisciplinary nature of tourism, its lack of a mutually agreed upon academic home, its publishing outlets, the career progression of academics, their disciplinary backgrounds, and many other issues fascinated me and gave rise to some empirical studies that were published in the literature. While this line of research answered some of my questions and generated some publications with interesting coauthors, I felt it was taking me away to read others' work in the area and two decades later returned to these issues with the cofounding of the Tourism Education Futures Initiative (TEFI) with Daniel Fesenmaier of Temple University.

TEFI came out of a serendipitous conversation with Fesenmaier at the TTRA conference in 2006 in Dublin. (My most interesting projects have emerged from serendipitous conversations with good colleagues.) We discussed the need for a shift in tourism education to reflect the seismic, socioeconomic changes in the world. We resolved to act on our conversation and invited a few colleagues and a futurist who were open to this idea to meet together. We first met at MODUL University in Vienna, Austria with about 35 like-minded educators and industry members. There we discussed various possible long-term (20–30 years) world scenarios that could unfold, and how tourism and tourism education would need to adapt. The outcome of the meeting was that however the world scenario unfolds, future tourism leaders will need to be value-based stewards of the destination. At the next meeting in Hawai'i, we defined that set of values: stewardship, ethics, mutuality, professionalism, and knowledge. Two more meetings were held with like-minded educators and industry leaders and a white paper that developed the framework further has been written (Sheldon et al forthcoming). John Tribe, Leo Jago, Karl Woeber, and Janne Liburd have been part of the Steering Committee helping move the initiative forward.

The goal of TEFI is now to provide an international forum within which tourism educators and industry leaders can develop innovative programs to promote global citizenship and optimism for a better world. The challenge is to create foundations and frameworks for educational programs that will be relevant 20–30 years from now. A first step is the creation of a value-based framework for educators that incorporates the five values mentioned above. TEFI continues to work on other critical issues for the future of tourism education, such as faculty development, industry partnerships, and student engagement. It is committed to help to produce responsible leaders and stewards for whatever tourism future may unfold.

Moving toward Sustainability

The final destination of my academic life is sustainable tourism policy. Many serendipitous events occurred along the way to build this interest. The international meetings I attended as interim dean were some of the most important. In particular, the meetings at UNWTO provided insights into the issues that developing countries were facing relative to tourism and development. Involvement in various international meetings, seminars, and think tanks, including a Destination Management Think Tank at UNWTO headquarters, and Tourism Policy Forums at George Washington University broadened my perspective of tourism in different parts of the world. I saw that melding academic research with political savvy was necessary to accomplish change. Collaborations on various sustainable tourism policy projects followed, such as those with Eduardo Fayos-Sola in Sri Lanka, Don Hawkins and Doug Frechtling in Washington DC, and Esteban Bardolet in Mallorca. This last research piece compared and analyzed the policy development of Hawai'i and the Balearic archipelagoes as mass tourism destinations (Bardolet and Sheldon 2008).

Trips to UNWTO in Madrid, followed by visits to Mallorca to work with Bardolet and teach in the Tourism and Environmental Economics Program at the University of the Balearic Islands Tourism, followed by a semester teaching sustainable tourism policy in Seville (my favorite city in Spain), have provided me with much cultural enjoyment and first-hand experience of tourism in Spain. It is a country that knows tourism well, and one that has captivated me. One of my most memorable visits to Spain in June 2008 was to receive the UNWTO Ulysses Prize for knowledge creation. It was an honor and an experience I will never forget.

Another serendipitous event affecting my move to sustainability was the TIM hosting of an annual lecture series on tourism sustainability sponsored by Bill Lane of *Sunset Magazine*. At the 2000 lecture by Bernard Lane, editor of *Journal of Sustainable Tourism*, Michael Seltzer from the Conference Board in New York approached me about an initiative called Business Enterp to host the next BEST Think Tank in Hawai'i in 2002. BEST's goal was to collect and disseminate best practices in sustainable tourism and to create teaching modules on it. The first meeting in South Africa had created modules on tourism marketing, planning and development, and human resource management. TIM and the East-West Center hosted the second meeting of the BEST group and the topics were tourism transportation and tour operations. The meeting brought many academics together with key people from Hawai'i's tourism industry; this inspired me to learn more about sustainability. I soon started teaching sustainability courses after the Think Tank.

BEST continued as an initiative under the Conference Board for one more year and held its third Think Tank on strategic management and events and meetings management at the INCAE Business School in Costa Rica, after which the Ford Foundation funding ended and Michael Seltzer left the organization. Not wanting to see this initiative fold, a few colleagues and I decided to launch it in a new direction and I became the chair of BEST in 2001. We redirected it into an education network called Business Enterprises for Sustainable Tourism Education Network (BESTEN), which holds annual Think Tanks at universities around the world on various subthemes of sustainable tourism. These Think Tanks differ from most tourism conferences in that they included sessions of open debate and meetings to design teaching modules and research agendas using the nominal group technique to consolidate the group's knowledge (www.besteducationnetwork.org). With colleagues such as Larry Dwyer, Deborah Edwards, Janne Liburd, and Leo Jago, the network continues to make substantive and practical contributions to the study of sustainable tourism. On a personal note, working with Larry Dwyer at these Think Tanks was an enjoyable challenge as we tussled to bring order to the thinking of energized and sometimes unruly groups of tourism academics. He and I also coedited a number of special issues of journals that included the outcome of these Think Tanks.

It was becoming clear to me from participating in BESTEN and other sustainability initiatives that the economists' toolbox would not alone further the qualitative development of tourism. While realizing that economic analysis could shed light on many tourism problems, I chose to broaden the scope of my teaching and research to encompass the more holistic study of tourism. Economics has been an important bridge from my mathematical beginnings to the more varied areas I now study. These include wellness tourism, corporate social responsibility in tourism, and tourism education futures.

My personal interest in well-being (spiritual, mental, emotional, and physical), self-discovery, and inner reflection naturally spilled over into my tourism interests. Since my early days at university in England, I have been attracted to understanding more deeply the growth of human consciousness and the connectivity of all life. My own spiritual path of meditation, yoga, breathing, and ayurvedic practices has also guided my life forward over the last 40 years. I have spent a considerable amount of time studying and teaching these practices (most recently with the Art of Living Foundation). Numerous trips to India allowed me to study more deeply the Vedic philosophies that have enriched me and also affected my career direction. Overall this path has brought a sense of wholeness, and a strong desire to make a difference. There is no doubt that this part of my life has provided a background from which my tourism interests expanded beyond economics.

Subsequently I started to write about well-being in a tourism context. Hawai'i has unique wellness resources and many tourists were visiting to improve their well-being through ecotourism, adventure tourism, visits to alternative practitioners or native healers, visits to sacred sites, volunteer tourism, spa tourism, medical tourism, and many others. The state was intrigued by this niche market and has developed it further in its destination strategy. I was instrumental in the founding of the Hawai'i Wellness Tourism Association to bring together the practitioners of wellness with the tourism industry. This proved a successful step in developing wellness tourism as a product in Hawai'i.

My interest in wellness tourism grew when Jafar Jafari and the Mallorcan government invited Robyn Bushell and me to assist in organizing a conference on wellness tourism as part of an innovation in tourism series. An outcome of this conference was the coedited book *Wellness Tourism: Mind, Body, Spirit, Place* for the series *Innovation and Tourism: Connecting Theory and Practice*, edited by Jafari (Bushell and Sheldon 2009). The book includes authors from different disciplines and begins to build a conceptual framework for the academic study of wellness and tourism. Continuing this line of research, in 2009 I visited Victoria University in Melbourne, invited by Leo Jago, director of the Centre for Tourism and Services Research, to contribute to the development of their wellness research program. I anticipate that my future research and writings will continue to reflect these and other interests. Topics such as corporate social responsibility that somehow contribute to the increased quality of tourism, and the well-being of the planet.

Networks

As I mentioned at the beginning, my academic journey has been a serendipitous one; one that has been inspired by many networks of people, organizations, and events. In particular I have benefited from the networks in TTRA, ENTER, PATA, UNWTO, BESTEN, International Academy for the Study of Tourism, and TEFI. They have all brought opportunities to work with fine people from different backgrounds, disciplines, and geographic locations. I was particularly honored when inducted into the academy at its biennial meeting in Savonlinna, Finland in 2003. The academy has provided meaningful interactions with the founders of our field, which have nourished me academically. Talks with Erik Cohen about how he identifies and approaches research topics, and with Valene Smith and Graham Dann about their research journeys, have injected me with renewed appreciation for the theoretical and interdisciplinary nature of tourism studies. In 2008, I was honored to be elected as the president of this prestigious institution and have worked with the fellows and especially the executive committee members Julio Aramberri, Larry Dwyer, Haiyan Song, Rick Perdue, Kaye Chon, and Jafar Jafari (founding president) to serve the academy and continue the good work of previous presidents such as Rick Perdue and Bill Gartner. The TTRA network was also very important to me, as I progressed through my career. The opportunities to serve on the board and to chair the awards program were gratifying experiences. TTRA's recognition of my contributions at the annual conference in Honolulu in 2009, with their Lifetime Achievement Award, was very humbling.

Other network connections have come through the manuscripts I have reviewed for about 10 different tourism journals over the years. Connecting to new ideas in these manuscripts has often inspired me to new projects and new ways of seeing things. Similarly the various opportunities to teach abroad in Spain at the University of the Balearic Islands and the International College in Seville, at the Vienna Institute for Business and Economics in Vienna, Austria, in Australia at Victoria University and Bond University, in Vietnam at Hue University, and others have enriched my life immensely. Networks have been very important to me throughout my career. Living on an island and working in a rapidly growing field has required cooperation. Collaboration through networks seems so necessary in the field of tourism with its complexity of issues and multitude of stakeholders. It may allow us to more successfully navigate our increasingly uncertain future; it has certainly been an important navigator of my career.

There have been some limitations to my academic journey. Perhaps the serendipity of which I write was a limitation in that I did not follow a controlled, linear trajectory of economic research in tourism. Perhaps I could have contributed more if I had—but life is rarely linear. Another limitation is that TIM had no doctoral program and subsequently I have only worked with a few PhD students. More doctoral students would have been stimulating, and may have kept me closer to being a pure economist. Another limitation is the geographic location of the islands being more than 2,500 miles from any other land mass. Trips to conferences for us tended to be more expensive and less frequent. But being in the islands has provided so many good opportunities. Hawai'i has been a wonderful place to study tourism with its cultural and environmental resources, its excellent professionals, and its many challenges to tourism development. Another limitation could have been being a woman in what was initially a man's world. But men colleagues have always treated me with respect, I never once felt held back, and now I also have many excellent women colleagues. Therefore, none of these potential limitations seem to have deterred me in any substantive way.

CONCLUSION

I have now retired from the University of Hawai'i, but the academy, TEFI, research projects, and teaching in select places will continue to engage me. It is difficult to imagine a life without the richness of the people, events, and ideas summarized in this chapter. I have sometimes questioned the research directions that I have taken (and sometimes regretted those that I have not taken). But most importantly, as I reflect on my career, I feel the privilege of being an academic and an educator, and value greatly the serendipitous flow of events and people that have entered my life have enriched it immensely.

Chapter 11

Theory, Econometrics, and Bridge Building in Tourism Economics

Egon Smeral
Austrian Institute of Economic Research, Austria

Egon Smeral is an economist at the Austrian Institute of Economic Research in Vienna and teaches at the University of Innsbruck and the Modul-University, Austria. Areas of research are applied economic theory and politics (especially in the fields of tourism economics, leisure and service sector economics), tourism forecasting and modelling, impact analysis and tourism satellite accounts, designing and evaluating tourism policies programs as well as marketing strategies. He is a consultant to the Austrian Ministry of Economics, family and youth board member of the International Association of Scientific Experts in Tourism; member of the International Academy for the Study of Tourism, the Travel and Tourism Research Association, the Tourist Research Center, the Deutsche Gesellschaft für Tourismuswissenschaft, and the International Institute of Forecasters. Further, he is coordinating editor of the journal *Annals of Tourism Research*, member of the editorial review board of the *Journal of Travel Research* and of the editorial board of the journals *Tourism Analysis*, *The Tourism Review*, *Anatolia*, and *Tourism Economics*. Email <Egon.Smeral@wifo.ac.at>

The Discovery of Tourism Economics
Tourism Social Science Series, Volume 16, 147–158

ISSN: 1571-5043/doi:10.1108/S1571-5043(2011)0000016014

INTRODUCTION

I was born in Vienna, Austria in 1950, a few years after World War II. There are only a few memories left of those times: Vienna was dark, gray, and in ruins; Austria was occupied by the Allied Forces, divided into four military zones. I remember the Four in the Jeep (both in reality and from later movies). In 1955, Austria regained its freedom and the Allied Powers left the country. What took place next happened at great speed: the *Wirtschaftswunder*, the Beatles, and the Roaring 60s came along, but so did the Iron Curtain and the Cold War. Vienna, 60 km away from the frontier of Western Europe to the communist East Bloc was a bulwark, a capital city full of dead-end train stations. During this time I went to school in Vienna and, by end of the 1960s, passed my university entrance exam. After doing compulsory military service in the fall of 1970, I started on a course of economics at the University of Vienna.

My favorite study fields were consumer and foreign trade theory (without then knowing that these research fields are important theoretical approaches to analyzing tourism and would later be useful milestones on my way to tourism economics), before I discovered econometrics as a discipline to apply to economic theory. From the microeconomic perspective, consumer theory at that time was strongly influenced by the neoclassical approach, whereas the macroview was dominated by Keynes and the post-Keynesians. The latter also greatly influenced monetary trade theory with their INTERLINK models (Klein 1971).

I ran through my study courses very quickly and started on my Masters thesis after three years (one needs a minimum of four years for a Masters degree in Austria). In my thesis, I analyzed the effects of exchange rate fluctuations on income and employment. Basically, I learned to model import and export functions and to perceive monetary foreign trade in a macroeconomic context. Through this I created a knowledge base that would later help me analyze and model international tourism.

Upon gaining my Masters degree, I wanted to get a university job, but there were no job vacancies. I was rather unhappy about this because I wanted to work for an academic institution and fulfill my dream of being a scientist. Then I had an idea for solving the problem: one of my examiners at the university was also the head of the Austrian Institute of Economic Research (a think tankwith an excellent international reputation; the institute was founded in 1927 by Friedrich von Hayek and Oskar Morgenstern). I asked him if there was any chance for me to join the staff of his institute. Without any hesitation (maybe because I had impressed myself on his memory), he accepted me. Two months later, I started on my first job at the newly built institute. It had spacious rooms, air conditioning, and—already—computers, thus successfully leaping into applied economic research. The advantage of being at such an institute is the access it offers to an enormous knowledge base (each room is manned with a specialist for a specific topic) and to a data base covering all of economics, both nationally and internationally. As a further bonus, I was permitted to study for my PhD on the side.

My first assignment at the institute was to do research into international economics, especially foreign trade. I had to analyze the current situation, write reports and papers for journals, participate in conferences, give presentations, and provide policy advice. Two assistants were assigned to me to do the number-crunching work, format papers, search for literature, etc. In my first years as an economic researcher, I investigated potential Austrian export markets at a country level; wrote papers about the export industry, current account problems, and exchange rate effects on foreign trade; and started to model merchandise exports and imports at a national and international level. From the very start, I had to deal with empirical facts and data; only the study of theories was not part of my job description. This working philosophy has not changed and will not change.

Because forecasting is one of the main business segments of our institute, I had to learn the different approaches and to apply them. Also I had to interpret the results of my research and translate them into practical policy advice. The knowledge thus acquired provided the foundation for future research and many publications. On the side, I looked around for an appropriate subject for my doctoral thesis and I decided on consumer theory, especially demand systems. This new orientation, in addition to foreign trade, forecasting, and economic policy advice supplied me with my fourth milestone on the way to tourism economics (and policy).

In my doctoral thesis "A Demand System for Austria" I analyzed the concurrent problem of consumption and saving by means of a consistent demand system, to which end I modified the linear expenditure system developed by Richard Stone and used it as a methodological base. In this system, saving takes, in terms of operationality, the character of a future consumer good and becomes an argument of the utility function. I demonstrated that the usual neoclassical assumption of utility maximization allows deriving a linear expenditure system of consumption and saving at given prices and incomes. Further, I pointed out the remarkable weaknesses of the linear expenditure system. These are the assumption of certainty and of a direct additive utility function (causing colinearity between income and price elasticities), as well as a disregard for major motives for saving.

In parallel to studying for my PhD, I wrote a paper about export modeling (Smeral 1979), where I modified the linear expenditure system and applied it to the merchandise exports of 18 industrial countries. I made efforts to get this paper published and I was successful. It was printed in 1979 and I had my first international publication in a highly ranked journal. In 1980, I was awarded my PhD and continued to work in the segment of export industries and international economics.

TOURISM RESEARCH

In 1982, Bruno Kreisky, at that time Austrian federal chancellor, tried to push through a prestige project: the building of a big modern international conference center in Vienna (designed to hold 15,000 participants). In order to justify this investment decision, he needed an impact study considering the value added and employment effects of the investment and the conference tourism it would generate. Our institute was to prepare this study. But who should do it? I remember it was late on a sunny afternoon when the head of the institute came in my room. He told me, "For this job we will apply the 'new' input-output table of 1976 and you should do it because you are good at modeling and like doing it." He also added, "As you know our tourism expert has left the institute, and we need somebody to take over his job, because in Austria tourism is a major contributor to the country's GDP" (at that time, tourism added significantly more than 10% to Austria's GDP, including direct and indirect effects). I was sorely disappointed because at that time tourism was almost the last research field that a (real) economist worth his salt would consider (I believe things have slightly improved since then, but there seems to be still much to do on the image held about this subject matter). I thought, what the hell is tourism? None of the economic textbooks, journals, and studies I had read over the last 12 years ever mentioned the word "tourism." It simply did not exist. My boss saw that I was disappointed and we did a deal, agreeing that I should spend half my working hours on foreign trade and half on tourism issues.

It took me several months to finish the impact study on the conference center, but it became another milestone on my way to tourism economics, dealing with impact studies. In these first years of my involvement with tourism, I tried to put it in the context of economic theory, but it was not easy as there was hardly any specialized literature and what there was did not really go into any depth.

In 1983, I went to the University of California at Berkeley for a sabbatical. My main goal was to put tourism in the context of economic theory. I started with monetary theory (which was very much in vogue at the time, and with it the "Chicago School"). Looking back, I have to say that it was a good practice for me, but that the effort was not very successful. I went back to the library to dig into this subject. I read a lot and lost my way, but then I discovered some publications that used econometrics to explain international tourism based on the modeling approaches of monetary trade theory and tourism consumption, applying a typical Keynesian consumption function (Archer 1976; Artus 1972; Bond 1979; Gerakis 1965; Gray 1970; Loeb 1982; Menges 1958, 1959; Quandt 1970; Schulmeister 1978). The interesting thing about this was that most of these publications came from nontourism researchers and a good part of the publications had been published in nontourism journals. Another point of interest was that the first econometric works about tourism were written in German (Menges 1958, 1959).Thinking over these discoveries, I began to see a bridge that would connect economics and tourism for me. There began to emerge (although I did have some doubts then) a research field that could be both interesting and new (at least in my eyes): tourism economics.

I returned to Austria in early 1984, I was immediately swamped with work consequent to a growing demand for tourism studies. There was no more time to analyze and write about foreign trade: as of mid-1984 all my working hours were given over to tourism research. My first major project work in tourism was a study for the Austrian Ministry of Economic Affairs about a long-term forecast for Austrian and international tourism. This study became my first tourism footprint, setting me up as a scientist in the country. The universities also discovered me and I started to teach tourism econometrics. The link got ever closer, and there came the day when I was made a university professor.

From the mid-1980s, I began to attend tourism conferences. The first big one was the 1985 conference of the International Association of Scientific Experts in Tourism (AIEST) in Bregenz, Austria. It was at this conference that I met Stephen Witt for the first time. We found that we more or less shared the same field—tourism demand forecasting—and we sat down to interesting discussions. We have stayed in contact ever since, meeting many times at other conferences and jointly doing a couple of publications in *Annals of Tourism Research*, *Journal of Travel Research*, and *Tourism Management*.

My next really big tourism conference was the 1986 Travel and Tourism Research Association meeting in Memphis, USA. This conference had another lasting influence on my life, because I met my future wife. She was from Vermont and worked for a tourism consultant firm. We stayed in contact. In October she visited Vienna for three wonderful weeks. The weather did its best; we had the Austrian equivalent of a lovely Indian summer. I visited her for Christmas in Vermont. She bought a one-way ticket and in January 1987 went with me to Vienna. We got married in October 1987. Soon we will celebrate our silver wedding anniversary. Incidentally, the slogan of Memphis was "Start Something Great in Memphis."

Ever since this 1986 conference, I have been an ever more frequent attendant of international tourism conferences, slowly becoming an established member of this international community. At these conferences I have met all the icons of tourism research and got appointed to the editorial boards of most of the key journals in tourism research. Now I am also a member of the most important international associations of tourism research.

From the late 1980s, my way to tourism economics has been developing along several parallel streams. First, in many publications, I brought together consumer and foreign trade theory. This development process was started in 1988 and finished by 2004 (Smeral 1988, 1994, 2000, 2004). The model can be viewed as a static partial model, which explains country-specific tourism imports and exports based on payment flows at constant prices and exchange rates.

Static partial models start out from a multistage budgeting process. For a decision to be of a multistage type model, it is necessary to break down the decision process (by time and by bundles of goods) and to assume that items of consumer goods can be aggregated. In contrast to a simultaneous approach, multistage decisionmaking and budgeting means that overall expenditures are first broken down by time, and then followed by the formation of budget groups, before the budget is assigned to individual items. In other words, after allocating the budget by time, it is next allocated by leisure-time goods and other consumer goods. After that, the budget allocated to international travel is separated from the budget for domestic traveling and the budget for other leisure-time goods. In a last stage, a distinction is made among destination countries (the expenditure streams are tourism imports of the origin country and tourism exports of the destination country). Allocation by time means that there are no habits, no regular returning tourists, and no dynamic aspects.

Key variables are the relative prices in a unified currency (tourism-weighted real effective exchange rates) and GDP variables as an indicator of income variables. In order to incorporate the range of other important explaining variables, dummy variables and specific trend variables have to be used. The model explains tourism imports by an income effect, a price effect, and special factors. Tourism exports in turn are explained by a demand and price effect, plus the effects of special factors. Each country included in the model is both a country of origin and destination. The (endogenous) variables explained by the model are the respective tourism exports and imports at constant prices and exchange rates.

In order to be consistent with the multistage budgeting process of partial demand models, the import expenditures (outbound) of a specific country should be allocated among the different destination countries. Unfortunately, the development of an optimal forecasting model on a global scale was limited by the fact that no systematic statistical information was available on bilateral payment flows between the key countries of origin and the destination countries. An admittedly imperfect way to bridge the gap between theoretical requirements and statistical realities was a special design of the export function.

In the export function, the explanatory demand variable for each country of destination is the weighted sum of imports, weighted by the country-specific guest structure by countries of origin for the specific destination country. Thus, each export function includes a specific demand variable that reflects the country-specific market demand structure of the destination in terms of overnight stays; in other words, the weighted demand variables reflect the special export market structures of the different countries.

The destination country-specific explanatory demand variable reflected through the weighted imports of the generating countries could be interpreted as a proxy for the foreign travel budget. The reduced model solution for the exports shows that the latter are in principle dependent on the GDPs and relative price variables, where, through weighting, the country-specific influences of the exogenous variables are approximated and the multistage budgeting process is simulated.

Drawing on this type of model outlined above, I prepared and published several long-term forecasting and impact studies. The impact analyses were mostly the outcomes of historical and political events (such as the fall of the Iron Curtain, German reunification, several EU enlargements, its eastern enlargement, and introduction of the euro). In addition to causal econometrics, I used univariate time series econometrics for forecasting, measuring forecasting accuracy and impact analysis such as the effects of the EU presidency (e.g. intervention models; Smeral, 2007a; Smeral and Wüger 2000, 2005, 2006, 2008).

In other impact studies such as those about a Guggenheim Museum for Salzburg and Vienna (Bilbao won this contest), the planned Vienna–Budapest

Expo for 1995 (rejected in a referendum), and sports events and casino gambling in Austria, I used input–output analysis, in some cases combined with multiplier analysis. In this connection, the study by Blackorby et al (1986) gave me the initial impetus to cope with these projects. Some 10 years ago, Peter Laimer from Statistik Austria and I developed a tourism satellite account (TSA) for Austria, later followed by regional satellite accounts for three Austrian states. For these accounts we do an update every year.

When it comes to implementing the TSA and pointing out the (real) contribution of tourism value added to GDP, I have always been very critical about the way it is done in practice (Smeral 2005, 2006). It should be considered that a major goal of the TSA project was to prevent the tourism industry from being dismissed as a minor economic player. Unfortunately, the TSA spans only those effects that are generated by the direct economic relationship between guest and producer and thus makes it difficult to compare tourism-related GDP in relation to the overall GDP, since the latter also includes indirect effects caused by economic interlinkages. Another problem arises from the fact that, in the TSA, expenditures from residents on business trips are accounted for as final demand. On the other hand, intermediate consumption is not considered in GDP calculation, resulting in a biased comparison of the value added to GDP according to the TSA. It is clear that in measuring the TSA-based contribution made by the tourism industry to national/regional GDP, results must be adjusted for indirect effects and intermediate consumption (as we did for Austria at the national level and for the three Austrian states). The adjustments demonstrate the enormous scope by which the tourism industry's contribution to national and regional GDP is underestimated, even when only its direct effects are considered, as is required by the TSA approach. Even when business trips by residents are included and thus make for a greater contribution of tourism to GDP, this fails to compensate for the downward bias produced by ignoring the indirect effects of tourism demand.

Looking back, I have to say that impact studies have kept me very busy for the last three decades and I see no end. Douglas Frechtling seems to have a similar history. Therefore, we decided to do a small survey (because the publisher did not allow more than 5,000 words) about impact measurement (Frechtling and Smeral 2010).

Next to impact analysis, forecasting has always been an important activity in my research work (and will continue to be so in the future). This can be seen from a technical/methodological, philosophical, and a policy adviser side (I have given tourism policy advice to the Austrian Ministry of Economic Affairs and the National Tourism Board for about 20 years).

Here the two latter sides may be commented on. Irrespective of the fact that forecasting is difficult, "It is always very difficult to predict the future on the basis of the past. Indeed it has been linked to driving a car blindfold while following directions given by a person looking out of the back window" (Harvey 1989:xi). Publishing a forecast might influence the behavior of the public to the point that statistical reality becomes modified (while we measure forecasting accuracy and discuss the forecasting performance of different models), this problem can be approached in three different ways (Smeral 1993).

One, we do not tell anybody our forecast. Telling nobody about the forecast we have done is not the point of applied social science, except when the scientist spends some time to test the forecast accuracy of the model before s/he starts publishing the results. Two, we publish our forecast. One may achieve an excellent forecasting accuracy without publishing the results, but without consideration of possible reactions by the public to the published forecast and their influence on the statistics resulting from their potential actions, forecast accuracy as measured afterwards could become very bad indeed. Actually, measuring forecasting accuracy makes sense only if there is no public reaction at all (to be cynical: why do we make forecasts if nobody reacts?). In most cases, there will be at least some reaction by the public to the published forecasts, which influences the actual values, the forecast accuracy, and the forecaster's reputation. In other words, one is mostly wrong, by definition.

Three, we publish our forecast and consider the feedback effects. This would improve—subject to the quality of the forecast model—forecasting accuracy, but we would need a very complex model which includes, in addition to the tourism industry, many other parts of the economy and society (related production sectors, politics, media, etc.). Also, even if we could build such a complex model, we are still faced with the limits of information about all the underlying reactions, feedbacks, and learning patterns. Furthermore, even if we attempted to construct a system dynamic model, it is in general very difficult to build such a model on an empirical basis (except in some special cases only). Regardless of whether such an almost perfect model is feasible, we have to deal with the paradox that, assuming feedbacks and optimization of the forecasting accuracy, the unpublished forecast value does not equal the published forecast value.

Growth theory was another research field that attracted my interest. Impressed by the work of Robert Solow and his intention to draw a parable of economic growth, I tried to formulate a parable of tourism growth

(Smeral 2001, 2003; Solow 1970). Solow described the building of a parable with the following words:

> Please keep in mind that we are dealing with a drastically simplified story, a parable, which my dictionary defines as fictitious narrative or allegory (usually something that might naturally occur) by which moral or spiritual relations are typically set forth. If moral or spiritual relations, why not economics? You ask of a parable not if it is literally true, but if it is well told. Even a well told parable has limited applicability. There are always tacit or explicit assumptions underlying a simplified story. They may not matter for the point the parable is trying to make; that is what makes parables possible. (1970:1–2)

My parable of tourism growth was partly based on the theoretical work of William Baumol (1967) and J. N. Bhagwati (1984a, 1984b). For this research project I focused on structural aspects, because these are important factors when it comes to explaining tourism growth (the Vienna School of Economics is influenced by structural thinking, which certainly had at least some influence on my scientific work). In this connection, crucial roles are played by the structural change in demand and differentials between productivity in tourism and in manufacturing.

The demand factor stimulates the rise of tourism demand and explains why tourism grows faster than the global economy as such, or why the income elasticity is above 1: tourism is a luxury good, and structural change in demand is a key factor for explanation. Once having achieved saturation in basic needs and durable goods, a growing economy has more money left to spend on, first, leisure and tourism services, and, second, on knowledge-based goods and services. As opposed to manufacturing, opportunities to increase productivity are limited in the tourism industry. Because of relatively fewer options to rationalize (as tourism services are typical embodied services), tourism services become more expensive in the long term than manufactured goods or other services, which weakens the demand-triggered growth effect (Smeral 2007b). Nevertheless, in sum, the demand effect is stronger than the productivity disadvantages. As a side effect of productivity disadvantages and the demand effect, employment grows as a share of total employment in the hotel and restaurant sectors, the core segments of the tourism industry. A further analysis showed that in the hotel and restaurant industry, in most cases, the greatest contribution to growth derives from quantitative labor input (Smeral 2009).

CONCLUSION

When I look back at about 30 years of tourism research, the impression grows that working as a tourism economist, using econometrics and models is seen as a more or less exotic activity by the other tourism-related disciplines: you think differently, you have your own language code, you fill numbers into equations to make forecasts, you use the word relatively (relatively) often, you attempt to quantify everything you get your hands on (if the information is qualitative, you try to make at least a ranking and/or you develop a model to define the distances), and at the end you come to the conclusion that the results should be seen with reservations only and that they could be very different from reality if certain assumptions fail to hold. Yes, we really are strange folks and difficult to understand.

The way tourism economists are seen might have changed somewhat in the last years as the global financial and economic crisis showed its teeth and bite into every economic activity, including tourism. Overnight, economic questions moved into the center of practical life and daily politics. In other words, tourism economics or economics in tourism is back in town and will be around for quite a few more years (because we are about to face the next recession in connection with severe financial problems) to analyze, forecast, and then summarize what we have learned about the changes in demand and supply patterns.

In retrospect, a few weeks after the collapse of Lehman Brothers Holding Inc. (which had to file for chapter 11 on September 15, 2008), I received a call from the Austrian Minister of Economic Affairs, asking me to prepare a study about the potential impacts of the global financial and economic crisis on international and Austrian tourism. I thought that the job was very interesting, but there was a time problem; they would give me only six weeks to do it. Arguments why this timeframe was inadequate (lack of data, research time too short, lack of literature, etc.) were ineffective. All they said was, yes, we know, but we need the study and we know nobody else who could do it in this short time. I accepted and delivered the study in early December 2008.

I learned a lot from this "all-hands-on-deck" situation. I found new data sources, started to build a new data base, changed econometric methods, and learned to see demand and supply patterns in a crisis from a different point of view. Summarizing my findings about the changes in demand behavior and forecasts, I produced three publications (Smeral 2009, 2010a, 2010b), and at this writing two more are forthcoming.

In dealing with the impacts of global financial and economic crisis, I found myself increasingly doubtful about whether (tourism) demand elasticity is really symmetrical—e.g. that elasticities in up- and downturns have a similar magnitude or that they remain stable across the business cycles. On a country level, I found empirical evidence that the relative fall in (tourism) demand during an economic downturn is more precipitous than the relative increase in demand during an economic upturn of a similar magnitude. But empirical evidence has also been accumulated for the opposite as much as for the symmetrical cases. In other words, the patterns of (tourism) demand elasticity during up- and downturns can vary from country to country. Finding answers to these questions will be my next major research project. I will start on it as soon I have finished this contribution.

Chapter 12

From a Random Walker to a Firm Believer

Haiyan Song
The Hong Kong Polytechnic University, Hong Kong

Haiyan Song is a chair professor of tourism at the Hong Kong Polytechnic University. He has a first degree in statistics and a PhD in economics. He has been involved in tourism research from 1997 when he joined the School of Management for the Service Sector at the University of Surrey, as a lecturer in tourism economics. Since then he has published more than 60 journal articles related to tourism. His main research interests rest in tourism demand modeling and forecasting, tourism impact assessment, competition issues in tourism, and tourism supply chain management. He has traveled extensively in China as well as in the rest of the world. With his passion for travel, he has a plan to climb all the major mountains within China when he retires from his academic expedition of tourism economics. Email <hmsong@inet.polyu.edu.hk>

INTRODUCTION

I was born in Weihai, a beautiful seaside city, which has become one of the most visited coastal tourism destinations in China, in September 1957, when

The Discovery of Tourism Economics
Tourism Social Science Series, Volume 16, 159–172

ISSN: 1571-5043/doi:10.1108/S1571-5043(2011)0000016015

China just started its Great Leap Forward Movement. My father was a navy officer in the People Liberation Army at the time, so that I was inducted to travel from the very beginning of my life, as I had to travel between the navy base and home on a regular basis with my mother. As a result, I was the only child in the family (I have two younger brothers) who do not suffer from any seasickness. At the age of 4, my grandmother told me that I would be traveling a lot and living in faraway places when I grow up, as I held the very end of the chopsticks when I started learning how to use them. According to a Chinese saying, if one holds the end of the chopsticks, he or she would be a traveler for life. This was the first time that I was inducted to travel forecasting, and this forecast proved to be 100% accurate.

The *Great Leap Forward* was a disaster for China as it led to the Great Famine (1958–61) in which more than 20 million people died. I survived, thanks to the rations provided by the government to the military personnel. For this, I owe my life to the Chinese Navy. Following the Great Famine was a 10-year Cultural Revolution (1967–76). When it started, I joined the Little Red Guards, given the fact that my parents were both from poor families. Many of my classmates and friends were not as fortunate as I was, as their parents were from rich families (landlords or business owners) before the founding of the People's Republic of China. Not only could they not join the Little Red Guards, their parents were often persecuted and sent to the countryside to be reeducated.

During the Cultural Revolution, normal education curriculums at all levels were suspended, as they were seen to be irrelevant to the communists' ideology and produced too many graduates who did not know how to work in the fields and factories. In schools, the biology course was replaced with agricultural studies in which students would have to spend considerable time in the countryside learning how to grow vegetables and raise pigs. Physics classes were called "Industry Technologies" and students had to learn mechanics and the structure of materials in the factories. The general education modules were mainly focused on Marxism, Leninism, and Mao Zedong thoughts. I was considered to be a good student. This was not because I was more intelligent than others but mainly because I was favored by the teachers due to my family background.

In 1975, I graduated from high school and was sent to a remote village in Liaoning Province, in the northeast of China, together with 50 fellow school leavers to receive further "education" from the farmers. The "education" meant hard labor. I had to learn how to grow vegetables, harvest crops, and plow the fields. The days were very long; every day we had to get up very early in the morning and return to the camp very late in the evening. The foods at that time were basically stewed Chinese cabbage, radish, and potatoes. Each of the youth laborers was only entitled to about half a liter of vegetable oil per month. So, the foods were tasteless without oil and meat. About one year later, I was selected by my fellow youth workers to be in charge of the catering department, as I had some connections through my father to purchase meat from the navy base. This was my first "industry experience" related to hospitality. At that time, the basic need for every youth worker was to get enough to eat, and the varieties of food and service quality were not important issues.

After chairman Mao died in 1976, Deng Xiaoping came to power in 1977. One of the first things he did was to reform the education system. He reintroduced the national university and college entrance examination. All high school graduates from the period 1966 to 1976 were allowed to take part in the national examination. In fact university places were very limited after the 10-year Cultural Revolution, and only a handful of these school leavers were able to score high enough to be admitted to the universities or colleges. I was one of the lucky ones who passed the entrance examination and was admitted to university. I left the Youth Camp where I worked for three years in the summer of 1978 and started my university life at the Dongbei University of Finance and Economics as a student specializing in statistics. During my university years, I took full advantage of the semester breaks and traveled to Beijing, Shanghai, and Hangzhou as a student tourist. I visited the Great Wall of China, Tiananmen Square, the Summer Palace, and the Forbidden City in Beijing, the Bund and the Old City Quarter in Shanghai, and the Ten Scenic Areas around the West Lake in Hangzhou. I consider myself to have benefited more than what I had learnt in the classrooms. Although the university and colleges returned to normal, the subjects were still heavily skewed toward political science (Marxism, Leninism, and Mao Zedong thoughts). My travel was an eye opener for me, as I saw the real beauty of the country, and interacted with real people who shaped my views about Chinese society under a tightly controlled political scheme. My university traveling experience actually stimulated my desire to travel even further afield.

I graduated from university in 1982, and was recruited as a lecturer by the same university upon graduation, as it was severely short of qualified teachers. Between 1982 and 1988, I traveled to a few more places in China and at the same time I worked hard to improve my English proficiency, as I was determined to broaden my personal perspective by going abroad. In fact, I had not studied English at all before I entered the university. My speaking and listening comprehension benefited greatly from the BBC and

Voice of America, which at that time were officially banned in China, as they spread capitalist views.

TOURISM RESEARCH

In 1988, I boarded a brand new Air China Boeing 747 to London and started my dream in overseas travel. I first studied economics at the University of York as a visiting scholar and was then awarded a PhD scholarship by Glasgow Caledonian University to examine the causes and effects of inflation in China. Once I started my PhD in Glasgow, I spent about £500 to buy a second hand Austin Metro, which was almost two months' of my PhD stipend. I started traveling with my family in Scotland. The European Cultural City of Glasgow, historic Edinburgh, mysterious Loch Ness, the soul-wakening landscape of the Scottish Highland, the golf resort of St. Andrews, and the remote but beautiful Isle of Skye all left us with profound memories.

First Encounter with Tourism Economics

My PhD study was on modeling and forecasting inflation in China using the latest econometric techniques, such as using cointegration, error correction, and time varying parameter models. The works on cointegration and error correction models were first published by Engle and Granger in 1987 when I started my PhD, so I was well equipped with these new techniques and my thesis benefited greatly from their application in modeling and forecasting inflation in China. Upon completion of my PhD, I was offered a job at the University of Abertay Dundee as a lecturer in applied economics. Abertay was a teaching university with very limited requirement for research. However, as a young academic, I wanted to advance my career through research and publication. At that time, I focused mainly on the Chinese economy in transition, and wrote a few articles on Foreign Direct Investment, aggregate investment, and consumption in China. One day when I was browsing the journals in the library, a review article written by Witt and Witt (1995) on tourism demand modeling and forecasting published in the *International Journal of Forecasting* caught my attention. The article reviewed published studies on tourism demand modeling and forecasting over a period of 30 years. One of the striking facts that I found from reading this article was that the methodologies used in the empirical studies had mainly been traditional regression analysis, although more advanced econometric methods were widely available in the late 1980s and early 1990s. I thought I had identified a research gap in the tourism forecasting literature, and started immediately to review the subject and collect data on tourism demand. During the course of the literature review, I became familiar with the works by Stephen Witt and Christine Witt who were leading academics and published widely in the area of tourism demand modeling and forecasting. One of their research findings was that the naïve no-change model tends to outperform most of the econometric and time series models. This research finding generated considerable debate on the validity of tourism forecasting research. The underlying message was that if more sophisticated econometric or pure time series models, such as the regression, Box–Jenkins, and exponential smoothing approaches cannot outperform the naïve forecasts, then what is the point of even considering using these sophisticated techniques in tourism demand modeling and forecasting? In recognizing this important issue, Witt and Witt, in their 1995 article provided a proposition for further research: the forecasting failure of the econometric and time series models in comparison with the no-change model might be due to the fact that the recent advances in econometrics and time series analysis were not used to identify the complexity of the data generating process in the tourism demand models.

Armed with modern econometric techniques, I collected the outbound tourism demand data in the United Kingdom and started to model the determinants of the UK outbound tourism demand to all destinations. In the study, I created a destination preference index, which reflects the determinants of non-economic variables in addition to the economic determinants, such as the income level of the UK residents, the costs of tourism in the destinations, the exchange rates, and substitute prices of alternative destinations. Cointegration and error correction models were used to identify both the long-run equilibrium and the short-run dynamic relationships between UK outbound tourism and its determinants. The results overwhelmingly suggested that the error correction models outperformed all the other competing models including the naïve no-change model. This was the first study that confirmed the proposition provided by Witt and Witt (1995). However, after the article was completed, I had some difficulty in getting it published in tourism journals. The article was first sent to *Annals of Tourism Research* and then to *Tourism Economics* for consideration of publication. In both cases, the paper was not favorably reviewed by the referees. The reviewers' reports indicated that they were unfamiliar with the new methodologies, as the main reason for rejecting the paper was that the techniques used in the study were not suitable for tourism researchers/practitioners. The paper was later submitted to *Applied Economics*, and it was accepted for publication with some small revisions in 1997 (it finally appeared in print in 1999 after a two-year wait). This was one of the few early studies that utilized modern econometric techniques in investigating tourism demand and has received a good citation since it was published (Song et al 1999).

Working with Great Scholars

In 1997, the School of Management for the Service Sector at the University of Surrey announced three openings. One of the positions was a lecturer in economics. In the announcement, it was specified that the candidate should have a strong quantitative economics background with some research experience in tourism. Since I had just completed a tourism research project, I thought I was qualified for the position. I submitted my application and was subsequently offered the job as lecturer in economics, which I consider to be an important milestone of my journey to tourism economics discovery. David Airey, who also has a background in economics, and Richard Butler, known for his life cycle model in tourism joined Surrey at around the same time.

When I settled down at Surrey, I was told by the then head of school, Michael Kipps, that Stephen Witt was about to take early retirement from the University of Swansea and would work part-time at Surrey. Since my research interests fit very well with his, I was asked by the school to pay Witt a visit in Swansea so that we could work out a collaborative research plan between us. I was so excited with this golden opportunity, as he was a big name who was widely recognized as the father of tourism forecasting. I still vividly remember my first meeting with him. It was a sunny day; I drove 173 miles to Swansea from Guildford. I was ushered to his office by his secretary. To my surprise, his office was extremely clean and tidy, which did not reflect a typical working environment of an econometrician. I further discovered that he did not even have a computer on his desk! To me, a computer to an econometrician is just like a rifle to a soldier, and I could not figure out how he had managed to publish so many articles without using a computer. Later on, I realized that he is not a foot soldier but a strategist who does not need to carry a rifle. He took me to a French restaurant in The Mumbles, a former fishing village in the outskirts of Swansea near to the university, where we discussed our research collaboration over some French dishes and wine. We decided to write a book on tourism demand modeling and forecasting using modern econometric approaches, as there was urgent need for such a book to better equip tourism researchers with the latest developments in forecasting techniques. We also decided to write a series of articles on the evaluation of the forecasting performance of a broad range of modern econometric models. I was extremely happy with the result of the meeting, and started my return journey to Guildford. Halfway through my journey, a lady drove her car into mine from behind. Although I had a fruitful meeting with Witt, my lovely Toyota was written off by the insurance company.

Witt joined Surrey as a part-time professor of tourism forecasting soon after our meeting in Swansea, and we started working on the book and the paper. The book, *Tourism Demand Modeling and Forecasting: Modern Econometric Approaches,* was published in 2000 by Elsevier. It received very positive reviews by both general as well as tourism forecasters. The following comments are extracted from two book reviews:

> This book is an excellent introduction to tourism demand modeling and forecasting from an econometrics point of view. Both topics, tourism demand and econometrics, are so well combined by the authors and so many different approaches are presented in such a short space ... the book may be of great interest to a wide range of audiences. (Pedregal 2001:297)

> This book is a very timely description and application of advanced causal forecasting methods for tourism series ... , and is very important in raising the level of technical expertise required to achieve accurate causal model forecasts ... as a text, the book pushes the understanding of tourism forecasting methodology out to currently accepted econometric standards, and must become a standard research reference work for econometric forecasting of tourism series. (Lindsay Turner 2001:578–579)

Witt was commuting between Guildford, Bornholm, and Melbourne during 1997–2003. So, our joint research was carried out via emails, faxes, post, and his periodical visits to Guildford. In the summer of 2002, he traveled from Bornholm to Guildford to work with me on a paper entitled "Forecasting Tourism Generated Employment: The Case of Denmark." On my way from home to Guildford for the meeting with Witt, my brand new Nissan Primera was involved in a highway pile-up. My car was the first of the five cars in the accident, and the car behind me was driven by a lady as in the previous accident. I was not sure whether these two car accidents were purely random events or meeting with Witt was a causal variable for the car accidents. As a forecaster, I naturally became very careful whenever the meetings with him were coming up. Either I paid additional attention to the cars and drivers around me or I simply used public transport to attend the meetings with him.

When I joined the University of Surrey, I was the only non-white academic staff member in the School of Management for the Service Sector. But I did not feel alienated in any way, as my colleagues were very friendly, supportive, and collegial. Michael Kipps, a food scientist, became the head of the school (1997–2000) shortly after I joined Surrey. He brought Witt to the school and encouraged me to work closely with him. Kipps understood my desire to develop myself as a young academic and provided every possible means for me to grow. I was given full autonomy to decide what to teach. Under his headship, I developed a postgraduate subject—tourism demand modeling and forecasting—which attracted 15–20 students every year. Witt and I co-taught that subject. Although the class size was small, the students had an opportunity to learn firsthand modern forecasting techniques, which strengthened their quantitative skills and benefited students when they graduated from the program. In fact, a few students who later contacted me said that they benefited greatly from the subject.

David Airey became the head of the school in September 2000 and stayed on until September 2002, before taking up the pro-vice chancellor position in the university. Airey is a typical English gentleman and fine scholar in every aspect. He was very fair and transparent in managing the school. I was most productive under his leadership, as I published my seminal *Tourism Demand Modeling and Forecasting: Modern Econometric Approaches* and about 10 articles (including the accepted ones) when he was the head of the school. Under his headship, I was also very much encouraged to interact with internationally renowned scholars, provided with funding to recruit research students and to attend important conferences, such as the International Symposium on Forecasting. Due to his encouragement and support, I was promoted to reader directly from lecturer, which is a rare case in British universities. To me, this was a major boost to my academic career, as I became more confident when I communicated with researchers around the world. This was also demonstrated by the fact that I was promoted to a personal chair in 2003 after Bob O'Keefe took the headship of the school in

October 2002. Working at Surrey for seven years, I achieved the highest possible career goal one possibly could dream of, thanks to the very supportive and collegial environment created by the great scholars and leaders.

One of the contributions that I made to the tourism forecasting literature during my tenure at Surrey was that I was able to demonstrate that advanced econometric models, such as the time varying parameter and dynamic error correction models can outperform the simple naïve model in terms of the forecasting error magnitudes and directional changes. I remember that I had a conversation with Witt about why I believed that the econometric models should do better than the naïve model in terms of forecasting tourism demand. The following was the reason that I provided in my discussion with him.

The naïve model can be better explained by a random walk process:

$$Y_t = Y_{t-1} + \varepsilon_t \tag{1}$$

where Y_t and Y_{t-1} are tourism demands at time t and $t-1$, respectively, and ε_t is a random error term with zero mean and constant variance.

If the naïve model indeed can always outperform the econometric models, we will have to be convinced that tourism demand follows a random walk process as described by Eq. (1). That is to say no other variables could be used to explain tourism demand apart from its immediate past. The random walk process has been identified to best represent the evolution of share prices by researchers in the finance literature. One of the properties of the random walk process is that the probability for right or wrong forecasts is 50/50, and that is why not many people become rich in investing shares. However, both tourism economic theory as well as our efforts in data analysis suggested that the tourism demand variables do not follow a random walk process. Some economic variables, such as tourists' income, prices, exchange rates, and marketing variables, do play a role in determining tourism demand. The main reason why the previous studies did not find the econometric models superior to the naïve model was the inability to identify proper econometric models.

In 2000 I was very fortunate in recruiting a very talented and hard working PhD student—Gang Li, a graduate from the Dongbei University of Finance and Economics in China. His thesis topic was related to modeling and forecasting the UK tourism demand in Western Europe using the time varying parameter approach. Not only did his research use cointegration and error-correction techniques in identifying the long-run equilibrium and short-run dynamic relationships, it also utilized the system-of-equations approach (known as the linear almost-ideal demand systems), together with the Kalman Filter, to examine the evolution of tourists' demand behavior over time. Gang was the first researcher who successfully demonstrated that this time varying parameter-error correction consistently outperformed all other econometric and pure time series models. This study in fact further confirmed the proposition put forward by Witt in 1995. Li graduated in 2003 and was employed by Surrey as a lecturer in economics. Since then he has been seen as a rising star in tourism demand modeling and forecasting. Since his PhD graduation, we have co-published a few articles on tourism forecasting using the time varying parameter technique. Our "Tourism Modeling and Forecasting: A Review of Recent Research" article (2009) was ranked No. 2 among all papers published in *Tourism Management* in terms of citations and No. 9 in terms of downloads (the data were retrieved from http://journals.elsevier.com/02615177/tourism-management/ on October 10 2010). Li is now a senior lecturer at Surrey, and will continue to shine in the field of tourism economics in the future.

Most, if not all, of my publications, including my first research monograph with Witt and Li concluded that the performance of the tourism demand models can be enhanced by introducing advanced econometric techniques. Especially the time varying parameter models tend to be superior to many other competing models, including the naïve no-change model when short- to medium-term forecasting is concerned. Since then the dominance of the no-change model in tourism forecasting performance has shifted to more advanced econometric and time series models, as demonstrated by many other studies. However, no agreement has yet been reached on which type of models would be likely to generate superior forecasting performance over their competitors in all situations. This provides tourism forecasters with an incentive to crunch more numbers, as tourism practitioners demand the forecasting principles and guidelines to be developed by researchers.

Moving Back to Asia

In 2001, I was granted a six-month sabbatical leave by the University of Surrey. In choosing the institution where I could spend my sabbatical leave, the School of Hotel and Tourism Management at The Hong Kong Polytechnic University was at the top of the list. The reason why I chose it was because I met Kaye Chon, the head of the school, at a conference in 2000, and he invited me to spend some time in his school as a visiting fellow.

I also learnt that he had just taken up the headship and embarked on an ambitious plan to turn the school into a leading institution in the world in tourism research and education. I was very much impressed by his dedication and leadership, and joined the university in 2001 as a visiting research fellow. After six months, before I returned to the United Kingdom, he asked me whether I would consider joining the school permanently. At that time, I had just been promoted to reader by Surrey, and wanted to accumulate more experience in a leading institution in Europe. So, I said that I would be very much interested in the offer, but maybe in a few years time. He was very kind in saying "please let me know whenever you are ready to join us." Of course, I continued my communication with Kaye Chon thereafter, and I observed everything that was related to the School of Hotel and Tourism Management. I noticed that the university was making a major impact on tourism and hospitality education and research in Asia.

Under Kaye Chon's leadership, The Hong Kong Polytechnic University was recognized as a leading institution in Asia and was ranked number 12 among all tourism and hospitality programs in the world in 2002. The impact was often known as the Asian Wave in the academic community. In 2003, I spent two weeks at the Institute for Tourism Studies, Macau, as a residential professor working with Stephen Witt on a research project related to forecasting the demand for Macau tourism. When Kaye Chon knew that I was visiting Macau, he called me and said that he would like to have a face-to-face meeting with me to discuss the possibility of me joining his school. So we fixed a date and time for the meeting in Macau. On the day when he said he would come to Macau, there was a heavy storm and the storm signal was raised to Amber. I thought he would not be able to come due to the storm. To my surprise, he said he was already on the ferry and asked me to meet him at the Mandarin Oriental Hotel in Macau. I was deeply moved by his determination in getting me on board. Therefore, I made up my mind at the meeting that I wanted to be part of his team working toward the goals that he set for the school: to become the top institution in Hospitality and Tourism education in the world. I resigned from Surrey one year after I was promoted to a personal chair and joined The Hong Kong Polytechnic University in August 2004, as chair professor in tourism and associate head of the school responsible for Research, China Affairs, Quality Assurance, and Administration.

Moving back from Europe to Asia after 16 years has been a very important change in my life and career in several respects. Firstly, I was born and raised in China, and have a natural connection to Asia in general and China in particular. So, I consider I was a leaf falling to its root. Second,

China has been developing so fast over the past 20 years, not only in terms of its economic growth but also its tourism development, and I wanted to make a significant contribution to this change. Third, the university has been playing a significant role in shaping the hospitality and tourism education and research in Asia under Kaye Chon's leadership, and being part of the team would be very rewarding.

Over the six years since I joined the university, I have seen the School of Hotel and Tourism Management progress to No. 4 in 2005, and this rank was further improved to No. 2 in 2009. I have successfully organized six China Tourism Forums, and established a successful academic journal, *Journal of China Tourism Research*, that provides an important channel of communication between the research from China and the West. Although my administrative duties have been very heavy, I still keep a strong interest in research. Over the past six years I have published about 50 journal articles and 5 books. About 80% of these publications are related to tourism economics.

There have been some perceptions in academic circles that our research on tourism demand modeling and forecasting had been too theoretical with limited application value. When we spoke at conferences and communicated with colleagues within the school regarding our research, one of the frequently asked questions was "what is the relevance of your research to tourism practice?" Therefore, one of the things that I wanted to do when I moved to Hong Kong was to integrate our research into tourism forecasting practice. Before I left Surrey, I was contacted by Ngoc Lee, senior adviser to the President of The Hong Kong Polytechnic University, who was in charge of establishing a Public Policy Research Institute at the university, and he asked me whether I would like to be a founding member of the Institute. To be the founding member, I would have to submit a research proposal to apply for research funding from the university. I was delighted with the invitation and submitted a research proposal on establishing a web-based tourism demand forecasting system for Hong Kong.

My proposal was approved by the university, which allowed me to utilize the latest advances in forecasting methodologies in the development of this system. I envisaged that this system should integrate the advantages of modern forecasting methods and scenario analysis and allows for a prompt judgmental contribution from a wide range of experts. At the functional level, a system should be a forecasting support system that is capable of providing quantitative tourism demand forecasts and allowing the users to perform scenario analyses or make their own "what-if" forecasts. Scenario analysis is an important and systematic method of studying the future, which incorporates uncertainty by including alternative future values for the influencing factors. At the technical level, the system could be seen as an information system consisting of a set of computer-based modules or components that supports tourism demand forecasting and scenario analysis. The purpose of establishing such a system is to deliver tourism demand forecasts and provide decision support to policymakers and business strategists via a Web browser. This system could also facilitate information sharing and communication, and bring considerable convenience to various users engaged in tourism demand forecasting at different locations. This web-based tourism demand forecasting system was formally launched in 2008 after three years' research and construction. The system can be accessed via www.tourismforecasting.net. Since its launch in 2008, the system has attracted considerable interest from both public and private sectors, as it has been visited more than 79,000 times. A detailed account of this system can be found in a recent article published in *Tourism Economics* (Song et al 2008).

Tourism economics is such as a broad discipline, and there are so many research directions that one can explore. In order to broaden my research perspectives, I started to read and write on such issues as tourism supply chain management, and destination competitiveness from tourists' satisfaction perspective. My research on tourism supply chain management is very much biased toward tourism economics, as I tend to look at supply issues and destination competitiveness from the perspectives of market structure, coordination and competition, information asymmetry, game theory, and demand management and forecasting.

THE FUTURE

In recognition of my contribution to tourism economics research, I was admitted to the International Academy for the Study of Tourism in 2005. This is a prestigious academic institution comprising renowned authorities in various disciplines related to tourism. In 2010 the International Council on Hotel, Restaurant and Institutional Education presented me with the "John Wiley and Sons' Life Time Research Achievement Award" at its annual conference in Puerto Rico, which signifies a new beginning of my academic career. It has been more than 10 years since I randomly stumbled into tourism economics, and it is time for me to think about what would be my new goals in tourism economics research. To forecast the future of a forecaster is always a tricky business. But in reflecting upon what I have achieved in the past and what would be my research in the future, I think I will continue my research in the following areas (listed in order of priority and level of involvement): leading in tourism demand forecasting research and practice; making significant impacts on tourism competitiveness research; contributing to the development of the emerging research area on tourism supply chain management; and continuing in research related to tourism in China.

Chapter 13

The Excitement and Value of Discovering Tourism Economics

Clement A. Tisdell
The University of Queensland, Australia

Clement Allan Tisdell joined The University of Queensland in 1989 as Professor of Economics and since the beginning of 2005 has been Professor Emeritus there. He was professor of Economics at the University of Newcastle (New South Wales) from 1972 to 1989 and before that he was at the Australian National University in Canberra from 1961 to 1972 where he completed his PhD in Economics, joined the academic staff and was then rapidly promoted to the position of Reader in Economics. Clem Tisdell has been fortunate to visit many overseas countries, universities, and institutions during his career and has forged diverse cooperative academic ties. His range of research interests is broad and he is a prolific author. He has been assessed (May 2010) by his IDEAS profile as being one of the world's leading economic researchers. The seeds of his discovery of tourism economics were probably sown in 1970 but his interest in the subject developed slowly and intermittently at first. However, by 1984 Tisdell's interest in tourism economics became firmly established and still continues. Email <c.tisdell@economics.uq.edu.au>

The Discovery of Tourism Economics
Tourism Social Science Series, Volume 16, 173–189

ISSN: 1571-5043/doi:10.1108/S1571-5043(2011)0000016016

INTRODUCTION

In outlining the way in which I came to discover tourism economics and to develop my research on it, I'll do so chronologically. Then I'll discuss why it excites me and the value I have obtained from my journey. I'll focus on my development that relates primarily to tourism economics rather than attempt an overall autobiography as some contributors to this series have done. Further information of a biographical nature is available in Dollery and Wallis (1996), Tisdell (1997) and Lodewijks (2007) plus references in this article as well as from the following websites:
http://en.wikipedia.org/wiki/Clem_Tisdell
http://www.uq.edu.au/economics/PDF/staff/Clem_Tisdell_CV.pdf
http://www.search.com/reference/Clem_Tisdell
http://www.uq.edu.au/economics/index.html?page = 15911
I have no idea who contributed the material for Wikipedia, and why, nor do I know who completed the item on the search website. Another pertinent reference is Tisdell (2007a) which attempts to classify and outline the way in which my published books evolved.

I begin by providing some background on my journey up until the end of 1960 (the completion of my undergraduate degree) and next I cover my relevant experiences at the Australian National University (the 1961–72 period). It was towards the end of my stay at the Australian National University that the seeds of my interest in tourism economics were sown. This interest sprouted after I joined the University of Newcastle in the Hunter Valley of New South Wales. I was there from 1972 to 1989 and it was in the 1980s that my interest in tourism economics became firmly established. It continued to flourish and was boosted after I joined The University of Queensland in 1989. After outlining these stages in my development, I discuss the excitement and value I feel I have derived from exploring tourism economics and then conclude.

My Early Years

I was born on November 18, 1939, in the country town of Taree in New South Wales, Australia. I was the eldest of 10 children, an equal number of boys and girls. Given my socioeconomic background, it was statistically highly unlikely that I would ever go to university, let alone write about tourism economics. I was officially given the name of "Clement" but I always thought it was "Clem" until I had to obtain copies of my birth certificate in order to apply in 1956 for a Teacher's College Scholarship of the NSW Department of Education. In my earlier years, I always used Clem as part of my *nomme de plume*. But as I have grown older, I have increased the frequency with which I use Clement.

I completed all my schooling at Taree Public School, which, in fact, was a state school of the NSW Department of Education. For me, it was a positive experience. I liked learning and my teachers were supportive of my efforts. I was encouraged to explore, to be constructively critical, and to back up my work with references and evidence. For me, these traits turned out to be a life-long asset. My experience also resulted in my placing a very high social value on education. I became supportive of well-designed state-sponsored educational systems and of access to free education in schools for all, as well as the provision of financial support for students pursuing university education, especially of those likely to perform well at this level. Hence, I tend to favor support of intellectual meritocracy in relation to this education because, in my view, it is likely to be a form of inequality advantageous to all. Therefore, it would satisfy Rawls' (1971) principle of justice. Rawls argued in favor of equality of income except for income inequality that can be expected to be advantageous to all in society.

The schoolteachers who influenced me most made me aware of the social and intellectual dangers of dogmatism and of jingoism. They also pointed out that rote learning and the repetition of ideas would stifle innovation and, consequently, intellectual and economic progress. One of my history teachers suggested that China lost its global leadership in relation to intellectual advance and scientific and technological progress for several centuries due to its development of an intellectual culture (which he associated with Confucianism) that was not supportive of new ideas and innovation. While this may or may not be the major cause in this specific case, I am firmly convinced of the importance of academic institutions fostering innovatory attitudes and the quest for new ideas by students.

I worry that many Western universities today are in danger of losing their earlier emphasis on making students think (Tisdell 2000a). Modern teaching techniques, large classes, excessive reliance on text books, and use of teacher evaluation procedures and scores discourage students and many of their teachers from searching for new ideas (Alauddin and Tisdell forthcoming). In economics, this tends to be reinforced by the mechanical application of mathematical and econometric techniques. These techniques all too often become a substitute for an in-depth assessment. I believe that the academic philosophy imparted to me by my teachers motivated me strongly to explore new fields in economics, including tourism economics.

My final year at Taree Public School was 1956. For me, this was a crucial year. I wanted to go on to university studies but knew that that would be impossible without an adequate scholarship (whether I would win such a scholarship depended on my final examination grades). I was fortunate to be awarded two scholarships: one to study law at Sydney University and the other from the New South Wales Department of Education to complete a degree to teach in secondary schools. I accepted the latter, because it paid both university enrollment fees and a living-away-from-home allowance, whereas the former did not pay more than university enrollment fees. I enrolled in the University of New South Wales and attended its Newcastle University College campus in the Hunter Valley, to study for a Bachelor of Commerce in Economics. Eventually, I obtained this degree with first class honors and the university medal.

My lecturers had been trained in the British academic tradition; they had either completed their education in Britain or in Australia, which then clearly followed existing British traditions. There was considerable emphasis on reading (very limited use of text books), presentation of seminars by students, and on essays displaying critical abilities. None of my classes touched on tourism but much that I learnt was later to prove valuable in my discovery and exploration of tourism economics. Since my university student years, Australian universities have become increasingly attuned to academic practices in the United States, which may have also brought about major changes in the way British universities operate. In my view, a new academic culture is developing that could retard intellectual progress.

Postgraduate Studies at the Australian National University

My final year at Newcastle University College was 1960. I was encouraged by my lecturers, especially Warren Hogan, to apply for postgraduate scholarships. I was successful—won a scholarship for Harvard University to cover fees, a scholarship and fellowship for the University of Pennsylvania, and a scholarship of the Australian National University. The latter was financially attractive but I did not look forward to further coursework that would be required if I went to the United States. So I went to Canberra and submitted my PhD thesis in economics in 1963. Fred Gruen and Trevor Swan jointly supervised my research.

My thesis was relatively theoretical and was published in 1968 by Princeton University Press (Tisdell 1968). There was nothing in it about tourism. However, in 1984, I did publish a tourism-relevant article (Tisdell 1984b) that drew on some of the theoretical ideas in this thesis and which was reprinted with some minor changes in Tisdell (2001). The content of my thesis was quite original and was underpinned by some philosophical discourse. Yet, I did not depart too much from the use of a standard economic framework. Several articles based on it (or an extension of this research) were published in leading academic journals and the philosopher Jon Elster took note of my contribution comparing one of my viewpoints about decision making with that of Descartes (Elster 1979:60–61). I only learnt about that in the early 1990s when a colleague at The University of Queensland brought it to my attention. Naturally, I was rather pleased. The rationality and decision making of tourists is receiving increased attention in my more recent research on tourism.

Lecturing in Economics at the Australian National University

I began lecturing in microeconomics in 1964 at the Australian National University and continued to do so (except in 1965) until mid-1972 when I took up a position Professor of Economics at Newcastle University in New South Wales. In 1965, I traveled around the world as a result of being awarded a postdoctoral scholarship of the Australian National University. The award was for one year, paid my airfare and provided an adequate living allowance. This was my first experience of international travel.

I spent the major portion of 1965 at Princeton University as a visiting fellow and a shorter period at Stanford University. In Princeton, my main contacts were William Baumol and Oskar Morgenstern and I also enjoyed some academic interaction with Fritz Machlup. I did not work on any specific aspect of tourism economics, but I wrote a paper (Tisdell, 1966) that dealt with aspects of game theory, for which I later found some applications in relation to tourism economics. Morgenstern was very supportive of my work. I also wrote a working paper on aspects of evolutionary economics and showed it to Baumol who felt (probably correctly) that it did not have a lot to say. However, I did return to evolutionary economics (1996a) and have considered evolutionary themes involving tourism in my work (1991:chapter 10; 2005: chapter 10). My discussions with Fritz Machlup were motivated by my interest in knowledge—its economic value and role in economic activity and development. This is a wide subject that has been of particular interest to the Austrian School of Economics. I cannot go into the details here, but it includes the economics of research and development and innovation, science and technology policy, as well as the role of knowledge in the coordination and management of economic activity. After I returned to lecture at the Australian National University in 1966, I received grants to undertake research on industrial research and development policy and studied, among other things, intellectual property rights. This research developed my interest in economic externalities and provided an opportunity for me in 1982 to obtain my first research grant to study specifically some economic features of tourism.

I received a stimulus in 1970 to begin a new line of inquiry when Trevor Swan (one of the supervisors of my PhD thesis) rang me to say that he had seen a recently published theoretical article of mine. He said it was very good but asked me to do something different (this article involved an extension of ideas in my PhD thesis). I then decided that I would study ecological and environmental economics and by 1972 I was already publishing in this area and have not stopped since. This interest of mine in environment and natural resources provided an important bridge to the development of my interest in tourism economics, particularly my interest in the connections among nature, environment, and tourism.

Professor of Economics at the University of Newcastle

In mid-1972, I left my position as Reader in Economics at the Australian National University to take up a position as Professor in Economics at Newcastle University (Australia). It was during this period that my interest in tourism economics became well established. My research output continued to expand on a variety of fronts. Ecological economics, agricultural economics, the economics of research and development policies, and science and technology policies all held my interest. I wrote some papers relating to the value of national parks from a recreational point of view (Tisdell 1974, 1977) and published a major work entitled *Wild Pigs: Environmental Pest or Economic Resource?* which included some material on the recreational hunting of wild pigs (1982) and, at about the same time, published a few articles on recreational hunting. However, I did not obtain a real breakthrough in the development of my emerging research interest in tourism economics until 1982.

About this time, Ken Tucker of the Research School of Asian and Pacific Studies of the Australian National University approached me about the possibility of participating in the ASEAN–Australia Joint (Economic) Research Project. He was the Australian organizer of research on the service (tertiary) sector and he was keen to have a contribution from me dealing with industrial R&D. Early-1970s onward, I had written extensively on the subject and had a book published in 1981 on Science and Technology Policy (1981). However, I thought it was time to move on to a new subject and I proposed to him that I should focus on tourism, a different service. He was reluctant at first but accepted the idea and I received a grant (covering 1982 and 1983) to study "Natural (and related) resources and the generation of international tourism in Australia and ASEAN countries." The results were published in a project paper (Tisdell, T1984c) with parts of the results being published in journal articles (1983a, 1983b, 1984a).

The research grant from the ASEAN–Australia Joint Research Project set me firmly on my journey in exploring tourism economics. While in the remainder of my stay at Newcastle, I did not receive any major grant to concentrate on tourism economics, a number of opportunities arose that enabled me to continue my research interest in tourism economics. Sometimes I could include some consideration of tourism as part of my wider project. For example, I received a research grant as part of the Australian Research Grants Scheme to study the "World Conservation Strategy and the Economics of Conservation." One aspect of this strategy was the view that wildlife tourism should be promoted in developing countries to provide them with economic incentives to conserve wildlife. Therefore, I gave some consideration to this aspect (1991:chapter 4, 2005:chapter 4).

In 1984, I received support from the East-West Center (Environmental and Policy Institute) for a project and in 1986 from the Resource Systems Institute of this Center in Hawaii for another project. The former project was my first opportunity to consider marine turtles and dugongs (1986b). After coming to Brisbane, I subsequently did much research on turtles and tourism and also completed a paper about the conservation of dugongs (1999b). In the second project, I focused on marine-based tourism in Southeast Asia and Australia and coordinated the research of several contributors. Some of the results were included in an edited volume (Tisdell et al 1988) published by the Institute of Industrial Economics and in a book edited by James Barney Marsh of the University of Hawaii (Tisdell et al 1992).

During the 1980s, I became Director of the Institute of Industrial Economics at Newcastle University after its founding director (Brian Johns) left to take up a government position in Canberra. I then expanded the interests of this institute to include tourism economics.

For a part of 1986, I was a Guest Investigator at the Marine Policy and Ocean Management Center, Woods Hole Oceanographic Institution, Massachusetts, USA. My work was partly funded by the Pew Foundation and I also obtained funds from the Johnson Endowment Fund to study marine policy in relation to marine resources and tourism management. I completed one paper with the director of this center (Tisdell and Broadus 1989) and planned to write an article with him about economic aspects of tourism in the Galapagos Islands. However, he was far too busy to be able to contribute to that. Apart from doing research, he had to manage the center and continually seek funds from donors to help finance it. The strain must have been considerable and he died unfortunately of a heart attack not that long after I returned to Australia. I did, nevertheless, eventually complete an article about tourism in relation to the Galapagos (1988c). Among other things, this led me to develop a critical view of the simplistic notions of tourism carrying capacity. Originally, however, I had in mind a rather different article: one to look at the demand for different tourist packages based on varied combinations of attributes or attractions. Later this type of analysis would become the focus of those studying choice experiments, but I did not proceed down this path. As a result of my visit to Woods Hole, I also published an article about Antarctica (1986a), but it was only after coming to Brisbane that I undertook a study of Antarctic tourism.

An important event for my progress with the economics of tourism also occurred when I was stationed at Woods Hole. I made a visit to Toronto to participate in a conference of the International Association of Social Economics. While there, I met Yushi Mao. He was then Professor of American Studies at the Chinese Academy of Social Sciences, an accomplished economist, and a visitor to Harvard University. After our initial meeting, we arranged to meet again in Boston and then in Woods Hole. We got along very well and when Mao left after visiting me in Woods Hole, he said he would get me invited to China. He had noted my interest in tourism economics and arranged for an article of mine on this subject to be published in China in 1987 (1987a). In 1988, I received an invitation from the President of Nankai University in Tianjin, China, to teach tourism economics to a postgraduate class; an opportunity which I took up in 1989.

Meanwhile at Newcastle University, I was expanding postgraduate studies in economics. Several PhD students arrived from developing countries and one, Rajasundrum Sathiendrakumar (who actually came from the United Kingdom after studying at Manchester University) decided to write his thesis on the role of tourism and fisheries in the development of the Maldives. He was my first PhD student to include tourism as a component of his research (others did so later). We published several articles about the development of tourism in the Maldives (Sathiendrakumar and Tisdell, 1985, 1989). I became interested in the development of tourism in small economies and have continued that interest.

In 1988, I was fortunate to be invited to the Economics Department at the University of Otago, New Zealand. On this occasion, I was awarded the position of William Evans Visiting Professor of the University of Otago. While in Dunedin, I observed that the royal albatross on the Otago Peninsula had become an important tourism attraction and that yellow-eyed penguins were increasingly popular. Therefore, I decided to do some research on the economic impacts of this tourism and its potential, and I was invited to present a paper on this subject at the Otago Museum (1988a). Little did I know that 20 years later that I would be invited back to Dunedin by the Yellow-Eyed Penguin Trust to do more research and update this paper for a conference to mark the 20th anniversary of the establishment of the Yellow-Eyed Penguin Trust.

During the latter part of my stay in Newcastle, David McKee of Kent State University, Ohio, came to visit me and then he came back again not long after I moved to Brisbane. He convinced me to be the coauthor of *Development Issues in Small Island Economies* and to contribute material dealing with issues in tourism development in small island economies (McKee and Tisdell 1990).

A Digression on Sustainable Tourism

Because of the way in which my interest in sustainable tourism developed and straddled my stay in Newcastle and in Brisbane, it is relevant to outline, as a side issue, how that interest arose. Around the mid-1980s, I started exploring the concepts of sustainable development and economic sustainability, and was an early contributor to discussions of these subjects. For example, I presented a seminar paper at the University of New England on sustainable development and this was subsequently published in *World Development* (1988b). During my interesting visit to South Africa in 1984 as a guest of the South African Department of National Education, I developed the economics sustainability theme further and published additional articles on this subject. The subject of economic sustainability became a continuing interest of mine and had an influence on my thinking about tourism economics. This is reflected, for example, in my article "Tourism, the environment and profit" (1987b) and in (1988c) and several subsequent publications; for example, in Chapter 10 of *Economics of Environmental Conservation* (1991, 2005). The first edition of this book was based, to a significant extent, on my lectures developed for Environmental Economics at Newcastle University but it was not published until after I transferred to The University of Queensland.

In the mid-1990s, I began exploring the subject of ecotourism as a possible way to achieve simultaneously environmental conservation and economic sustainability. Several of the papers resulting from this research are reprinted (2001). They included articles prompted by my visits to China (1996b) and by my visits to Brazil (1998), mainly to the University of Pernambuco in Recife. Much of my more recent work on tourism economics continues to be motivated by sustainability issues, particularly efforts to achieve specific goals relating to environmental and ecological sustainability. For example, relationships between tourism and nature conservation, including conservation of biodiversity, remain important issues for me.

Professor of Economics at The University of Queensland

In 1988, I was "headhunted" for the position of Professor of Economics at The University of Queensland. Not long after this offer came, Bond University also tried to recruit me as professor of decision sciences. At the interview for this position, the selection committee was, among other things, particularly supportive of my interest in tourism economics. In any event, I decided to take the position at The University of Queensland in Brisbane starting in February 1989. It was expected that I would immediately take over as Head of the Economics Department (had considerable experience in that regard having been departmental Head at Newcastle University for 10 years). However, an opportunity for me to visit China in the first half of 1989 had evolved. Apart from the invitation to come to give lectures in tourism economics at Nankai University (Tianjin) in the first part of 1989 (a consequence of my meeting with Yushi Mao in the United States), the Academy of Social Sciences in Australia provided me with a grant to establish contacts with the Chinese Academy of Social Science. This was an opportunity too good to miss. George Kenwood kindly agreed to stay on as Head of the Economics Department at The University of Queensland for another six months. Therefore, I was given permission to go to China by The University of Queensland to lecture at Nankai University and establish contacts in China.

I enjoyed my stay in China and lecturing there on tourism economics, despite the political unrest at the time due to the democracy movement. In a way, however, this unrest also added to my excitement, despite the unfortunate events that eventually unfolded. I found my students to be enquiring and bright, particularly Julie Wen who would later come to Australia and complete a PhD focusing on tourism and China's development. As a result of my visit, I began writing and publishing papers on tourism in China, some jointly with Julie Wen. In 1993, I published a book based on my lectures in China (which not only included those given in Tianjin but elsewhere in China). Chapter 12 of the book (1993) is entitled "Foreign Tourism: Benefits to China and Contributions to Development" and contains some original ideas. After returning to Australia, I looked for further opportunities to do research on economic aspects of tourism development in China.

Having completed a study at the request of the Australian Centre for International Agricultural Research (ACIAR) on the economics of giant clam culture (which included a small component on tourism and this culture), ACIAR was supportive of my request to undertake another project. Some funding was obtained for the period 1993–95 for the project "Economic Impact and Rural Adjustment to Nature Conservation (biodiversity) Program: A Case Study of Xishuangbanna Dai Autonomous Prefecture, Yunnan." Research was conducted in cooperation with the Southwest Forestry College in Kunming and, among other things, attention was given to the development of ecotourism in Xishuangbanna State Nature Reserve and its economic impact on local communities. Several publications emerged, a number of which were jointly authored by Xiang Zhu, my Chinese coresearcher. In addition a number of chapters, (1999a) drew on results from this research. Also as an outcome of this experience, I recommended to Julie Wen when she came to The University of Queensland to complete a PhD that includes Yunnan as one of the important foci of her study of tourism development in China, which she did. Eventually, this study resulted in a jointly authored book (Wen and Tisdell 2001).

Beginning in the early 1990s, I became interested in India's economic development and joined the International Institute of Development Studies headquartered in Calcutta as a lifetime member. My colleague, Kartik Roy, was active in the institute. A conference was organized in Bhubaneswar, Orissa, India in 1987 focusing on tourism and development in general, as well as on tourism development in India. This resulted in the publication of two edited books (Roy and Tisdell 1998; Tisdell and Roy 1998). I was surprised to learn recently from a website that the latter book, *Tourism and Development*, is one of my books held by a very large number of libraries.

From 1994 onward, I was fortunate to receive several relatively modest grants to support my research and wildlife-based tourism. In the period 1994–95, a grant was received in conjunction with Derrin Davis to study "Recreational Scuba Diving in Marine Protected Areas: Impacts, Economics and Management." Davis and myself completed several joint papers on this subject and he completed a PhD thesis based on this study. Another PhD student (Darrian Collins) had commenced by 2000 studying the socioeconomics of outbound tourism from Australia. There was no specific funding for this research, but it resulted in several joint publications (Collins and Tisdell 2002). Collins' thesis was entirely focused on tourism. Earlier Biman Prasad, another PhD scholar, had included tourism as part of his study of development issues in Fiji and a revised and updated version of this research was published in 2006 (Prasad and Tisdell 2006). I was also able to convince Ranjith Bandara (who came from Sri Lanka to complete a PhD) to take an interest in aspects of tourism in Sri Lanka and we published several articles jointly as well as a book (Bandara and Tisdell 2010). I developed a particular interest in elephant orphanages as attractions and we considered their role in the conservation of Asian elephants (Tisdell and Bandara 2009). So along with my PhD students, I remained very active in studying topics in tourism economics.

In 2000, I had a visit from China by Dayuan Xue. He is a natural scientist with a special interest in biodiversity conservation. At the time, he was convinced that insufficient consideration was being given to nonmaterial and nonuse values in the conservation of nature in China. He proposed a joint paper to examine the tourist and biodiversity value of a biosphere reserve in China. This was published in *Tourism Economics* (Xue et al 2000) and was selected for the "*Tourism Economics* Award for Journal Article Excellence" in the year 2000. In the letter accompanying the announcement of the award in 2001, it is stated "among the criteria used in making the Award are the value of the papers' contribution to original research, the quality of its argument, the coherence and concision of its presentation, and its contributions to the academic reputation of the journal."

In 2001, I was fortunate to be a visiting professor at the University of Zurich, Switzerland, jointly in the Institute of Environmental Science and the Department of Geography. During that time, one of my contributions was to give lectures to students on tourism and the environment. This was the second opportunity I had to lecture on aspects of tourism and it helped to maintain my interest in tourism and the environment.

From 2000 onward, I received a couple of relatively small but very useful grants as principal researcher from the Sustainable Tourism Cooperative Research Centre (STCRC). These gave me my first opportunity (as principal researcher) to collect primary data in Australia relating to the economics of nature-based tourism. Although a shared grant was received from the STCRC to study the role of economics in managing wildlife tourism, the funds were utilized by Derrin Davis and it was essentially a desktop study.

As it transpired, I had to complete the STCRC report for this study because he left academia suddenly.

Clevo Wilson joined the School of Economics at The University of Queensland as a postdoctoral fellow in 2000 and we began joint research on the economics of nature-based tourism. He participated in the "Sea Turtles and Ecotourism" project (2000) and in the Economics of Wildlife Tourism' project (2001–04), both of which were funded by the CRC for Sustainable Tourism. The research made use of surveys of tourists visiting attractions: the Mon Repos turtle rookery near Bundaberg, Lamington National Park, the Antarctic Peninsula, and studied glow worms as attractions at Springbook National Park. The results of this research were published and two separate reports of the CRC for Sustainable Tourism (Tisdell and Wilson 2002, 2004).

In this period 2001–02, I was also involved as a joint researcher in a project funded by the University of Brunei where I had established several contacts as an external advisor. I did write some articles related to this project (2003), but the project did not proceed as planned, because the leading researcher from the University of Brunei was transferred to a public service position outside the university. This resulted in the cessation of the project. The University of Brunei is operated as a part of Brunei's public service system.

By 2001, I was keen to do research on the economics of conserving Australia's tropical wildlife. The University of Queensland gave me and Clevo Wilson a grant in 2002 to undertake preliminary research on this subject and to prepare a submission to The Australian Research Council for a Discovery Grant. This application (with Clevo Wilson) for a Discovery Grant to provide funding in the period 2003–06 for the project "Economics of Conserving Australian Tropical Wildlife: An Analysis of the Role of Economic Valuations, Property Rights and Commercialisation" was successful. This was an important grant for me, because it enabled primary data collection and theory to be combined. We included a tourism component in the research proposal, but as a subsidiary (but not insignificant) theme. We had to obtain a covering letter from the director of the CRC for Sustainable Tourism to state that this component did not overlap to any significant extent with the mission of this CRC. Presumably, this was to stop "double-dipping" for funds. This funding was useful for sustaining my research (for a limited period of time) after I became Professor Emeritus 2005.

Apart from the books already mentioned, two concentrating on tourism economics appeared in this period. Edward Elgar approached me to compile and edit a book on tourism economics for his *Critical Writings in Economics* series. This involved surveying the literature on tourism economics and selecting articles that, in my view, had played a pivotal role in the development of tourism economics (2000b). It was a challenging task but it did provide me with a comprehensive overview of the development of tourism economics. I decided not to include many of my own articles in that collection, because I did not want to take advantage of my editorial position and I was not sure that any were really of critical importance for the development of tourism economics. In any case, a year later, Edward Elgar published a collection of my essays in *Tourism Economics, the Environment and Development* (2001). This has proven to be one of the most popular of my books and is stocked by many libraries globally.

Professor Emeritus

My academic life did not stop when my status changed from Professor of Economics to Professor Emeritus at The University of Queensland. The fact that I no longer had to attend meetings, respond to bureaucratic reporting, and give lectures gave me more time for my research and writing. The down side was that I had fewer resources to support these activities. Nevertheless, the Discovery Grant from the Australian Research Council continued for a couple of years after my status changed. While many of the discoveries made possible by that grant were published, much of the primary data relating to tourism economics only became available toward the end of funding for this research. At that time, remaining funds were insufficient to enable papers to be completed using this data. However, last year (2010), I had revisited these data and have written up the results for some chapters for a manuscript to be published by Edward Elgar (Tisdell and Wilson forthcoming). Finishing my contribution to this manuscript is one of my main projects at present. Some of the findings will be supportive of tourism economics based on behavioral economics and critical of some models of tourist decision making based on neoclassical economics.

In 2005, I completed a second edition of the *Economics of Environmental Conservation*, which included a chapter on tourism and the environment. This edition was given the Choice Award of the American Libraries' Association in January 2007. Edward Elgar had also requested me to edit another book in his *International Library of Critical Writings in Economics Series*; one dealing with the economics of leisure. This book (2006), in two volumes, was intended to complement my other book, *The Economics of Tourism* (2000b) in this series. It was a difficult project, because I found many gaps in the economic literature dealing with this subject. For example, there was little or no coverage by economists of significant leisure activities (such as the economics of gardening as a hobby, nor of the keeping of pets) and the economics of industries that cater for leisure activities had been neglected by economists, as I noted in my overview of *The Economics of Leisure*.

In 2006, I visited Mauritius to participate in a workshop arranged by professors from the University of La Réunion (notably Jacques-Marie Aurifeille and Serge Svizzero) with whom I had had previous contacts. During that time, I gave three lectures to undergraduate students dealing with environmental issues. One was on tourism economics. The students seemed very interested in these talks and took the opportunity following the lectures to discuss with me topics raised during the lectures.

In 2007, I unexpectedly received an invitation from the Yellow-Eyed Penguin Trust (New Zealand) to update my 1988 study of the development of wildlife-based tourism on the Otago Peninsula, particularly in relation to the yellow-eyed penguins (1988a) and to prepare a paper for presentation at a conference to mark the 20th anniversary of the trust. I was most enthusiastic about this update and it provided me with some new insights about tourism economics (2007b, 2007c, 2009).

My recent assignments were to write a keynote address for the 3rd Australian Wildlife Tourism Conference (September 1–3, 2010), to make progress in preparing a "Handbook on Tourism Economics," and to finish my contribution to the manuscript for *The Economics of Nature-based Tourism and Conservation*. Preparations for a *Handbook of Tourism Economics* have progressed and this book is expected to be published by World Scientific in 2012.

Why Tourism Economics is Exciting and Valuable

Forty years ago, when I first began exploring my interest in economics and the conservation of nature, I had no idea that it would result in my discovery of tourism economics and lead to the journey I have taken so far. In recent years, exploring tourism economics has become a passion, a hobby, and, one might well say, virtually an obsession. Although I never have had large research grants for projects exploring tourism economics, as time went on, I did get sufficient funding to do fieldwork and collect primary data and do other than desktop studies. This gave me the opportunity to use direct observations to assess and develop theories. I enjoy this and find it exciting, especially as some of the results of this research are supportive of new developments in economic theory, such as those associated with behavioral economics and psychological economics, bounded rationality, and transaction cost theory.

Tourism economics has also appealed to me because of its interdisciplinary nature, the considerable scope it provides for heterodox approaches to problem solving, and especially the openings it gives to me to communicate with nonspecialists. My discovery of tourism economics has enabled me to explore a wide range of issues, for instance in microeconomics, welfare economics, international economics, and development economics. Furthermore, I have become increasingly aware of the limitations of mainstream economic methods of valuation of resource use, the multidimensional nature of valuation, and the limitations of human reasoning in resolving valuation issues. This is not to say that no progress in these matters is possible, but we should be humble in assessing our achievements.

As a result of my interest in tourism economics, I have been able to visit so many interesting and diverse places. These include Xishuangbanna in China (staying in forestry camps, traveling to the Laotian border, and meeting local minority groups), the Sundarbans in Bangladesh and India, parts of Orissa, the natural attractions of Brunei, the Otago Peninsula in New Zealand, and much more. Very often one small encounter sparks curiosity and leads to more research. For example, on a visit to Brunei, I once saw a troupe of proboscis monkeys at sunrise in the treetops on a mangrove-fringed island in the bay near the Sultan's Palace. These are one of the wildlife attractions of Brunei. Later, I coauthored an article about the conservation of proboscis monkeys and orangutans (Tisdell and Swarna Nantha 2008) and have become involved in research studying the economics of conserving the orangutan. As in the mathematics of chaos, one small incident can alter the evolution of thought and research and result in its following an unpredicted and unpredictable path. This adds to the excitement that comes from exploring unexpected ideas and creates diversity in thought which in turn generates enthusiasm.

CONCLUSION

For me, the discovery of tourism economics and my journey in this field has both been exciting and valuable. The nice thing about the subject area is that there is still a lot to discover so there is still plenty of room for others to obtain the excitement of discovery in this expanding field of study.

It might be observed that I have never taught tourism economics, except as a guest lecturer. This is because I have always been employed in departments (schools) of economics and normally this field is believed to be too specialized to be part of their curriculum. The teaching of the subject usually occurs in schools of tourism and recreation. Nevertheless, tourism economics could be a valuable elective if made available in some schools of economics. I must, however, admit that if I had been expected to teach the subject on a regular basis, it would probably have jaded my appetite for exploring tourism economics. It would have no longer been a hobby and a spontaneous interest. Had I been required to teach tourism economics regularly, I would probably have lost my enthusiasm for tourism economics, especially since in academia considerable external supervision and monitoring (management?) of courses, in the name of accountability, has occurred. While accountability is in principle good, it involves costs: it limits experimentation and invention and generates transaction costs. As a result, the generation of new ideas is adversely impacted and the effective amount of funds available for research in fields, such as tourism economics, is reduced, because the costs of administration eat up a large segment of the funding pie. There is a danger that the same malady may beset modern universities as Joseph Schumpeter (1942) predicted might happen to large business companies as market economies develop, namely that they will be crippled by bureaucracy.

Chapter 14

Solving Little Math Problems about Community Tourism

Timothy Jay Tyrrell
Arizona State University, USA

Timothy Jay Tyrrell is professor in the School of Community Resources and Development in the College of Public Programs and director of the Center for Sustainable Tourism at Arizona State University, USA. He is also emeritus professor in the Department of Resource Economics in the College of Resource Development at the University of Rhode Island where he spent most of his career. He has taught graduate and undergraduate courses in econometrics, dynamic modeling, statistics, research methods, and tourism planning and assessment. His publications employ mathematical and statistical methods to evaluate the community impacts of tourism. He is a member of the Travel and Tourism Research Association, the International Association of Scientific Experts in Tourism, the International Association of Tourism Economists, and Hospitality Sales and Marketing Association. Email <Timothy.J.Tyrrell@asu.edu>

> Life is good for only two things: discovering mathematics and teaching mathematics (Siméon-Denis Poisson (1838)).

The Discovery of Tourism Economics
Tourism Social Science Series, Volume 16, 191–198

ISSN: 1571-5043/doi:10.1108/S1571-5043(2011)0000016017

INTRODUCTION

While my life has been good for other things, discovering and teaching mathematics have always been close to the top of my list.

We moved a lot when I was young—by my count 30 different houses in my first 30 years in eight different states in the eastern United States. During sixth grade my family moved twice: once from Louisville, Kentucky to Elgin, Illinois and once again across town in Elgin. At each of the three schools I attended that year, the teacher seemed to be just introducing "story problems." By my third exposure to the topic, I thought I was "king" of the story problem. I am still doing story problems—solving little math problems in economic theory or statistics, and now they all relate to community tourism. I always liked solving little math problems, but until recently did not enjoy writing about the solutions. I had intended to include some mathematics in the text of this biography since certain solutions provide reference points for turns in my professional path, but the editors had other ideas.

I did not really want to work for a living the way my father did—in so many places, for so many different employers, and receiving so little satisfaction (from my perception anyway). I once calculated that I would need a million dollar savings account in order to live off the interest (one of my earliest little math problems). Since that was not going to happen, I came up with Plan B: make a living at the thing I most probably would want to do after I retire. Since I enjoyed college at the University of South Florida where I was exposed to computers, economics, and the academic lifestyle, Plan B was to become a professor. The latter has worked out very well.

Just Algebra

Brief comments made to me and about me at different times as a student have had significant influences on my path. The first was made by an advanced calculus professor at University of South Florida in the margin of one of my hastily completed mathematical proofs: "this is just ALGEBRA," he said. Clearly I had missed the idea of the exercise and fallen back to my mathematical comfort zone. That is when I realized that I really liked algebra. These days I no longer do "just ALGEBRA" but I certainly do a lot of it.

I started as an accounting major at University of South Florida and, after earning only a "C" in intermediate accounting, became an economics major. Economics seemed to be the ideal major for me: completely devoted to solving story problems. Unfortunately, I did not keep very good account of my credits toward the economics degree and in my senior year I found out that I was three social science elective credits short of graduation. My solution was to change my major to mathematics where all my math electives became major credits and all my economics credits became social science electives. I graduated on time and that last minute change of major turned out to be an asset in landing my first job as a computer programmer at Oak Ridge National Laboratory in Tennessee. The alternative in 1969 was to enlist in the military and serve in the Vietnam War. That war influenced the lives and career paths of many friends and family members.

Electricity Demand and Food Consumption

At Oak Ridge National Laboratory, I was a first-generation programmer (punch cards, 1,536K of available memory on an IBM 360, debugging machine language codes, without screen controls and verifying codes on a hand-cranked Merchant calculator). Because of my economics coursework, I was invited to work in 1971 on the first-ever National Science Foundation energy project. My job was that of a statistical programmer to work with a recent Berkeley PhD, Duane Chapman, to estimate electricity demand models for the United States. Up until that point, most economists had found electricity demand to be inelastic with respect to price and predictable simply from population growth. At that time the only statistical software other than what we wrote ourselves was part of BMDP, a statistical package for biological sciences. We collected data for all the states for 25 years and estimated models for residential, commercial, and industrial customer demands, experimenting with seemingly unrelated regressions and instrumental variables methods to estimate distributed lagged models and variable elasticity models. This was great fun and exciting work. I was sent to the Library of Congress to collect data and invited to speak at an MIT conference about projections of electricity demand where I secretly enjoyed being introduced incorrectly as "Dr. Tyrrell."

While at Oak Ridge National Laboratory, I pursued a part-time Masters degree in economics at the University of Tennessee, which took entirely too long (seven years). My first coauthorship was for a *Science Magazine* article describing our electricity demand modeling results (Chapman et al 1972). We were arguably the first to suggest that electricity in the United States was price elastic in the long run. With this I was introduced to art of professional writing, and use of dummy variables, logarithmic transformations, and distributed lagged models.

With the support from Duane Chapman and his colleague from Berkeley, Timothy Mount, I received a teaching and research assistantship for PhD at

Cornell University in agricultural economics. I only took one course about agriculture "Ag Marketing"; most of my courses were in economics and statistics. I met my wife while teaching the lab section of a linear programming course. Carol (now my wife of 30+ years) was the smartest person in the class and helped me understand a subject I had never studied before. Mount guided me through the PhD program and I completed a doctoral thesis entitled "An application of the multinomial logit model to predicting the pattern of food and other household expenditures in the Northeastern United States." I used my Oak Ridge National Laboratory programming skills to create a maximum likelihood estimator for the multinomial logit model and got a supreme thrill when it actually converged on a solution one evening in the basement of Warren Hall. The dissertation won an honorable mention with the American Agricultural Economics Association, although I did not hear about that for several years after graduation. Two papers were published out of the dissertation. One was based on the linear logit estimation of a nonlinear expenditure system (Tyrrell and Mount 1982). The second one was based on the application of a solution by Joseph Lagrange (1736–1813) to the problem of interpolating between tabled values. Because of computer algorithms, interpolation is not a subject of much interest anymore, but the Lagrange's method provided an elegant approach to modeling the composite effect of the ages of all household members based on an underlying cubic polynomial effect of age on consumption. The algebra of things always had my greatest attention.

Never a Great Economist

In 1978, I interviewed for faculty positions at the University of Rhode Island (URI) and several other places. Chapman told one search committee that I was "a great technician but would never be a great economist." He was probably right, but after he said so I quickly stopped using him as a reference. His candor helped me recognize my weaknesses, but unfortunately discouraged me from professional writing.

I accepted my first academic appointment as assistant professor in the Department of Resource Economics at the URI. We lived in Wakefield, Rhode Island, a rural community near the Atlantic Ocean and a 10-minute commute to the university. We raised two children, Matthew who still lives in the area and Emily who now lives in Vermont. For 27 years, I taught graduate econometrics, dynamic economic models, and an undergraduate tourism economics class. I was promoted to associate and later professor mostly on the basis of my teaching and service to the community. The URI had no tourism or hospitality program, and my tourism economics class was always underenrolled because it was too mathematical for most undergraduates seeking an easy undergraduate elective.

TOURISM RESEARCH

I began to study the tourism industry in 1980, two years after I arrived at URI, as part of a National Oceanic and Atmospheric Administration (NOAA) investigation of the economic impact of the Amoco Cadiz oil spill on the tourism industry of Brittany, France (Grigalunas et al 1988.) What started as a simple econometric analysis of the disturbance in the trend in tourism industry employment growth in Brittany due to the spill, ended as a lesson in the complexities of the tourism industry at the community level. I began to imagine how my ability to solve little math problems might be useful in tourism economics, and found great support from the industry and newfound academic tourism colleagues. Encouragement from John Hunt (then at University of Massachusetts), Mark Okrant (Plymouth College, New Hampshire), Rick Purdue (Virginia Tech), and many members of the Travel and Tourism Research Association cemented my professional path to tourism.

I obtained a contract with the Rhode Island Department of Economic Development in 1983 to monitor the economic impacts of tourism on the state and each of its 39 cities and towns. This involved solving math problems associated with reconciling national, state, and local data over months and years to estimate a monitoring model that, unbeknownst to me, contained the elements of a tourism satellite account. (Eventually I would estimate one for the state.) As part of the state-funded project, I also estimated the economic impacts of tourism events and welcome centers on local communities. Over the 22 years that I held the state contract, I made a great many tourism industry friends and attended every Travel and Tourism Research Association conference, but I did not publish in the professional literature as much as I should have. The latter was partly because of Chapman's prediction and partly because I was happy enough just solving little math problems for appreciative tourism industry friends.

An Important Collaboration

My interest in publishing was rekindled by collaboration with a highly talented URI graduate student in 1992. Rob Johnston (currently professor and director, George Perkins Marsh Institute, Clark University) knew just how to position applied math solutions in the professional literature. He inspired me to write and read literature that I had avoided. Over the decades since, we developed a close friendship and great research partnership. Our first joint effort encapsulated results from about 20 economic impact studies of tourism events written for the Rhode Island Department of Economic Development. A standardized framework had emerged over time that allowed us to compare the impacts of events and even make credible forecasts.

Three little math problems emerged when implementing the framework. First was how to separate expenditures associated with the activities of the event and its location. We treated that problem in the paper pretty effectively. Another problem was how to track expenditures from origin to destination. We came up with a pretty good solution to that problem also, but it was never published. A third problem was how to estimate the number of visitors at an event when there was not a fee, a single gate, or a single venue. That is, how does one combine multiple indicators of attendance (activities such as food sales and traffic counts) with survey estimates of the proportion of each type of visitor that participated in each activity to derive their underlying number?

Our solution was to treat the unknown numbers of visitors as coefficients, proportions as regressors, and activities as the dependent variable in a regression framework. We were able to publish several applications of this model (Johnston and Tyrrell 2003; Tyrrell and Johnston 2002; Tyrrell et al 2004) even though an eminent econometrician later pointed out that our claim about the unbiasedness of our estimator was false (Johnston and Tyrrell, 2005a).

During the same period, we developed a procedure for estimating the expenditure impacts on state tourism of a welcome center stop using pre- and postvisit survey data (Tyrrell and Johnston 2003). In the same year, we edited a special issue of *Journal of Travel Research* on the economic impacts of tourism (Tyrrell and Johnston 2006). We learned a great deal about the breadth of the field that year and made some lifelong friends.

I ran a consulting business (we wanted to call it "Impacts R Us," but settled on "Impact Research Associates"). It never made any money, but it did provide many opportunities to solve real tourism industry and community development problems. One of our successful projects was sponsored by the Southeastern Connecticut Tourism District (now defunct). In that we developed a model to estimate the impacts of tourism on municipal revenues and expenditures (Tyrrell and Johnston 2009). The contribution of this model was that it separately estimated three types of primary impacts of tourism growth (changes in residential population, industry employment, and visitor traffic) rather than assume that the product of employment growth and a fiscal impact multiplier would describe the spatial distribution of impacts. This separation of impacts enabled us to more precisely measure the different impacts on the 21 communities in contrast to the standard multiplier analysis which treated all tourism growth the same.

Tourism for the Public Good

Our most successful research collaboration was a dynamic model of sustainable tourism based on the transformation of a classic two-equation fisheries management model. It won the 2005 Charles R. Goeldner Article of Excellence Award (Johnston and Tyrrell, 2005b). In it we abstracted about planning objectives, constraints, and the resilience of community environmental qualities to derive a dynamic model of sustainable tourism for the tourism industry and another for community residents. Our comparison of the two models demonstrated two basic results for sustainable tourism: (a) that in all but the most rare of circumstances, there is no single, universal sustainable optimum and (b) a policy that maintains overly pristine environmental quality may be just as unsustainable—from the perspective of either the tourism industry or residents—as a policy that causes excessive environmental decay.

The development of the model, which is represented by two basic equations, also dictated follow-up research into the community objective function (Tyrrell et al 2010) and the community resilience equation (Tyrrell and Johnston 2008). We have also recently formulated a quantifiable "triple bottom line" that focuses on the relative contributions of tourism to social, environmental, and economic dimensions of community quality of life.

The community quality of life aspects of tourism development have been in the back of my mind since my study of the impacts of the Amoco Cadiz oil spill in 1980. There have always been social or environmental backstories associated community economic impact studies, but these have always been beyond the scope or resources of the research investigation. In the past decade, I have reexamined my assumptions about the fundamental goals of community tourism development and embraced a new perspective: "community development using tourism" to replace "tourism development in the community." This allows reduction, redesign, and elimination of tourism to be considered as community development solutions and focuses increased attention on direct social and environmental impacts of tourism. One application of this approach, where I was most excellently mentored by colleagues at Virginia Tech, resulted in a paper examining the nature of the value of tourism (Perdue et al 2010).

CONCLUSION

My current position as a professor, in the School of Community Resource and Development in the College of Public Programs at Arizona State University (ASU) is the direct result of turning attention to the role tourism plays in community development. Many colleagues thought I was personally crazy to leave my URI professorship in the idyllic, coastal rural Rhode Island community after 27 years and move to the urban desert in Phoenix, Arizona to start again. But ASU has enabled me to pursue my goal to developing a research center entirely devoted to "Tourism for the Public Good." Marketing the idea of "public good" to the tourism industry and marketing "tourism" to community development foundations have been very challenging, but I think that if I can formulate these challenges as little math problems, I will be able to solve them, at least conceptually. "With me everything turns into mathematics" (Rene Descartes, 1650).

Chapter 15

Regional and/or Tourism Economist

Norbert Vanhove
Katholieke Universiteit Leuven, Belgium

Norbert Vanhove received his Doctoral degree in economics in 1961 at the Erasmus University of Rotterdam (cum laude). From 1979 to 2000, he was director-general of the Regional Development Authority of West-Flanders and WES (Westvlaams Ekonomisch Studiebureau), market leader in tourism research in Belgium. He was and still is involved in several teaching assignments: College of Europe: European Regional Policy (1967–2001), University of Antwerp and KULeuven: Economics of Tourism and tourism management (Since 1990); guest professor at several universities (UIB Palma, Venice, Savonlinna, Lausanne, Sion, Sao-Paulo, Rio de Janeiro). He has been a tourism consultant in several countries: Egypt, Indonesia, Argentina, Thailand, Slovenia, Rwanda, the Netherlands, and Belgium. He is member of several international tourism organizations: Tourist Research Centre: secretary-general since 1965; AIEST: vice president from 1994 to 2010; founder fellow of the International Academy for the Study of Tourism; International Association for Tourism Economics (IATE). He was honored with several awards and distinctions. One of them is the nomination as Grand Officer in the Order of King Leopold II. Email <norbert.vanhove@skynet.be>

The Discovery of Tourism Economics
Tourism Social Science Series, Volume 16, 199–216

ISSN: 1571-5043/doi:10.1108/S1571-5043(2011)0000016018

INTRODUCTION

I was born in 1935 in Torhout, a provincial town, at 20 km from Bruges, in the Province of West-Flanders, the most western part of Belgium. It was a small center with an agricultural population. At that time, there was no tourist office, or not until the 1980s that the town council decided to set up a discrete one. Torhout has a few touristic attractions: a town hall, a roman church, and the Wynendale castle. The latter is known for two historic events. The first relates to World War II. King Leopold III of Belgium signed in this castle in May 1940 the capitulation agreement with the German army. Wynendale castle also reminds us of Countess Mary of Burgundy (1457–1482), daughter of Charles the Bold and Isabella of Bourbon. She married Maximilian I of Habsburg (Maximilian of Austria). Mary died accidentally at the early age of 25 during a hunt with falcons on horseback in the domain of Wynendale castle.

My parents were respected farmers. The farm was since the middle of the 16th century (or earlier) in the hands of the family on my mother's side. I was the first child of a family of 11 children. Tourism did not belong to the vocabulary of the Vanhove family. However, my parents made their honeymoon trip to Lourdes in France. Tourism activities were restricted to visits to family and friends and occasional excursions.

From my early youth on, I had to work on the farm during my free time and school holidays. I milked hundreds of cows manually. At the university, during the study period before the exams (we had a one-month exam preparation time), I got up at five o'clock and worked for two hours at the farm before starting my studies. It was hard work. I learned to respect the work of my parents and of many people who earn their living with their hands. I also became aware that welfare should be earned. I finished my university studies in economics at the University of Ghent and passed with "great distinction" or *magna cum laude*.

A VOCATION AS REGIONAL ECONOMIST

A few days later professor, André Vlerick, founder of the famous Ghent–Leuven business school, asked me to become his assistant and to join the seminar of economics, specializing in regional economics, a subject with which I was familiar. My MSc thesis was an economic monograph of my hometown. My methodology was considered as original; one year later, the thesis was published in book form (Vanhove 1960). I collaborated in regional studies in the Province of East-Flanders. While this was not a very exciting job, Vlerick knew how to stimulate his collaborators and had many international contacts. One day during my first working year, he offered me a two months' work placement at the headquarters of Socony Mobil Company (now Exxon Mobile) in New York. To save on my travel costs, I flew Icelandic Airlines. This company was not a member of IATA, at that moment a special type of cartel for air carriers. This was my first experience with long-haul tourism. It was a long trip. It took me 27 hours to fly from Luxemburg over Iceland to New York. I arrived late and was obliged to go straight from the airport to the chief economist of Socony Mobil. I remember two things from this meeting: that I was very tired and that the man was astonished that I could speak four languages. "This can be very useful in my department," he said.

My stay in New York was exciting in many respects. The work interested me and the city was a real confrontation. I had never seen such a cosmopolitan and multicultural city with so many attractions. To me, New York is a "beautiful monster." Vlerick encouraged his collaborators to take up international studies and undertake PhD studies. It was an unwritten rule that each of the scientific assistants was offered one year's study at an American university. As early as 1960, he offered me such an opportunity. However, I preferred to spend one year working and studying at Netherlands Economic Institute (NEI) in Rotterdam, a leading Dutch economic research institute with a department of regional economics. Jan Tinbergen, the first Nobel Prize laureate in economics, and Leo Klaassen, world-known regional economic scientist, were at that time NEI directors. To my great surprise, Vlerick was enthusiastic about my proposal.

I started in January 1961 at the NEI. This was a unique opportunity to prepare a PhD thesis. I chose "The Efficiency of Dutch Regional Economic Policy" as my research theme. Dutch regional policy was an example in Europe at that time. He arranged the academic procedures in a minimum of time. The challenge could start; I worked day and night for several months. After a few weeks, I submitted the first chapter of my thesis to the promoter or supervisor who, a few days later, invited me to discuss it with him (this was unusual to me). I received many suggestions and he greatly stimulated my thinking on the subject. Further, he wanted to introduce me to various administrations and regional authorities and offered logistic support for multiple regression calculations. I was very lucky to have such a helpful and resourceful supervisor. Furthermore, my quantitative research very soon confirmed my central working thesis (all of which seemed like a dream). My public defense of my thesis was held on December 14 at the Nederlandsche Economische Hoogeschool (now Erasmus University) under the chair of Rector H.W. Lambers. In the Netherlands, the defense of a doctorate is always a special academic ceremony with respect for traditions. I passed with *zeer veel genoegen* (very high honor), the second highest degree.

Very soon, I was faced with two dilemmas. Klaassen offered me a part-time professorship at the Nederlandsche Economische Hoogeschool, combined with a research task at the NEI. After long discussions with my wife and friends, I declined. This has not influenced our good relationship. We published several times together and became close friends. Our best-known joint publications were the two editions of *Regional Policy: A European Approach*. This was mainly based on my teaching task at the College of Europe, a famous postgraduate institute for European studies in Bruges. The second dilemma was the presence of Olivier Vanneste, director West-Flemish Economic Council/West-Flemish Study Office (WER/WES), at my doctorate. I knew him from my student days. He helped me several times with my MSc thesis. Much earlier, he had spoken to me about a new tourism research within WER/WES in Bruges. The presence of Vanneste in Rotterdam was for some Belgian people at least unexpected. Was he scouting for a possible new collaborator?

Start of Tourism Research at WES

After the NEI period, I returned to the University of Ghent. I had some difficulties in adapting myself to the old environment. I was convinced that at that moment, the University of Ghent was not my future. Vlerick himself was paying more and more attention to his business school and less and less to the macroeconomic department. On the other hand, I was greatly indebted to Vlerick for all the support in my short career. However, he himself was suspicious about the presence of Vanneste at the occasion of the PhD ceremony. This and other things created some personal tensions between us.

Several weeks later, Olivier Vanneste phoned me for an appointment in our house in Bruges. He came back to the tourism project he had evoked months before. The Governor Knight Pierre van Outryve d'Ydewalle and president of WER/WES had thought of starting a tourism research department in WES.

The Province of West-Flanders was the most important tourism area of the country with the Belgian Coast and the old city of Bruges as major attractions. In the Province of West-Flanders, tourism was a vital economic sector. This also became evident in the study by Vanneste and Declercq (1955) "Kust en Hinterland" (The Coast and its Hinterland). One of the many recommendations of this analysis was permanent economic and market research. The province made money available to start with a new department within the WES organization. Vanneste asked me to start such a new department. I hesitated, for my knowledge of the tourism industry was zero. Vanneste did not see this as a handicap. He would guide me through the jungle of the tourism world. Finally, I accepted in 1962 the challenge, since regional economic analysis and development were the core business of WER/WES.

Tourism research for a region without data and for an industry that was reluctant to research was not a simple matter. During the first four years, the tourism research activities were totally orientated toward the Province of West-Flanders. Each year, we would focus on a number of topics, including domestic market, the market of the neighboring countries (United Kingdom, France, Netherlands, and West Germany), and comparative price level. All these studies were published in a special series and discussed with the industry. In this way, we informed the industry and received feedback.

One interesting study was an econometric analysis of the domestic tourism flows per county to the coastal area. I published an article "Binnenlandse toeristenstromen naar de Belgische Kust" (Domestic Tourist Flows to the Coast) about this study in "Tijdschrift voor Economie," a scientific review of the university of Leuven. In 1967, this contribution was awarded with the biannual prize of economics from the respected "Vereniging voor Economie" (Association for Economics).

Year after year, we proposed four research facets to the National Tourism Board and Westtoerisme (The Provincial Tourism Board). They made research funds available. After nine years of investigation, I disposed of a lot of data and ideas and proposed to my director (meanwhile I was deputy director of WER/WES) to prepare a book on the Belgian Coast. He was very much in favor. The book, more than 500 pages, was ready in a minimum of time. WES published *Het Belgisch Kusttoerisme: Vandaag en Morgen* (*Belgian Coastal Tourism: Today and Tomorrow*). The focus of the publication was on a new competitive tourism product for the coast. The publication got a lot of attention in the public and private tourism industry of Belgium and was awarded the Pro Civitate Prize for 1972. Furthermore, the organizer of the prize, Het Gemeentekrediet van België, published the French edition: *Le Tourisme sur le Littoral Belge Aujourd'hui et Demain* (*Collection Sciences Sociales 3*, 1974). From the very beginning, I was also expected to develop a tourism production index for the coast and its hinterland. The idea behind this was to collect data and to get a much better view of the evolution of the industry.

Tourism Production Index

Tourism arrivals or nights are, for many regions, not a good indicator of the tourism performance. Destination data about nights and arrivals are very often unreliable or only relate to hotel nights. Camping, rented apartments, second homes, and other accommodation forms are very often not considered. It is also well known that official tourism data totally neglect day visitors. Furthermore, the official data are only available long after the tourism activity took place.

These were the reasons why the WES started in 1962 with the development of a tourism production index for the region West-Flanders in Belgium (coastal region, Bruges, and hinterland area). The aim was dual: to collect data covering all aspects of the tourism business in the region and to be informed quickly about the performance of the tourism industry. The WES Tourism Index is similar to an index of manufacturing production. Each category of the index is given a certain weight factor; within each, a weight is attributed to the components of the category. The number and variety of the components is a guarantee to cover all measurable aspects of the tourism activity of the region. The results were published no later than four weeks after each month of tourism production. This was possible due to a performing data collection system, the good participation of the industry, and the use of a representative sample in the major components.

The WES index was produced monthly for the months April–September of each year. Although the index was considered to be the only reliable measuring instrument to measure the performance of the industry in the region, the production stopped in 2001 for financial reasons. The concept can be an example for many other tourism regions.

In the 1960s, the Belgian market was a very important market to the coast and the Belgian Ardennes. Nobody had a clear view about that market. WES proposed to the National Belgian Tourist Office (Commissariat Général au Tourisme) to finance a first national holiday survey according to the rules of scientific research. We organized a national random sample with 3,000 interviewees. To our surprise, there was a great enthusiasm for the project. We got logistical support from the National Statistical Office (interviews and computer help for data processing). At that time, such a research was original and an example in Europe. For the first time, there was a clear and correct Picture of the Belgian tourism market. We got a lot of information, and I prepared a scientific publication: *Het vakantiepatroon en de toeristische bestedingen van de Belgische bevolking* (*Holiday pattern and touristic expenses of the Belgian population*). This book too was translated into French: *Structure des Vacances et Dépenses touristiques de la Population Belge*. The industry showed a real interest in the results and urged WES to repeat this study on a regular basis. Up to this very occasion, WES organized biannually a national holiday survey with 6,000 interviews for the summer (short) holidays and a similar number for the winter (short) holidays. This research is one of WES' showpieces.

WES as a National and International Institute

By the end of the 1960s, WES enjoyed a reputation in tourism research at the national level. The staff had grown and the geographical area of West-Flanders was now considered too limited. The tourism industry in Belgium as a whole also became more research minded.

One international event worked in favor of WES. The relationship between Belgium and the former colony Congo deteriorated. This had an impact on the cooperation between the two countries. Belgium preferred to spend a larger share of development funds in other countries. There was a tense relationship between the Netherlands and Indonesia. There was a linguistic link between Flanders and Indonesia (the older civil servants of Indonesia spoke Dutch) and this put Indonesia on the shortlist for development aid. Vanneste, director-general of WES, was charged with a consulting mission in Indonesia in 1970. The Indonesian government expressed an interest, among other things, in regional development and tourism development in particular. One of the big problems of the Indonesian government was a lack of skills. Who in Belgium could provide the necessary support for human resources in regional and tourism development? WER/WES had the knowledge.

The Belgian Minister Scheyven, responsible for international cooperation, asked WES to start a training project in Bruges and Indonesia. During more than 20 years, Indonesian staff (10 per year) were sent to Bruges for a nine-month training course in regional and/or tourism development. The participants were prepared to work in the provincial tourist office or in the newly created *Bapeda* (a kind of regional development authority). WES also sent several teams for one month to the national training center in Bali to upgrade operational skills. I was the team leader of two teams. This brought me in contact with the famous SCETO report for the tourism development of Nusa Dua in Bali. We helped the provincial authorities with the implementation of the study. Many years later, Nusa Dua became one of the most successful comprehensive tourism projects in the world. This project respected Balinese architecture with great success.

The Nusa Dua study encouraged me to pay more attention to a macroevaluation of tourist project and to apply cost-benefit analysis (CBA) to tourism. One vital point of a CBA is the identification of the cost and benefit items that should be considered. For this purpose I developed a scheme that can be used in any project. This also avoids confusion between positive and negative externalities, side effects, indirect effects, impact on other firms, etc. We distinguish four levels of costs and benefits: project or paymaster's level, "unpaid" level, "underpayment" level, and side effects.

The first is the microlevel, also called the project or paymaster's level (in other words, which pays the project). The other three levels are related to all kind of externalities. Some costs or benefits are unpaid. Taking into account that a free lunch does not exist, the society is paying those items in one way or another. For certain items, the paid costs or benefits are estimated at a too low value or are underpaid. Finally, a tourism project may have a negative or positive impact, respectively, on competitors or complementary firms.

The strategic tourism-marketing plan for Belgium and for the different macroproducts (Coast, Ardennes, Art Cities, and Green Flanders) that we prepared in cooperation with THR (a Spanish consulting directed by E. Bordas) was another highlight of the tourism research activities. With the experience of this extensive marketing plan, WES was charged by the European Commission to prepare a strategic marketing plan for Argentina. THR was our subcontract, with WES as subcontract to THR for similar studies in Guatemala and Peru. Several other strategic marketing plans followed.

In 1993, WES was invited by the Inter-American Development Bank in Washington to carry out a study on "The competitive situation of tourism in the Caribbean area and its importance for the region's development." Several public and private clients had problems in reimbursing their loans. This was a great honor for our institute. WES developed its own tourism competitive model. This study was very well accepted by the bank.

Director-General GOM/WES

As already noted, WER/WES were two organizations with one management. The director and the deputy were active in regional development for the Province of West-Flanders and were involved in research. Our basic philosophy for an efficient regional development was research, conception, strategy, coordination, and implementation. Research was a WES task; the subsequent phases were the responsibility of the economic council (WER). In 1976, WER was transformed to GOM-West-Vlaanderen (Regional Development Authority for the Province of West-Flanders) with a public statute. In 1979, I succeeded Olivier Vanneste as director-general, when he was nominated governor of the Province of West-Flanders. More than before, my job moved from regional economic and tourism research to regional development. For more than 20 years, I combined the two functions. But tourism was my favorite field of interest. How could I combine research and development? One must have a special work attitude and discipline and I could rely on a lot of experience and a good team of collaborators. Tourism and regional economics were always interwoven in my career.

During all my research activities, I tried to keep a good relationship with the tourism industry. We relied on their input and support. The respect was reciprocal. In 1974, I was awarded the Jean Walckiers Prize and in 1985 with the Positive Prize of the Touring-Coach; prize awarded by the European Union of Publishers for Touring-Coach Tourism (Caredit).

Vice President AIEST

First, a few words about Association Internationale d'Experts Scientifiques du Tourisme. It finds its origin in an initiative of the Heads of the two Swiss tourism research institutes founded at the universities of St. Gallen and Berne in 1941, Walter Hunziker and Kurt Krapf. After the end of World War II, both felt the need to make known the fruits of their scientific work to a wider circle of colleagues, and to resume the broken threads of international scientific relations in tourism, in order to develop them as well as the scientific work related to tourism itself. The inaugural meeting of association took place in Rome on May 31, 1951. It is as such the oldest scientific organization in tourism. The counterpart in the United States is Travel and Tourism Research Association founded in 1970. Today, the Association Internationale d'Experts Scientifiques du Tourisme has 400 members in 50 countries all over the world. As such, it is a genuine international scientific society. This is an interdisciplinary network of experts, whose members include specialists from different disciplines (economics, business administration, geography, sociology, and other) who have a particular interest in tourism.

Its aims, as they were outlined and laid down at the outset and drawn up in Article 3 of the bylaws, have proved themselves and remained unchanged in that form to this day. Accordingly, the association endeavors to foster friendly relations among its members; promote scientific activity on the part of its members, in particular, by developing personal contacts, providing documentation, and facilitating exchange of views and experience; support the activity of scientific institutes of tourism, or other centers of research and education specializing in tourism, and to develop relations between them as well as between them and the members of the association; and organize and cooperate in congresses and other meetings and courses on tourism of a scientific nature.

Therefore, AIEST may be considered as being the international catalyst of scientific activities in tourism. The association does not itself directly engage in tourism research and education, but it endeavors to foster them as much as possible within the limits of its possibilities and those of existing institutions. Because of strict observance of its scientific character and the intensification of research and education in tourism, AIEST has been able to develop in a most gratifying way and has acquired a position of respect. Four focal points mark its activities and development: the annual congress, the tourism review, the documentation, and the network of experts.

I became a member of AIEST in 1965. At the time, I was its youngest member. My first contact with the association was in Budapest, Hungary in 1965 on the occasion of its annual congress. It was my first visit to a communist country. I do not have happy memories of that congress, particularly that. Traveling in an Eastern European country was not easy. One had the permanent feeling of being checked and supervised. The congress took place in the famous Gellert hotel and we were told that all rooms were provided with monitoring equipment. Furthermore, the congress was not good. The German professor Sauermann was very upset and made a speech of one hour to express his dissatisfaction. His proposal was to drop the letter "S" from the acronym. His intervention was debatable, but he was right. My boss was dissatisfied with the standard of the papers as well, and urged me to take the floor. This was my first, unprepared intervention. I had the feeling it was appreciated by the members. From the next year onward, AIEST congresses were restructured with success. In the following years, I attended about 40 AIEST congresses in all continents.

I was an active and sometimes a critical member within the organization. Nevertheless, I was invited several times to present a basic report (seven in total), to act as general reporter or to chair sessions. Basic reports of which I was proud included "Interrelation between Benefits and Costs of Tourism Resources: An Economic approach" (1982), "Tourism and the Architectural Heritage: Promotional, Economic and Fiscal Aspects" (1984), "Tourism and Economics: What Remains from a Long Research Tradition" (1994), "Globalisation of Tourism Demand" (1996), and "Externalities of Sport and Tourism Investments, Activities and Events" (2003). Furthermore, I was for a very long time member of the Editorial Board of the scientific journal *Tourism Review*, the official journal of the AIEST. When Emerald took over the review, I was on the new Editorial Advisory Board. In 1990, I was elected as a committee member. In 1994, I became vice president until September 2010. I worked with two great presidents, first Claude Kaspar and later Peter Keller.

During the long period of my membership, the AIEST has changed. From a purely European organization, it has become an international network. Due to globalization, this movement was inevitable. On the other hand, we have probably lost contact with some European roots. Of significance is the upgrading of *Tourism Review*. Due to a partial referee system, the changed outlook and the efforts of Emerald Group publishing, this review can compete with other well-known scientific tourism reviews. The annual congresses are always well developed, with quality proceedings. Up to 2008, they were always published before the congress, which I favored. I also worry about the decreasing participation in its annual congress. There are many reasons for this outcome. First, there are too many organizations and congresses, coupled with proliferation of tourism journals. Second, the simple "call for papers" formula is degrading the level. A congress theme needs a few keynote speakers, from either the industry or academics, who present comprehensive reports. Third, young tourism experts are more interested in specialized topics. Fourth, local organizers can no longer rely on generous sponsors, which make the congress fees rather high. Finally, most tourism experts nowadays have real travel experience. Congresses in attractive tourism locations become less appealing. As departing vice president, I recommend the new AIEST Committee to renew contacts with the operators in the tourism industry. The mission of TTRA can be inspiring: "The Travel and Tourism Research Association is committed to improving the quality, value, effectiveness, and use of travel and tourism research and marketing information. TTRA seeks to improve the industry through education, publications, and networking activities."

Secretary-General Tourism Research Center

The first Tourism Research Center meeting took place in 1965 in Bruges. I was in charge of the organization. My director Olivier Vanneste, one of the founders of the Tourist Research Center (TRC), was at the moment of the event taken ill and I was obliged to do the honors. I remember quite well, as a young researcher, my first meeting with Alfred Koch, René Baretje. Jozef Ramaker, and Maurits Tideman, the founding fathers in Hotel Portinari. The number of participants was rather limited. We had no need of a large meeting room.

In 1980, on the occasion of the 25th TRC meeting that took place in Bruges, Rik Medlik stated that the TRC

> was founded in the mid-1960s by a small group of researchers who felt the need to meet and exchange experience of research in tourism. Their decision at the time was largely a reaction to larger organizations and their conferences, in which participants tended to talk at each other from the platform rather than confer and discuss.

Rik Medlik was very polite. The origin of the TRC was to some extent an expression of dissatisfaction with the working of AIEST. A number of its members working in tourism research were of the opinion that AIEST was not the ideal platform to discuss methodological aspects in depth. One should recall that the background of AIEST members was quite diverse in its earlier years and in no way comparable with the present membership. The so-called revolt was prepared for the first time in 1963 on the occasion of an AIEST congress in Switzerland. I use the term "revolt" because the president of third time, Prof. Hunziker, did not favor the idea of starting a new club. In 1964, the opposition of Prof. Hunziker was less pronounced in the meeting of Bregenz and the rebels decided to start the following year with the TRC. It should be noted that Bern and St Gallen did not belong to the "rebels." The forces of reaction were not against AIEST, but were of the opinion that close to or within it there was a need for an annual exchange of research among a limited number of tourism researchers. According to the original bylaws, "The Tourist Research Centre was formed in 1965 to promote exchange of research experience and other forms of cooperation among its members." In the late 1960s, it came to an agreement with the president of the AIEST. He could live with the existence of the TRC, provided its members are also members of AIEST. Claude Kaspar and Jost Krippendorf became members in 1969.

The TRC mission is twofold: to promote exchange of research experience in tourism as well as other forms of cooperation among its members. Members work in higher education and in other centers as independent researchers and consultants. Their background is in economics, other social sciences, and in related fields. They share a common interest in a wide spectrum of tourism research. New members who can demonstrate a record of significant involvement in tourism research are admitted. They should be accepted by the general assembly of the TRC. In order to fulfill its aims and to function effectively, the TRC restricts membership to 25 members (excluding honorary members), with not more than 3 members per country and not more than 2 members per center. The working language is English.

A regular annual meeting, organized by members in different countries, is the main activity of the TRC. The Vienna meeting in 2010 was its 45th. But for most members, the network extends beyond the meetings, and also provides contacts for information and mutual assistance with their studies on projects. Importantly, its members see the center as a club, while mutual understanding, respect, and friendship have grown among them. The TRC has no formal status and for a long time had no membership fees. It had a difficult start, but gradually it took off. The success of the TRC club is based on a number of factors:

- TRC has strict meeting guidelines: presentation of the paper, length of presentation and discussions, etc.
- The members agreed to exclude nonactive members. The rule is "Membership will be normally terminated if a member has been absent from the annual meeting for two consecutive years without good reason or for three consecutive years for any reason." The membership rule works; a few people were excluded.
- There is exchange of research and research experience among the members.
- TRC is one of the few organizations where always the top of the research institutes are present and not young inexperienced collaborators.
- TRC is mainly composed of research institutes in tourism.
- Last, but not least, TRC is a club of friends. The half-day excursion and the friendly dinners have contributed to that friendship.

A while back, I went through the reports of the annual meetings. The point that struck me most forcibly was the evolution in the topics of the papers presented. In the beginning, the focus was on holiday surveys and physical planning. However, today, topics include strategy, marketing aspects, destination management, image, consumer value, environmental aspects, and other topics. However, a second and even more important fact is the tremendous increase of the volume of research activities in the institutes of the members.

Vienna 2010 was the 45th meeting, and, so far, TRC has gathered in 33 different European cities from Swansea to Istanbul and from Östersund to Barcelona. In 1972, the TRC was to meet in Dubrovnik. The late Serdjan Markovic organized the meeting in Easter week. Unfortunately, we were confronted with a serious smallpox epidemic in Yugoslavia. At the very last moment, Markovic informed me that it would be wise to cancel the meeting. I tried to inform the members. Unfortunately, I had only the telephone number of the member's institute and so I could not reach all of them (mobile phones did not exist then). The inevitable happened. Four members traveled to Dubrovnik. Fortunately, the destinations could have been worse. In the following week, I received very disgruntled letters.

In its 45 years, the TRC has had 74 elected members; most of them were active members for a long period; six colleagues have attended up to 20 and more meetings. One member, the secretary-general (TRC has no president), has organized and attended all 45 meetings. Sometimes it is said that TRC is unknown. That is correct; but it never aimed to be known and TRC is linked to AIEST (a TRC member is supposed to be an AIEST member; http://trc.aiest.org). The TRC is an organization with extremely low administration costs.

International Academy for the Study of Tourism

In 1989, Jafar Jafari informed me that he had the idea of starting a world academy of tourism and invited me to join the new organization. Jafari was not unknown to me. He was in Turin in the 1970s, one of my students who followed a summer school course organized by the IUOTO, the predecessor of UNWTO. He was a very distinguished participant. Later on, we met each other regularly at AIEST congresses. The academy was established in Madrid 1989. It is an international organization created to enhance both theoretical and practical research in the field of tourism. Its membership is comprised of highly accomplished tourism researchers from throughout the world. The goal of the academy is to further the scholarly research and professional investigation of tourism. Related objectives include encouraging the application of tourism research findings and advancing the international diffusion and exchange of knowledge about tourism.

I accepted the invitation and considered it as recognition for my work in the tourism industry. It is a great honor to be an academy member. Other founding fellows included J. Aramberri, D. Butler, G. Dann, W. Eadington, C. Goeldner, N. Graburn, J. Jafari, D. Nash, D. Pearce, K. Przeclawski, J.R. Ritchie, and V. Smith. The founding fellows were honored at the occasion of the 20th anniversary in Mallorca in June 2009. Presently, the academy has about 80 members (admission to the academy is competitive and requires majority of voting members).

The biennial meetings are the main activity. In the beginning, it was impossible for me to attend the conferences. I could not combine it with my function and my commitments to AIEST and TRC. Later on, I attended a number of those biennial meetings. It is a favorite occasion to meet colleagues across the globe in pleasant circumstances and to exchange research papers and documents.

I was also present on the occasion of the founding meeting of International Association for Tourism Economics in the Balearic Islands in 2006. I was opposed to another association. Proliferation of organizations should be avoided. The voluntary efforts of a number of tourism economists were stronger than common sense. Perhaps the younger generation is more interested in specialization. In any case, its first congress a year later in Palma de Mallorca was a great success: very good participation and many excellent papers.

Teaching Tasks

My teaching activities started in the mid-1960s at the College of Europe, a postgraduate institute specialized in European studies. My first course was "Methods of Economic Analysis" as support for other economic courses and related papers. Regression, input-output analysis, and CBA were always on the menu. I considered myself as one of the beneficiaries of the course. Those methods were very helpful in tourism research. At the end of the 1960s, regional economic policy was more and more on the agenda of the European Commission. Professor R. Regul, director of the Economics Department, urged me to teach "European Regional Economics." This course, offered in 1980, was the basis of the publication *Regional Policy: A European Approach* (Vanhove 1999). As already noted, Leo Klaassen was the supervisor of my doctoral thesis, as coauthor. The book was translated into Greek (Vanhove and Klaassen 1980). There followed a second edition in 1987. After the death of Leo Klaassen, I prepared a third edition in 1999. With a change in the direction of the economics department at the College of Europe, regional economic policy was no longer in the curriculum.

In 1990, J. Van den Broeck, professor at the RUCA (Rijks Universitair Centrum Antwerpen, nowadays incorporated into Antwerp University), insisted on teaching "Economics of Tourism" and a few days later I received a second call for the "Management of Tourism" course in the newly created structure with a distinction between "majors" and "minors" (there was a 'minor" of tourism). The school could not find a professor answering to the requirements for that course. After much hesitation (I already had a demanding job), I accepted the proposal on the condition that both courses took place on the same afternoon. The preparation of a course guideline is the first task of a professor teaching a new course. Although I had a long research career in tourism, I was surprised by the shortage of handbooks on the subject of economics in tourism. Most handbooks at that time focused on management aspects of tourism, more particularly the marketing theme. My friend, the late professor Rik Medlik, referred me to a publication of Mathieson and Wall (1982); however, he suggested that I should myself write a handbook on the economics of tourism. Many years later, I responded. After my retirement, I prepared a new handbook, which was the result of continuous improvement and revision of course guidelines. The outcome, *The Economics of Tourism Destinations* (2005), is different from previous publications on the subject. First, this book emphasizes new aspects such as measurement of tourism (tourism satellite account), supply trends, competition models, the macroevaluation of tourism projects and events, and the role of tourism in a development strategy. Second, an effort is made to deal with many different economic aspects of tourism in a single publication. Third, each chapter seeks to combine theory and practice. Fourth, the economics of tourism destinations is a central theme of this publication. A second edition of the book appeared in 2011.

After the reform of the university structure in Antwerp, a pre-master program in tourism started within the School of Management. Most participants already had some working experience and were strongly motivated. Teaching economics of tourism was a real pleasure. Due to reforms of higher education in Flanders in the Bologna context, the Antwerp tourism program moved in 2004 to the University of Leuven and was transformed into a Masters in tourism. I still enjoy my teaching activities in the oldest Belgian university.

An Active Retirement

During my 10 years of so-called retirement, three activities have occupied much of my time. The first one was completely unexpected. Olivier

Vanneste, former governor, and Jean-Luc Dehaene, former prime minister, president of the board of directors of the College of Europe, asked me to take responsibilities with respect to the new campus site for the College of Europe in Bruges (fundraising and supervision of the construction works). Later I also became the treasurer of the College of Europe, which was not unknown to me, and I had many contacts with the business world as former director-general of the Regional Development Authority. This project was a challenge. A big restoration project in Bruges without financial resources is not a simple matter. Thanks to the support of several authorities and more than 60 companies, we succeeded. The first phase of the project Verversdijk was operational in 2007; we hope to finish the second and last phase by the end of 2012.

My second postretirement activity is linked to tourism. Besides my duties in Louvain, TRC and WES, as member of the board, tourism was never far away. I was also involved in training sessions in Ecuador and Cambodia, teaching tasks in several universities (Spain, Switzerland, Finland, Iran, and Italy), attending conferences, and from time to time participating as keynote speaker in conferences.

My research activities have a low profile. However, I focus more on the topic of competitive destinations. This is a central theme of the second edition of my tourism handbook. Based on several competition models and my own experience, I reached a formulation of Ten Commandments for competitive destinations. I published them for the first time on the occasion of a special publication to celebrate the 60th birthday of Dr Hansruedi Müller of Bern, whom I greatly admire. We consider 10 very important factors that determine the competitive position of a destination: macroeconomic factors, attractions, innovation, strategic planning, positioning and branding, destination management, strategic alliances, making tourism a leading industry, quality management, and accessibility.

My third activity seems surprising, but is not. I love gardening; I am the son of a farmer. Unfortunately, the harvest of my orchard each year creates a big distribution problem.

CONCLUDING REMARKS

My career was a permanent combination of tourism and regional economics, of theory and practice. But they complement one another in many ways. Tourism takes place in regions and destinations. Theory without an eye for practice is unforthcoming.

Many friends have asked me "How is it possible to combine so many tasks?" First, one should have good health and, second, you need the support of your wife. In my case, both requirements have been fulfilled. Good health depends on many factors. Sports is one of them, and my cycling and tennis keeps the balance between spirit and body. But above all, one should have a certain working attitude. I got the fundamentals of this attitude during my youth on the farm. On the professional front, I am proud with the official recognitions for my work, culminating in the nomination as Officer in the Order of the Crown (1994) and Grand Officer in the Order of King Leopold II (2005).

Chapter 16

On the Road to Tourism Economics

Boris Vukonić
University of Zagreb, Croatia

Boris Vukonić, until recently was full professor of economics of tourism at the Graduate School of Economics and Business, University of Zagreb, Croatia. He has acted as consultant of tourism development in Egypt, India, Afghanistan, Bangladesh, Tanzania, and Guyana and has been a member of the Education Council of UNWTO. His tourism research interests include travel agency operations, marketing, destinations development, religion, and tourism and political relations. Besides articles and conference contributions, his publications include 34 books on tourism. In 2004, he established Utilus, a private business school of tourism and hotel management in Zagreb. He is editor-in-chief of the academic journal *Acta turistica nova*, and is on the editorial boards of several others. He is also the resource editor of *Annals of Tourism Research* and emeritus member of the International Academy for the Study of Tourism. Email <vubor@efzg.hr>

INTRODUCTION

Today, when I look back at my life in and with tourism, which relates to the greatest number of my years, a question immediately comes to mind: what could I have done, what could I have been engaged in, and what could I have

The Discovery of Tourism Economics
Tourism Social Science Series, Volume 16, 217–229

ISSN: 1571-5043/doi:10.1108/S1571-5043(2011)0000016019

lived from had I not experienced, accidentally, and not of my own will, an encounter with tourism? This is very difficult for me to answer when tourism has given me so many beautiful moments (but there have also been some less beautiful ones), when it has utterly and completely occupied my professional interest, so that I cannot even imagine another life or a different preoccupation than the one that has accompanied me through almost my entire life.

My interest in tourism came out of the blue, and was to a large extent the consequence of the general circumstances in which I lived. Many would find it odd that I have lived in four states (the Kingdom of Yugoslavia, the Independent State of Croatia, the Socialist Federal Republic of Yugoslavia, and the Republic of Croatia), while still continuously living in the same city: Zagreb. If we put aside my childhood period, I spent most of my life in the now former state, the Socialist Federal Republic of Yugoslavia (known by many as Tito's Yugoslavia), so it is not surprising that my professional life and work were also marked by the doctrine of that state, and also by the answers to the numerous questions raised by the political, economic, and other circumstances of the time. However, it was also an intriguing challenge to observe and explain the living conditions that were very different from those that prevailed in the greatest part of Europe.

Tourists of various profiles had been arriving in the area of the former Yugoslavia from as early as the 18th century. However, these were sporadic, individual visits, sometimes in groups, prompted by curiosity and inspired by the specific natural characteristics and attractions of the area, as well as by the wish to acquire new experiences in the somewhat "wild" region of the Western Balkans. Tourism, or "foreigners' trade" as we literally translated the German term *Fremdenverkehr*, was a topic of discussion even before World War I. Real tourism trade was mentioned just before the outbreak of World War II. Tourists would mainly travel to the Adriatic Coast, visit spas, or view the rare natural attractions (such as the Plitvice lakes, the Krka waterfalls, the Brijuni islands, and more), as well as see some of the cities and towns of specific historical and cultural value (Dubrovnik, Zagreb, Varaždin, Hvar, Split, Poreč, Rovinj). However, this trade did not bring any substantial economic benefit.

Consequently, it may be said that the economics of tourism in former Yugoslavia actually was "discovered" by World War II. In fact, Yugoslavia came out that war devastated in every respect. The country was in ruins, the traffic infrastructure had suffered great damage, industry had been decimated, and agriculture had almost completely been destroyed. After initial economic assistance provided by the West, Yugoslavia, as a country with a socialist ideology, turned toward cooperation with the former Soviet

Union and the countries of East Europe. However, very soon, it severed political and, consequently, economic ties with its Eastern neighbors. Without any connections with the West and lacking a well-planned development policy, Yugoslavia found itself on the verge of economic collapse. In that period, tourism appeared as the light at the end of the tunnel. It was a powerful and promising economic industry, capable of securing a flow of foreign currency that would make it possible for the country to engage in trade in the international market, and—more importantly—to procure basic funds to provide for the local population. Thus, tacitly and without a coherent policy, Yugoslavia latched onto tourism, although not yet completely aware of its positive economic effects that tourism would have for the future development of the country.

Another very important fact should be added to help understand when and how tourism economics was granted citizenship of the former state of Yugoslavia. In a state with a Marxist economic doctrine and which renounced private property (except for small crafts workshops), the entire economy belonged either to the state or to the society. For this reason, tourism could not be seen in the shape of a large number of private businesses, and thus discussed in terms of their interests and potential contribution to the national economy. Rather, any branch of the economy, including tourism, was approached from the viewpoint of macroeconomics and general state interest. This, then, is the answer to the question that many colleagues of mine generally ask: how is it that in the area of former Yugoslavia at the beginning of the 20th century, the country and its economic experts were already considering and discussing tourism economics and its macroeconomic effects?

My Beginnings

I mainly owe my own interest in tourism to three people: Mijo Mirković, who established the postgraduate study of tourism economics at the Faculty of Economics of Zagreb University (1962); Ivo Žuvela, who persuaded me to enroll in this program immediately after completing my studies in economics; and my father, who answered my plea to continue funding my education following graduation from the Faculty of Economics. However, let me start at the beginning.

My secondary school education at the Classical Gymnasium in Zagreb, which focused on social disciplines, played the main and probably decisive role in the choice of my career. This is where I acquired a respectable knowledge of history, geography, literature, and culture, fields which I found extremely useful later on because they facilitated my understanding of tourism and laid a solid foundation for research and generally broadened my horizons. These perspectives enabled me to gain a more comprehensive understanding of tourism than many tourism experts whom I met later and whose papers I read. I was also assisted in this endeavor by my father's voluminous library, from which I gained much understanding that significantly exceeded my school knowledge.

The choice of economics for my studies was preceded by a great disappointment when my desired study of architecture had been denied to me due to my poor knowledge of secondary school mathematics. However, at the very beginning of my studies in economics, I was confronted by mathematics as a course, and, to my greatest surprise and joy, I was able to handle it successfully. For a moment, this revived my hope of studying architecture, although in the end I was not diverted from the path of economics.

At the beginning of my studies in the late 1950s, former Yugoslavia was implementing an intensive reconstruction policy aimed at rebuilding the country demolished during World War II. Industrialization, modeled on that of the former Soviet Union, was the preferred direction for the national economy, and this was also the model on which the teaching curriculum of the Faculty of Economics, in which I had enrolled, was based. There was very little (or certainly not enough) room in the curriculum for other areas of revenue creation. Thus, within the teaching plan for the study of economics, everything began and ended with macroeconomics and industrial economics. During the four years of my studies, tourism was never even mentioned, and scant attention was given to tertiary activities.

The entire economic theory that we studied at the time was based on Marxist thought, so that the other lines of economic theory were mentioned only in very general terms, and many world-renowned economic scholars remained completely unknown to the students of my generation, as did awareness of their contributions to general economic theory. For example, we heard of the names and works of Alfred Marshall or John Maynard Keynes for the first time when a former professor of political economy returned to the Faculty of Economics from her study visit to the United States. Unfortunately for me, this happened at the time when I had already graduated from the Faculty of Economics. This short overview of the "controlled" understanding of economics is intended to help grasp the topics that later caught the interest of tourism scholars in the former state, as well as my own.

Soon after my graduation in 1962, I enrolled in the postgraduate study of tourism economics at the same faculty of Zagreb University. Thus, my encounter with this term and concept of tourism coincided with the foundation of this postgraduate study. Such ignorance of tourism in a person with a degree in economics was not surprising, since foreign tourism did not exist in Yugoslavia at that time. This was also due to the fact that, except for those from Eastern European socialist countries, foreign tourists encountered significant difficulties when entering former Yugoslavia. A change in the general awareness of tourism occurred when the national political establishment cut its close ties with the Soviet Union, soon comprehending that the development of tourism would bring foreign currency into the country. It also understood that the lack of foreign currency was one of the most serious economic weaknesses of the country. The fact that the national currency (dinar) was not convertible hindered imports, which eventually led to a great shortage of a variety of goods (especially food) on the domestic market and imperiled the entire national economy.

Around the beginning of this period, I completed my Masters in the field of tourism economics, which was also the moment that marked my professional interest in topics that seemed crucial for a better understanding of the role and significance of tourism in the national economy, particularly in the environment where I lived and worked. My first paper, also published outside the country (in former East Germany), attempted, although very tentatively, to explain why the market concept must always be included in discussions on the development of tourism. I claimed that Yugoslavia counted on tourists from countries with a market economy and that it must, therefore, use market tools to attract them to Yugoslav tourism centers (or at least to keep them informed). The paper, published in the Yugoslav national journal *Turizam*, was translated into German. This was logical, since East Germany was proclaiming more or less the same economic doctrine as Yugoslavia, which ignored the existence of a market, including a tourism market, and with it all the instruments that regulate market relations.

Changes in the Environment

The arrival of the first foreign tourists in former Yugoslavia was for me the earliest confirmation of the words of our lecturers during my postgraduate studies. I was most impressed by Srđan Marković's lectures, so that today I can claim that his views in particular shaped my understanding of tourism, and consequently made me want to begin my career by working at the Institute for Tourism in Zagreb, whose founder and director Marković was.

Unfortunately, this did not happen, so I began my professional career in the Croatian Urban Planning Institute at the very moment when it began to work on large projects: spatial plans, among which the largest project was the South Adriatic Project, cofunded by the World Bank, and involving experts from the most famous research institutes at that time in Europe—METRO from Paris, Shetland & Cox from Great Britain, and many others. For me, this was a huge and invaluable experience that guided me throughout my professional life, and also created a great interest in and love of planning and programming tourism development.

One valuable insight that I gained was the concept of small spatial units that behaved like small macroeconomic units in the tourism market, and the awareness that specific tourism complexes were beginning to be viewed from the perspective of their individual cost effectiveness. Under the influence of the foreign partners who participated in the project, the importance of the tourism market and its research was acknowledged for the first time in professional circles in Yugoslavia at that time. This led to a new dimension in understanding tourism, its economics and the effect that the industry had on the national economy. This encouraged me to devote my efforts to the more specific research of economic matters.

However, my first individual papers did not deal with tourism planning, but with the operation and economics of travel agencies. This happened by chance, as did a large part of whatever I started in tourism. Namely, I began to work in a travel agency. At that time, the secondary school curricula were undergoing numerous changes, which also affected the teaching plan of tourism in secondary schools. I was asked, as a person working in an agency and who met all the other professional requirements, to write the first textbook on travel agencies in our country. Thus, in 1972, my first textbook appeared under the title *Organizacija i tehnika poslovanja putničkih agencija* (Organisation and Business Techniques of Travel Agencies). This was an excursion into microeconomic issues, but an excursion that lasted quite a long time due to the lack of other authors or their interest in the operations of travel agencies. Later, this publication, in an amended and revised format, now as a university textbook, went through eight editions. For a long time, the field of tourism was associated with my name and a certain professional reputation.

In the period between 1973 and 1978, I edited a column on tourism in the journal *Kreativne komunikacije* (Creative Communications) in Zagreb. This involved a series of longer and shorter papers dealing with the micro and macro aspects of tourism development, with special focus on the development of tourism in former Yugoslavia.

The publication of one of my first books, *Turizam i razvoj* (Tourism and Development), should be understood as a fuller contribution to the economic research of tourism. The book was published in Croatia in 1987 as a result of my efforts to identify as precisely as possible, by using measurable indicators, the real strength of certain factors to which professional literature most often referred in texts to prove the power of tourism and its effect on the economy. By applying a statistically significant stepwise regression analysis and by gradually excluding from the analysis the factors with lesser statistical significance, I discovered that three factors were of special importance for the development of tourism: the political circumstances and potential turbulences in the environment, the dominant religion, and the extent of the state's indebtedness. I wrote a more extensive paper on this topic (with coauthor Š. Tanković) entitled *Snaga utjecaja pojedinih faktora na razvoj turizma* (1986) (The effect of specific factors on the development of tourism).

The favorable reception that *Turizam i razvoj* had in the Croatian professional public encouraged me to continue my research, which led to the production of several books in the following years. *Turizam i religija* (1990) and *Turizam u vihoru rata* (1993) were first published in Croatian and then in English under the titles *Tourism and Religion* (1996) and *Tourism in the Whirlwind of War* (1997), respectively. The former in particular attracted relatively wide attention, also owing to the fact that when it was published it was the first such extensive scientific study on this topic published in the world. Unfortunately, I have never written the awaited study on the relative effect of national indebtedness on the development of tourism, primarily due to the dissolution of Yugoslavia and the war that lasted until 1995. These events imposed other topics that became a priority for the development of what was now Croatian tourism, and which led me personally toward other areas of research.

However, in the meantime, I published a number of shorter texts. In the period between 1993 and 1996, I published 99 columns dealing with tourism topics in the journal *Ugostiteljstvo i turizam* (Catering and Tourism), many of which were also entirely or partially published as reprints in other tourism journals and in the daily press. In the same period, I was regularly presenting my thoughts on tourism economics at many local and international events. At an international conference held on the occasion of the 75th anniversary of the Faculty of Economics of Zagreb University in 1995, I made my observations on tourism economics in *Turizam kao područje istraživanja i edukacije na Ekonomskom fakultetu Zagreb* (Tourism as a Field of Research and Education at the Faculty of Economics in Zagreb).

I advocated that the subject matter that formed part of the university course of tourism economics be revised. Focusing on a multidisciplinary approach to topics, and particularly to contents, my proposals for the course were very different from what had been the practice until then. Unfortunately, I was not successful in my endeavors, probably due to the usual difficulty that some Croatian university lecturers have in accepting novelties, preferring to keep to the established and traditional methods of particular disciplines.

FOCUS ON TOURISM ECONOMICS

Given the aforementioned resistance, in the following years I made the decision to elaborate a comprehensive and reasoned view of the term "tourism economics." However, I had already expressed part of my thoughts at three professional conferences on tourism. First at the "Tourism and Transition," held in Dubrovnik in 2000, I spoke about the "Microeconomic aspects of macroeconomic problems in Croatian tourism." A year later, at the Second Professional Conference on the "Theory of Economics for Faculties of Economics in Croatia," held in Osijek in 2001, in a paper entitled "Uloga nastavne discipline ekonomika turizma u obrazovanju hrvatskih turističkih kadrova" (The role of the teaching discipline of tourism economics in the education of Croatian tourism personnel), besides the discipline of tourism economics itself, I expressed my views on the very term "tourism economics."

On another occasion, I outlined some historical reminiscences on the use of the term in the area of former Yugoslavia at the international conference "Rethinking of Education and Training for Tourism" in a paper entitled "Tourism at the Graduate School of Economics and Business, University of Zagreb from 1962 to 2002." Finally, in 2003 I presented more extensive views on tourism economics at a professional gathering at the Croatian Academy of Sciences and Arts in Zagreb entitled "The study of tourism: A contribution to the discussion on higher education in Croatia). All three presentations focused in particular on the concept of tourism economics, and only then on the teaching of tourism economics, which for a long period had an important role in the formation of higher education staff who occupied key positions, first in Yugoslav, and then also in Croatian tourism. What, then, were these different opinions about tourism economics that I advocated and for which I became known, at least within the framework of my own country and the academic community? I shall try to elaborate this first through some general statements, and then concentrate on specific answers.

As much as this may sound a bold claim, economic theory was for all this time barely concerned with tourism. This was the case not just in the area of former Yugoslavia, but also in most countries in the world where tourism theory was well developed, even when the strong growth of the service sector had changed the general views on economic theory in relation to the global economic driving forces of modern society. So we can only consider it a paradox that tourism itself was in fact observed and studied from its earliest beginnings mostly for its economic effects, as was highlighted in the works of nearly all tourism scholars, even those who in their early works had not always been happy to accept such views. Even this was not enough for macroeconomic theory to deal more systematically with the tourism phenomenon.

A probable reason for this might be that tourism, particularly in the form of a scientific discipline, in spite of its economic effects, was seen in many communities more as a sociological, even anthropological and cultural, than as an economic phenomenon. This is probably not the only or the most important reason. The right answer might be found in the fact that the theoreticians who shaped modern economic theory did not leave the smallest space for a phenomenon whose significance had grown by the end of the 20th century to become the most important industry in the world. In the history of the study of economic theory in the world up to now, this was really inconceivable.

It was quite clear, however, from the very beginning, that any expenditure that generated economic activity was worthy of macroeconomic attention, and thus the superficial interest of tourism economists evolved into more serious interest as soon as the objective economic consequences of this trade were firmly recorded within the GNP of countries around the world where tourism was well developed. At a global level, this was accentuated by the interest of less developed or underdeveloped countries in the potential positive economic benefits that tourism development may bring to such places. This, of course, broadened and increased the motivation around the world to study the economic consequences of tourism development, and greatly boosted the sphere of economic research and analysis of tourism.

In some places, this led to the emergence of a special scientific area—tourism economics—which set out the general economic characteristics of tourism and the consequences of its development as a fundamental matter of interest and research. In other places, such a development did not necessarily lead to the formation of a special scientific discipline; rather, the research was conducted within the framework of an overall study of this phenomenon, but very often at specialized tourism-oriented research and educational institutions. To understand tourism, and especially its economic development effects, it is probably more important that such research actually existed and was constantly enhanced than to know whether it took place as part of an autonomous scientific discipline.

For a long time, the economically and tourism developed West did not show serious interest in the macroeconomic discipline which would observe and study tourism from a macroeconomic perspective. It is difficult to determine the reasons for this, because they were probably numerous and differed from situation to situation and from country to country. The West satisfied its economic interest in tourism by studying individual sectors, or economic operators in the tourism market. If the reasons are sought within the acquired theoretical understanding, it may be concluded that this was mostly for reasons of ownership, since private property has a fundamental significance for the overall socioeconomic structure of so-called free-market countries. This was the same significance that social property had for countries belonging to the socialist and communist socioeconomic system. The dominant understanding of general ownership, whether state or self-government, focused on the effects at the level of the entire system, thus at the level of individual states. On the other hand, the exceptional economic and political interest in foreign currency inflows, where there had previously been an absence of currency funds, intensified the macro interest in tourism as an industry that generated significant foreign currency. This is how it probably happened that the postwar emergence of the discipline of tourism economics first happened precisely in East European countries which had an important tourism resource, had developed a relevant tourism trade, and had achieved appropriate economic effects.

What, however, remained disputable was the very content of the term. Namely, tourism economics became synonymous with the very concept of tourism, and as a teaching discipline it became the general framework for studying all the phenomena that influenced the development of tourism, even those that had no economic content. Obviously, the identification of tourism economics with the concept of tourism itself makes no sense. It is far more logical to assume that economic topics are brought together under the common name of tourism economics. But then it would not be clear what to do with concepts such as management, marketing, promotion, etc. if they were not already covered by the term "tourism economics." This was the case in former Yugoslavia, and all the authors who wrote about tourism under the title "tourism economics" analyzed and researched the overall phenomenon and wrote about it under this umbrella term. However, this model ignores the multifaceted nature of tourism and the need for it to be studied in a multidisciplinary way. Such a situation required more detailed research and the presentation of complete and corroborated views. I published most of my views related to this issue in *Ekonomika turizma: nesporazumi i nerazumijevanja* (Economics of Tourism: Misunderstandings and a Lack of Understanding) in the journal *Acta Turistica Nova* (2007).

CONCLUSION

What, therefore, belongs to the body of tourism economics as a specialist economic discipline? I have already explained what does not belong to it. The economic tourism industry is primarily

> a collection of service-based activities across a variety of industrial classifications and consumer expenditure categories that generally are not otherwise grouped together … Tourism does not have a unique base as an industry, but encompasses widely disparate firms and organizations from many industries which serve customers with a variety of incomes, tastes, and objectives. (Eadington 1991)

Following this, I consider in this context that we could say that there are a large number of "cconomic interests" outside "tourism economics" which basically belong to microeconomic disciplines and to managerial economics.

Following up on this conclusion, in my opinion the area of interest of tourism economics primarily involves the study of the basic rules and categories that help us to better understand the nature of the economic functioning of tourism. The acquisition of these theoretical macroeconomic tenets will affect our capacity to predict certain consequences, which is generally very important in the economic sphere. All the otherwise numerous economic functions of tourism have two things in common: tourism expenditure as a common material resource, and the effects on revenue as a direct or indirect economic goal. The subject and interest of the scientific discipline of tourism economics should be built on these principles.

Since tourism may broadly affect socioeconomic relations, and since there is a need for systemic solutions within national economies, for suitable economic policies for individual countries and the international community as a whole, tourism has all the necessary characteristics to be a subject of macroeconomic analysis. In such a context, tourism economics as a specific scientific discipline could be defined as a part of economic science that describes, analyzes, explains, and finds connections between phenomena and relations in tourism from the perspective of their macroeconomic effects and repercussions. The analysis is mostly confined to the long-term effects of tourism, especially aggregate tourism expenditure, its multiplying effects, the possibility of increasing employment, investments in tourism, but also increasingly the other macroeconomic consequences that its departures from a country or narrow region bring to the emitting country or region. Such views have been additionally enhanced by the principles of globalization. This interest was broadened by the interest of less developed or underdeveloped countries around the world in the possible positive economic benefits that the development of tourism could bring to their areas. Indeed, I have witnessed this myself by traveling to different developing countries as an UNWTO and UNDP tourism development consultant.

Although tourism economics predominantly deals with macroeconomic issues, in one of its parts, it also studies the microeconomic aspects of tourism development. Starting from the position that any expenditure that generates economic activity is worthy of attention from a macroeconomic perspective, it may be concluded that this is precisely why the scientific interest of economic disciplines in tourism grew into serious interest at the moment when its objective economic effects were strongly marked in the GNP of national economies of (receptive) tourism countries throughout the world. These are the very consequences that I see as the fundamental subject of the study of tourism economics.

In this sense, the first Croatian lexicographic publication in the area of tourism, *Rječnik turizma* (2001) (*Tourism Dictionary*) explained the term "tourism economics" as "part of the science of economics which analyzes, explains, and relates phenomena and relations in tourism from the point of view of their effects and repercussions."

I have to admit that after the publication of the first scientific journal in Europe titled *Tourism Economics*, edited by Stephen Wanhill, I hoped that other tourism authors would deal with the concept and the very definition of tourism economics, but this expectation has never been met. Even after Tisdell's *Economics of Tourism* (2000b), of which I had justified expectations, everything has remained within the old and traditional frames: all topics with economic content are still considered as tourism economics. The last hope in these terms appeared when L. Dwyer and P. Forsyth announced their edition of *International Handbook on the Economics of Tourism* (2000).

However, these editors also continued on the well-trodden track, including topics such as marketing and management among the list of topics of tourism economics.

If this chapter at least prompts other authors to think and study tourism economics as a concept and academic discipline within the study of tourism, then, as far as I am concerned, it will have achieved its purpose.

Chapter 17

It is the Project that Counts

Stephen Wanhill
University of Limerick, Ireland
Bournemouth University, UK

Stephen Wanhill is professor of tourism economics, University of Limerick and emeritus professor of tourism research, Bournemouth University, designate professor of tourism economics at the new University of Neapolis, and a visiting professor at the universities of Nottingham and Swansea. He is a director of Global Tourism Solutions (UK) and his principal research interests are in the field of tourism destination development. To this extent he has acted as a tourism consultant to a number of UK planning and management consulting firms, and has undertaken a wide range of tourism development strategies, tourism impact assessments, and lecture programs, with an emphasis project studies from airports to attractions, both in the United Kingdom and worldwide, covering some 50 countries. Email <stephen@wanhill.force9.co.uk>

INTRODUCTION

In January 1945, the American forces landed on the Island of Luzon in the Philippines, although the turning of the tide in the Pacific campaign had begun with the battle of Midway in June 1942. The Russians captured Warsaw. In Western Europe, the Allies were concentrating on squeezing out

The Discovery of Tourism Economics
Tourism Social Science Series, Volume 16, 231 246

ISSN: 1571-5043/doi:10.1108/S1571-5043(2011)0000016020

Hitler's Ardennes offensive, commonly known as "The Battle of the Bulge" prior to crossing the River Rhine. For the European theater, the turning of the tide began with El Alamein in October 1942 and Stalingrad in January 1943. My contribution to this month at the closing stages of World War II was limited to appearing on the planet, but little one would have thought that nearly 18 years later, after some 6 months at the Royal Artillery Depot in Oswestry, I would be joining Rhine Company at the Royal Military Academy Sandhurst to continue my journey as an artillery officer in the British Army.

In retrospect, like many others of my generation, I was influenced by the late Victorian period and the turbulent first half of European history in the 20th century, which had affected my family chronicle. My father served in the police fire service in Portsmouth during World War II, a city which was bombed heavily because of its naval base. My paternal grandfather had served under General Kitchener in the reconquest of the Sudan. His first battle was Omdurman that took place in 1898 and brought the war with the Kalifa and Mahdist army to a close. It also happened to be the first battle of a future eminent statesman, Winston Churchill, who took part in the charge of the 21st Lancers. From Sudan my grandfather went to South Africa to take part in the Boer War and completed his military service in India (where my father was born) during the Great War 1914–18. My maternal grandfather's military experience was confined to World War I. He went to war in August 1914 with the British Expeditionary Force that sailed for France. He was part of the famous retreat from Mons to the Marne; I am the proud possessor of his Mons Star, which, like the medals of my other grandfather and various memorabilia, bring me into contact with a period of history that is now confined to museums and literary texts for many people.

The 1950s were, in the main, a period of austerity for most people in Britain, and it was not until the 1960s that the country started to "swing." I still have my ration books, which I once lent to our research secretary in Bournemouth for her young son to take to his school, when they were re-enacting what it was like to be a child evacuee in World War II. They certainly impressed the teacher, who naturally asked where they had come from. Upon being told, her response was: "Well, he must be very old!" After 65 years of relative peace and economic growth in Europe, which has filled the shopping malls, it is difficult for the current generation to appreciate how little we had. But it is a good lesson in the economic futility of war, in that it can rapidly destroy the capital stock of a nation that has been carefully husbanded over generations.

In terms of my education, I was the product of the Grammar School of that era: "O" levels were completed at 15 years of age and "A" levels when one was 17. It is regrettable that today's "mix-and-match" of sixth form subjects was not available then. The choice was science, language, or humanities. History was always a favorite subject in junior school; it gave me context about the way we were, so this was a happy choice for an "A" level, but a new challenge presented itself, which was economics that was only studied in the sixth form at that time. To this I added geography, whereas mathematics would have been preferred, but was not an option. Although I deliberated on the military applications of mathematics at Sandhurst and in the Royal Artillery, further progress in mathematics had to wait until I was at university. Given my interest in history, it is not surprising that I took to economics, since it gave me insight into the way society functioned. It also had a remorseless logic that governs the way one looks at the world: it is often forgotten that in early economic treatises the mathematical theorems that we are familiar with today, covered the same ground but were written in words rather than algebra.

By the time I was in the sixth form, I was already accepted for Sandhurst. In the era of the "Cold War," the need for armed forces offered a challenging profession for a young man, and we now know from archive material how close we came to making it a "Hot War." The most memorable event of this early period was the Cuban Missile Crisis in October 1962.

Royal Military Academy Sandhurst

In my day, Sandhurst was a two-year course which one entered at the minimum age of 18 years, so after my "A' levels, rather than "click my heels around" at school, I simply enlisted as an ordinary soldier (gunner), as noted above. This gave me useful insights into the background of the range of young men that I would have to command at a later stage in my life. I learnt to study the progress of the principal UK football teams, although rugby was my preferred winter sport.

It was in January 1963 that I officially became a junior officer cadet, which happened to be one of the coldest British winters of modern times. So in good army tradition, along with my comrades in Rhine Company, I learnt to shovel snow. In field exercises, sitting in a slit trench at the dead of night was to say the least "bracing": I recall our company instructor, Captain Brown, who was a Gordon Highlander, saying that he had never been so cold since he was in the Korean War 1950–53. Never mind, the army needed fit young men and made sure that they were. Apart from compulsory military instruction, for example, assault course training, all kinds of sports were available at Sandhurst and I was eventually able to be a member of the

British Army Judo Team. In my last year, I was privileged to add parachuting to my list of military skills.

At that time, the curriculum at Sandhurst was much broader than it is today. Other than military courses (platoon, company, and battalion operations and administration), we were also encouraged to maintain the academic disciplines studied at school and add to our examination portfolio. These subjects were taught by civilian instructors, many of whom had some armed forces experience in the past. One might reflect that given the issues of pupil control in the schools nowadays, it must have been none too onerous a task teaching a set of disciplined and polite officer cadets. In all this, of lasting benefit to me was the study of military history under the guidance of some of the best scholars of the time: Sir John Keegan was a young lecturer in my spell at Sandhurst. It brought me back in touch with one of my favorite school subjects and over the years I have acquired a reasonable library in this field. To the general reader, this may seem rather specialized, but in many instances from the past, the fate of nations has turned on the outcome of a battle. In 1759, on the Heights of Abraham, outside Quebec City, it took about 20 minutes for Canada to change from being French to British, and they are still arguing about it. Now that the last Tommy, Poilu, and Fritz have left us, there is considerable general interest in the Great War 1914–18, and incredulity at the casualties that were sustained by the combatants, something that affected every town and village in their respective countries.

Military instruction in my time at Sandhurst was concentrated around attack and defense. We had some instruction in counter insurgency, but the troubles in Northern Ireland, which were to occupy the British Army for more than 30 years, were not yet on the horizon. Withdrawal or retreat were covered in the Sandhurst syllabus, but were not subjects to be considered as high on the agenda, which probably accounts for most retreats in the history of the British Army being somewhat shambolic affairs, apart from the masterly withdrawal from Gallipoli in 1916. I completed my course at Sandhurst in December 1964, and, at the age of 19, I was commissioned into the Royal Artillery, pejoratively nicknamed by the infantry arm of the service as "drop shorts" or "long range snipers."

Active Service

After a short course in gunnery, I joined 22 Light Regiment Royal Artillery in Germany, which was designated for active service in Malaysia. At that time, the Federated States of Malaysia—Malaya, Singapore, and North Borneo—were in confrontation with Indonesia, then under the rule of

President Sukarno. Our tasks were to defend the airfields of the Royal Air Force with our radar-controlled guns, and to work with local units on patrolling borders. It is on such regimental duty that one comes across the lessons that they never teach at Sandhurst, namely:

- Your enemy invariably attacks on one of two occasions: either when you are ready or when you are not ready. Irrespective, either is inconvenient and generally a nuisance.
- Never share a slit trench with someone braver than you.
- Do not look conspicuous: it draws fire and irritates the people around you.
- Anything you do can get you shot, even doing nothing.
- Look unimportant, they may be low on ammunition.
- If the enemy is in range, so are you.
- Incoming fire has the right of way.
- The only thing more accurate than incoming enemy fire is incoming friendly fire.
- Make it too tough for the enemy to get in and you will find it difficult to get out.
- The easy way is always mined.
- If your attack is going well, you have walked into an ambush.

This confrontation was closed down in mid-1966, and the question for 22 Light Regiment was where to next? Given our experience with jungle terrain, some felt that it would be Vietnam, but Prime Minister Wilson refused President Johnson's request for British involvement. Early that decade, Prime Minister Macmillan, based on the British experience of the Malayan Emergency in the 1950s, advised President Kennedy not to get involved. As a colonial power it was much easier for Britain to deal with Malaya, by simply granting the national mood for independence. America was not in that position in Vietnam and ended up backing a distinctly "dubious horse." Having helped the Allies against the Japanese in World War II, Ho Chi Minh expected independence for Vietnam and resisted strongly the return to French colonial rule in the postwar settlement. In the time of the Cold War, the prevailing political theory was the "Domino Effect" relating to the expansion of communist dictatorships, and this drew the United States into Vietnam.

University Days

As the end of the Indonesian affair came into view, the UK economy was going through its periodic financial crisis and there was a run on sterling as an international currency. Government cutbacks were on the way to "balance the books" and 22 Light Regiment was ordered back to "Blighty." With nothing new on the horizon, I managed to persuade the Ministry of Defence to second me to a remarkable institution (the University College of North Wales, Bangor) that was situated on the edge of the Menai Straits, across from the Isle of Anglesey. Up until relatively recently, the University of Wales was a federal university of five colleges: Aberystwyth, Bangor, Cardiff, Lampeter, and Swansea, but the expansion of the UK university sector has seen these establishments set up as universities in their own right.

I first came across Bangor while climbing in the nearby mountains of Snowdonia on an army outward-bound course, and its range of activities made it an ideal place for someone with my background to study. In Bangor, I was able to indulge my interest in economics under Duncan Black, who pioneered work on social choice before Kenneth Arrow's great work, *Social Choice and Individual Values*. With a student body of around 3,000, Bangor was a very personable place: it would be hard for today's students to imagine a final-year economics group of five undergraduates only.

Joining the Business Community

With my detachment to Bangor complete, I returned whence I came, only to be greeted with a depressing situation. Locked into military barracks with no budget for training, I spent as much time as I could playing judo at various competitions, but I could see that I was going nowhere fast. Moreover, officers senior to me were getting rather demoralizing letters from the Ministry of Defence encouraging them to go, which was difficult given that they were married with families to look after. After a year of this, as a single person and with no guarantee that I might not end up in the same situation, which is a prospect facing those currently serving in Afghanistan, I opted for a parting of the ways and struck off into civilian life to ply my trade as an economist, on the way picking up skills in econometrics at Southampton University, and the London School of Economics where Dennis Sargen and James Durbin were giving their master classes.

Practising one's trade as an economist in commercial life was not that easy. I ascertained from the Ford Motor Company that firms mainly saw economists as "soothsayers" to forecast demand, and it was Bernard Corry of Queen Mary College who convinced me that in view of multiple objectives and criteria, public sector economics was the right path to follow, as it gave opportunities for a whole range of economic skills. Armed with this information, I was fortunate to join an excellent engineering consultancy, Sir Alexander Gibb and Partners. They were based in Tothill Street in London, a short walk from the Houses of Parliament. There was a reason for this, for when the firm began in the late Victorian period, in order to build a structure, such as a bridge or dam, one had to have an Act of Parliament. I was placed in the Transport Division, which brought me into contact with docks and harbors, roads, and airports. It was the latter that drew my attention to tourism: at that time, airports were seen as communication hubs, for which the economic justification was saving business travelers' time. The reality was somewhat different: passenger movements for all purposes were growing and leisure trips faster than any. However, it was difficult to convince HM Treasury of the merits of developing airports for "a bunch of holidaymakers," which is probably why the Roskill Commission on London's Third Airport did not, with hindsight, produce the most rational answer of developing a new airport at the mouth of the Thames, so as to avoid fully loaded 747s taking off and landing over Central London.

My time with Gibbs lasted until 1975, though latterly on a part-time basis, for I was "bitten by the academic bug" and went back to Bangor, this time under Jack Revell, to whom I am forever grateful, to undertake a PhD in regional econometric modeling of the Welsh economy. At Gibbs, I became skilled at project evaluation from the wider perspective of cost-benefit analysis as well as the commercial feasibility study. Projects are basic units of human activity that unfold over time and are the realization of development strategies on the ground, which is the explanation for my chapter title. However, they do require patience due to the need to mobilize resources and planning consents, so I warn my students that it may take several years before one see the fruits of a feasibility study. There are only two projects that I can recall that give one the benefits at the beginning and the costs at the end: one is crime and the other is having an "affair." This interest in project evaluation and finance has remained with me to this day and is the subject of the core module I give to the MA International Tourism class at the University of Limerick.

TOURISM RESEARCH

It was at my second time around at Bangor that I met two further lifelong friends: Brian Archer and John Fletcher, both authors in this volume. Our subsequent career paths have been closely linked, so I will try to pick out material that will not be too repetitive for the reader.

It was Brian that brought me fully into tourism when we undertook work for the Ministry of Finance in Bermuda to build an input–output table in order to provide an economic "map" of tourism for policy decisions. The tourist trip is a complex product and every sector sees it in a different way, from hotels to attractions. Hence, without a "map" how might tourist authorities find their way through the jungle of opinions as to what should be done? My experience has taught me that our political masters are particularly susceptible to anecdotal evidence. The media like simple answers that give one-line headlines, which result in policy decisions that are at best half-right and sometimes plain wrong. It was Mark Twain who said, "Suppose you are a Congressman; then suppose you are an idiot. Ah! But then I am repeating myself."

However, as a professional, one does not "mix it" with politicians, but bear in mind that their objectives for a project are often different from one's own and they have an electorate to address. It is often difficult to trust them, so let them earn trust by their actions: every project needs a champion and if one is able to enlist their support, they can be most helpful. One serves them well by stopping them making electorally damaging mistakes, but note that when it comes to a choice between "murder" or "suicide," politicians commit "murder" every time. It was the Liberal leader Jeremy Thorpe who said of Prime Minister Macmillan after a rather brutal sacking of ministers: "No greater love hath a man than to lay down his friends for his life."

At Bangor, I joined the staff full-time at the end of 1974. I taught third-year undergraduates public economics and econometrics, with project appraisal being reserved for the Masters' students. I continued to work with Brian Archer, but to my chagrin found that by the time I had completed my PhD, he had gone to be head of the department of Hotel, Catering and Tourism Management at the University of Surrey. One year later, I joined his unit.

The Surrey Experience

By now I had determined that of the two professional attributes of tourism practice—marketing and development—it was the latter that should be my future path in the "subject." Although the two subjects are overlapping in terms of knowledge acquisition, marketing is very much a day-to-day operational subject, whereas tourism plans and projects are only demanded now and again. This makes it possible for an applied tourism economist, as I now was, to continue with my academic vocation, yet at the same time "practise" what I preached.

What I found was that the more important tourism becomes to an economy, the greater tends to be the role of government and the greater the interest it shows in helping investors. This is easy to see when comparing the attention given to tourism by the Southern European states *vis-à-vis* the Northern European countries. The state has an important role in the provision of infrastructure, as tourism tends to follow infrastructure rather than lead it, hence the need for tourism planning.

A more recent approach, particularly for peripheral areas, is community tourism development, where the state acts to develop partnerships by bringing the fragmented elements of the industry together. This is advocated, as the "joined-up" approach to government and at a national level is the idea behind setting up a tourism forum to bring all the different interests together. What makes this possible is the flexible technology of tourism, unlike the fixed production functions of manufacturing. As an example, high-rise hotels in cities and low rise in rural areas may be considered, which make it possible to reformulate projects to be acceptable to all parties.

Over the years I spent at Surrey, I gradually added to my experience of tourism policy and projects, from transport through accommodation and restaurants to attractions, the latter forming the bulk of my interest today. One aspect of our skills that Brian Archer and I had conspicuously missed out on was food and beverage practice. Thus, during my first year at Surrey, Brian and I partnered each other for two terms under our Head Chef Willi Bode. What the other students made of this generally I do not know, but some did come and ask us for advice in the belief we were working chefs from outside of the university. Willi's view was that if one understood how to cook at the Ritz standard, it would be easy to make the grade at McDonalds. There is the story of an employee of McDonalds visiting Paris who has dinner at a fine restaurant. Afterward the waiter brings him a platter of cheese on which he spots a fine Camembert. He exclaims, "Well I am damned! I did not know that these French guys make Camembert too!"

Parliamentary Advisor

In 1985, based on our applied tourism work in Wales, Brian Archer and I were appointed as specialist advisors to the UK Parliamentary Select Committee on Welsh Affairs, which was undertaking an enquiry into tourism. With Brian's important university commitments, it fell to me to take on the lead role and I stayed "on the books" until 1989. This gave me valuable insight into the workings of the House of Commons, the most "exclusive club" in London. It has only 650 members, shortly to be reduced if the current Boundary Commission that draws up parliamentary constituencies has its way. Being a member of parliament (MP) is a very individual job: one is very much alone. I like the story of an MP who is finishing a campaign speech with the request that his audience should vote for him, when a man jumps up and says, "I would rather vote for the devil." "Quite so" rejoins the candidate, "but in case your friend declines to run, may I count on your support?"

As an MP, one's primary objective is to hold the seat, for without it he cannot be a member of that most exclusive club. Politics is a difficult profession and if one ever sees an MP that pleases everybody, then he or she is neither seated on the left or the right. They are likely to be lying horizontally with bunches of flowers around them.

Most people are aware of published tourism policies, but inside policy gives an added dimension, not without an element of humor. Political parties influence the government of the day through the preparation of a manifesto, which it is the job of the minister to steer through parliament. The pressure groups on parliament to form policy are many. They range from the government itself, the European Union, various statutory bodies, trade associations, trade unions, individual industries, clubs, and ordinary people. Typical activities undertaken are receptions at the House of Commons, representations to government, meetings with senior civil servants, individual lobbying of MPs, and evidence to parliamentary committees.

Within the House, tourism issues may be taken up during debates on the floor of the House or during question time. However, as every student of politics knows, the work of parliament is done in committee. The floor of the House is a debating chamber, where the subject matter is of little relevance; the object is to score a point off the opposition. If a debate is flagging, the speaker of the House will often call on members known for their wit and humor to address the chamber. Some are feared for their ability to put down the pompous, and prime minister's question time is often an occasion not to be missed. As Sir Winston Churchill once said, "In war you can be killed only once. In politics you can be killed many times."

Select committees may take up a range of matters as the subject of enquiry, and these are agreed beforehand so a timetable for the parliamentary session is prepared in advance. To some MPs, this is a way of making a reputation, while to others it is a chore, but better than any alternative job they may be asked to do. Tourism issues may be taken up by the All Party Parliamentary Committee on Tourism, or select committees. The latter are serviced by a clerk, assistant clerk, and up to two specialist advisors. A committee will conduct its enquiry in three ways: invite written memoranda, take oral evidence, and undertake fact-finding tours. A committee will also receive unsolicited memoranda and further memoranda after fact-finding tours.

Specialist advisors are not essential: MPs may feel sufficiently confident to manage the enquiry themselves with the aid of the clerk. The task of the specialist advisor, as I understood it, was to offer advice on soliciting memoranda, expert witnesses, and proposing fact-finding tours. But I was soon made aware that I also had to write out MPs' questions for the evidence sessions and provide briefing notes. The final assignment was to draft a white paper, which is a short report carrying a series of recommendations.

The reality is that in making recommendations, the committee can only act within its sphere of influence, otherwise it can appear foolish. It might be very beneficial to have a Disneyland in South Wales, but the "Yea" or "Nay" of this is not within the gift of the committee. Memoranda must be given in a formal manner as the committee draws its recommendations from the evidence it receives, so if project X is not mentioned in the white paper that is because the committee was not formally told about it or given any supporting evidence. I found that many memoranda that were received were just positional papers, interesting in themselves, but contained no prescriptions that could be cited in evidence for any recommendations.

Oral evidence is record verbatim by stenographers, so taking evidence outside the House is expensive, and is only justified as public relations. Witnesses are given copies of the questions in advance, but there is no guarantee that MPs will stick to them. Many have "bees in their bonnet" as a result of "armchair" rationalization and continue to press the point, despite evidence to the contrary. As Churchill once commented about the MP George Wyndham, "I like the martial and commanding air with which the Right Honourable Gentleman treats facts. He stands no nonsense from them."

With the media present, the combative nature of some of the exchanges may produce headlines for some MPs, but usually serve no useful purpose. With expectations raised, it becomes impossible to have a discussion of the issues without them appearing in the press as a major row. MPs with legal training can turn these evidence sessions into a courtroom drama, with ordinary witnesses being made to look fools. It is a shame that political reputations are being made at someone else's expense. On the other hand, bureaucracy is conscious of its image and it is important that it is called to account. Journalists are always amused that the public believes what they write, given the thinness of the evidence on which their contributions are made. Prime Minister Balfour once remarked on newspapers, "I have never put myself to the trouble of rummaging through an immense rubbish heap on the problematical chance of discovering a cigar-end."

Fact-finding tours run the risk of being categorized as "junkets," but are necessary if MPs are to convey awareness about the subject. They also have an important public relations aspect, but are hectic as everyone wants to meet the committee to make their views known. This impacts on the length of the tour, because to miss out people gives rise to offense. MPs do tend to give the impression that they have a "magic wand," with the result that the clerk and advisors may get "lumbered' with some chief executive's "too difficult file."

Generally speaking, to be accepted, the recommendations of select committees have to fit into a tourism strategy that is structured around tolerable political criteria, rather than tourism needs. It should be remembered that the "status quo" in politics is a powerful force to be reckoned with and the government of the day is unlikely to accept recommendations that are politically contentious, in respect, say, of its manifesto or require significant legislative changes or are likely to upset the Treasury. Therefore, it is not surprising that tourism professionals in the United Kingdom are often frustrated by the direction of government policy, which may be described as "the art of the possible" within the context of the various interest groups. At best, the practical outcomes of select committees are improvements to policy and at worst they are a damage limitation exercise, filtering out "bizarre" ideas.

Cardiff University

In 1990, I took over as head of department in Surrey, while Brian Archer went about his pro vice chancellor duties. At the same time, I had an enquiry from Cardiff as to whether I would like to move from being a professor in Surrey to a research chair in what was to become School of Consumer Studies, Tourism and Hospitality Management. This was a new challenge that I duly accepted, and at first, under the leadership of the Principal Sir Aubrey Trottman-Dickenson, things went well. I was appointed by the secretary of state for Wales to the board of the Wales Tourist Board. The board consisted of six members and a chairman, who was at that time the former England cricket captain Tony Lewis. Unsurprisingly, my responsibility was for the research and projects divisions of the board. I cannot speak too highly of the professionalism of my colleagues and the lasting friendships that have endured to this day.

Within the confines of this volume, I can only give a flavor of how the board's project division worked. Under the terms of Section 4 of the UK 1969 Development of Tourism Act, the board is permitted to take equity shares, give grants, or offer loans in support of tourism investments. The schemes administered by the board are all discretionary, and in general terms consideration can only be given to feasible ventures for which a need for board assistance can be demonstrated. All projects must, in addition, be available to the general public when completed and be likely to attract tourists to Wales. Because financial assistance is discretionary, the board is able to change priorities in accordance with its current development plan. Irrespective of the board's development strategy, the conditions of the 1969 Act and internally provided ministerial guidelines dictate that every project should be submitted separately for approval. Significant schemes going before the board will have an appreciation or a project report prepared by the officers of the board's Development Division. Smaller projects will have similar appraisals but are dealt with under officer-delegated powers and are matters of report to the board.

The format of the project report is structured under the following headings: general, management, the project, financial appraisal, marketing, tourism impact, and recommendations. At each stage, there are likely to be officers' comments for guidance. The general aspects include a brief introduction, followed by the project name, its location, description, delegated authority as necessary, who the applicants are, project priority, say, historic town or rural community in accordance with the board's development strategy and a note on any previous application or assistance given, together with summary monitoring data. The management section will include details of the experience of the applicants, their qualifications and those of key staff, any training needs deemed necessary, and details of the existing business in which the project will be placed. Next follows a description of the project and the costs involved. The object of the financial analysis is to identify whether the project is operationally generating a surplus toward meeting its capital expenses and to detail the funding shortfall where support is necessary from public sector moneys. The tourism impact section gives consideration to on-site job creation, analyzed by full-time, part-time, and casual employment; on-site grant cost per job, this being a key performance indicator for the board; the average wage; multiplier effects; and the ability of the project to attract tourists and not displace market share from other establishments.

By the time a submission comes before the board for approval, the recommendation should normally be favorable, though conditions may be imposed on the applicant in respect of training, marketing, requirements to reveal all sources of finance, revisions as to costings, various legal matters, and so on. All aspects of the project are considered, but, ultimately, the accountability for public funds lays stress on the economic criteria.

Bournemouth and Bornholm

The arrival of a new principal, Sir Brian Smith, saw the end of my tenure in Cardiff. A new strategic plan saw a reversion to core disciplines that gave no future for my school, even though we were making a considerable surplus. The school was put on a program for closure: some staff were made redundant, others were transferred to a neighboring institution, and myself, along with a few colleagues, were marked down for the Business School. It was a decision that smacked more of university politics than vision and personally reminded me of the remark made by the American humorist Dorothy Parker on seeing the children's Halloween game "Ducking for Apples": "Change one letter and it's the story of my life!" Hence, I was in quite a receptive mood when I received in late 1994 an invitation to go to Denmark to take up the post as director of the Unit for Tourism Research, at the Centre for Regional and Tourism Research, situated on the resort island of Bornholm, in the middle of the Baltic Sea. In 1995, I also had the opportunity of joining Peter Jones' school at Bournemouth University, and in the end we negotiated a split appointment that was mutually agreeable to all sides. I took with me the journal *Tourism Economics*, for which planning started with my publishing friend, John Edmondson, in 1994. A year later, I was joined in Bournemouth by former colleagues, Chris Cooper, John Fletcher, and John Westlake, who set up the International Centre for Tourism and Hospitality Research as part of what is now the School of Tourism at the university.

The focus of the research program in Bornholm was tourism in the peripheral areas of Europe, principally in the northern or cold-water climates. The funding came from the Danish Research Council for the Social Sciences (SSF) and included a number of other Danish research institutes and the Copenhagen Business School as partners. The list of agreed projects included patterns of demand for tourism in peripheral areas; tourism and the environment—the innovation connection; tourism models; community tourism development; tourism, education, and the labor market; managing extended service experience—quality, productivity, and profitability among small firms; strategic development of tourism in peripheral destinations; summer house tourism; outdoor recreation and tourists; local and regional economic consequences of tourism; optimal forms of government intervention in tourism development; and cultural tourism.

Our funding permitted us to bring in scholars from outside Scandinavia from time to time, which served to give the center a truly international flavor. Our success gave rise to a second program, but this time it was led by Wolfgang Framke at Roskilde University. The logic behind this stipulation from the SSF was to ensure knowledge transfer, since we were a research institute and not a university. Nevertheless, we still had a healthy range of projects to undertake, including internet commerce for hotels; yield management in the restaurant sector; the economic evaluation of flagship attractions; management of destination infrastructure; creative innovations in attraction development; free riders in tourism; tourist expectations and experiences of the Billund region; virtual product development among Danish hospitality businesses; forecasting tourism-generated employment in Denmark; and image formation, guidebooks, and tourism.

All told, I spent eight years on my half-time appointment with the center. I got to know Denmark, Finland, Norway, and Sweden fairly well and made lasting friends and acquaintances among my academic colleagues. As is well known, Scandinavian societies score highly in the United Nations' Happiness Index, and given that the tourism business attracts very sociable people, including academics, one can imagine that I look back on my time there with great fondness. Yet, the region is not always as united as it seems from the outside: the bonding process does involve each country telling jokes about the other. One of my favorite stories is about a Dane that goes to Finland and is taken out to a bar by his Finnish colleagues. At social gatherings in Denmark, there are certain conventions when having a drink with one's hosts, but to the Dane's surprise nothing is said for a good hour. Thinking, that as the guest, he should perhaps take the initiative, our Dane picks up his glass and toasts his hosts. Upon this, a Finnish colleague leans over and says, "Excuse me, have you come here to drink or to socialize?"

Retirement

At the end of 2002, my time at Bornholm was complete. There was to be no third program, and I reverted to full-time with Centre for Tourism and Hospitality Research, where I had been researching and lecturing on the Masters' programs since their inception. In 2003, I was invited by Jim Deegan to spend a semester with the National Centre for Tourism Policy Studies at the University of Limerick. The Centre is within the Kemmy Business School, and although I had undertaken projects within Ireland previously, my continuing relationship with it has opened up a whole new range of research.

I formally retired from Bournemouth University in January 2005, and took emeritus professor status, although I stayed "on the books" for the research assessment exercise. My enthusiasm for the ever-burgeoning world of tourism continues, with the result that I hold a portfolio of appointments, including (since 1994) a directorship of Global Tourism Solutions. The company produces local area statistics and project evaluation studies. We have five directors and seven staff, ably led by the CEO David James, who used to be director of tourism for Scarborough in Yorkshire.

CONCLUSION

One day I must stop, but it is hard to do so when our business is a major demand driver of the creative industries in a modern economy. Over 200 years ago, at the time of Adam Smith, the received opinion was that such activities, whatever their important intrinsic merits, were a diversion of otherwise productive capital and labor into essentially unproductive work.

Looking back over the last 40 years, it is plain to see that the global growth in tourism has made nonsense of this idea, but it is unfortunate that this attitude persists even today in the political systems of the advanced economies. It is a modern form of Ludditism that bemoans the passing of manufacturing jobs and toys with protectionism, and fails to recognise, either through ignorance or in the cause electoral advantage, that, broadly speaking, for 10,000 years we had agriculture, but capital widening and deepening displaced people from agriculture into manufacturing, which lasted for 150–250 years, depending on when the modern economies industrialized.

The same process in the last 40 years has displaced labor into the service sector, now styled by various writers as the knowledge economy, the creative economy, or the experience economy. By this we mean economic activities producing symbolic products with a heavy reliance on creativity and intellectual capital as primary inputs, and, naturally, for as wide a market as possible. This is where the future lies and it is time to update the economic textbooks, which continue to emphasize the production of commodities.

Epilogue

INTRODUCTION

I could attempt to summarize here the contributions in this volume, but I confess that I do not see much to be gained by this. The authors have told their stories with eloquence, perspective, and humor. It would be gratuitous of me to attempt to summarize or provide additional explanations, since the authors' words can speak far more eloquently for themselves. Readers can judge for themselves the diversity of scholarship represented by the contributors to this book. They make it clear that tourism is a global force for economic and regional development. Tourism development brings with it a mix of benefits and costs, and the growing field of tourism economics is making an important contribution to tourism policy, planning, and business practices.

Some major developments in techniques have occurred since the initial forays into tourism economics. For example, the development of tourism satellite accounts (TSAs) provides economists with data that was unavailable to our pioneer researchers. TSA provide an internationally recognized and standardized method of assessing the scale and impact of tourism-related production and its links across different sectors. They also provides a comprehensive database that identifies tourism's role in an economy and provides a rigorous and reliable basis for drawing comparisons between tourism and other sectors in terms of their contribution to the economy, as well as international comparisons. They also provides an invaluable tool for measuring and monitoring the development of tourism and assessing its economic contribution. Such information is necessary for the making of efficient and effective policy decisions to guide the future development of tourism. Since TSA allow the industry to be better included in the mainstream of economic analysis, it may be expected that more research will now be undertaken on tourism's economic contribution to a destination. The research literature may now be expected to contain more studies that compare and analyze the contributions that tourism and its component industries make to key variables, such as GDP, value added, and employment.

TSAs provide policymakers with insights into tourism and its contribution to the economy, providing an instrument for designing more efficient policies relating to tourism and its employment aspects. As a result of basing more of their research in analyzing data from TSA, the outputs of tourism economists should become even more relevant to the information needs of destination managers. Worldwide, regional governments are developing tourism plans to maximize the opportunities for income and employment growth resulting from an expanding tourism industry. Extensions to the TSA methodology present economists with opportunities to investigate tourism's contribution to subregions. This has traditionally been a neglected research area given previous data limitations. Other extensions of the TSA methodology include estimation of the wider flow on effects of tourism across the economy (indirect effects). There is also substantial scope for using the TSA methodology as a structure for more detailed breakdown of the information it provides. This includes areas such as tourism's use of human resources and its contribution to capital formation.

Another relatively neglected research topic has been measures of tourism productivity at the industry level. TSA can be used to develop performance indicators such as measures of productivity, prices, and profitability for the tourism industry as a whole. They can also be used to explore performance in individual sectors. Researchers now have the data to explore the performance of individual tourism sectors or of the entire tourism industry relative to that of other industries, domestically and internationally. The role of information and communication technology, which has had a growing impact on tourism promotion, marketing, and sales, is yet to be researched in detail for its effect on firms' productivity. It is interesting to reflect that the Internet was not even imagined when the contributors to this volume began their careers.

Economic impact analysis has engaged tourism economists for decades as illustrated in many of the chapter contributions. A major objective of estimates of tourism's economic impacts has been to inform policymakers as to the appropriate allocation of resources both within the tourism industry itself and between tourism and other industry sectors. Perhaps more than in any other area, tourism economists seem to remain uncritically wedded to an assessment method based on input–output multipliers that projects exaggerated economic impacts for shocks to tourism demand. Given the advances in computable general equilibrium (CGE) modeling over the past two decades, tourism economists now have the opportunity to play a much more important role in providing information that destination managers can use in policy formulation. CGE models consist of a set of equations that characterize the production, consumption, trade, and government activities of the economy.

CGE models recognize resource constraints and consider the demand, price, and income effects flowing from government policies and structural changes in the economy. They incorporate all input–output mechanisms; they incorporate mechanisms for potential crowding out of one activity by another, as well as for multiplier effects. CGE models can guide policymakers in a variety of scenarios arising from a range of domestic or international shocks or alternative policy scenarios. They can be tailored to allow for alternative conditions such as flexible or fixed prices, alternative exchange rate regimes, differences in the degree of mobility of factors of production, and different types of competition. CGE models are helpful to tourism policymakers who seek to use them to provide guidance about a wide variety of "what if?" questions, arising from a wide range of domestic or international expenditure shocks or alternative policy scenarios (Dwyer, Forsyth and Spurr 2004). In tourism, very interesting results have emerged using this technique in areas as diverse as tourism taxation, the impacts of special events, policies in response to human-induced tourism crises (terrorism), and other crises affecting tourism destinations (such as SARS, foot, and mouth disease), and tourism development as a means of poverty reduction. As well as enhancing our understanding of tourism's impacts on both developed and developing economies, CGE modeling is now being used for the economic impact assessment of special events (Blake 2005). Tourism economists have an important role to play in researching the effects of the workings of labor markets, government subsidies, and taxes on event impacts, as well as the distributional effects associated with large events. Given that government funding agencies are now demanding that event evaluation be undertaken using state of the art techniques, it can be expected that evaluation of special events will increasingly incorporate CGE modeling of the economic impacts and cost-benefit analysis of the wider economic, social, and environmental effects.

Climate has a major influence on destination choice. Human-induced climate change is an externality on a global scale that, in the absence of policy intervention, is not "corrected" through any institution or market. Climate change is perhaps the greatest market failure the world has seen. It presents a global challenge that requires a long-term worldwide solution in order to avoid environmental, social, and economic dislocation. One of the fundamental challenges for tourism into the future is to adapt to climate change and to meet the responsibilities that all industries have in respect of mitigating greenhouse gas emissions. TSA provide the opportunity for tourism economists to contribute to our understanding of the "carbon footprint" associated with the tourism industry. The advantage of using the

TSA to estimate the carbon footprint is that it ensures that the measure is comprehensive, and incorporates all emissions from all industries that comprise tourism. If the relationship between industry production and greenhouse gas emissions is known, as per environmental accounting frameworks that are being increasingly developed, then it is possible to calculate the emissions that are due to tourism as measured by its output in the TSA. Estimation of tourism's carbon footprint represents a starting point for the development of industry strategies to mitigate and adapt to climate change. Tourism can and must play a significant role in addressing climate change as part of its broader commitment to sustainable development and the United Nations Millennium Development Goals <http://www.un.org/millenniumgoals/>. Economic analysis can contribute to our understanding of the different types of issues raised by climate change, in policy formulation, and in analyzing the implications for tourism.

A reading of the contributions makes it clear that a primary role of these pioneers, in addition to their contributions to the research literature, was to provide advisory services to developing countries and regional organizations interested in implementing sustainable tourism activities. Much of the literature today appreciates the importance of developing tourism "sustainably." Increasing attention is being given to the balance among economic, environmental, and social goals (what is known as the triple bottom line), social intragenerational inequity and the relationship of tourism with poverty in destinations, and responsible tourism that is sensitive to the conservation of natural and fragile environments. Whatever the precise meaning of "sustainable," an essential element of a sustainable tourism industry is economic viability. It is sometimes forgotten that the concept of sustainability has an economic dimension alongside its social and environmental dimensions. Economic efficiencies result in less use of resources with potentially less adverse social and environmental impacts from their use. Tourism development is fundamentally driven by business. However, governments play a significant role as partners in tourism development to an extent which is not replicated in most other industries through their extensive engagement, by all levels of government, in tourism planning and strategy, marketing, infrastructure development, land use planning, and responsibility for parks and public and natural attractions, and through their role in managing environmental and community impacts of tourism. The more comprehensive is our understanding of the economic issues associated with tourism, as reflected in the decisions made by operators and policies enacted by destination managers, the more able are economic efficiencies to be achieved in the overall objective of sustainable development of the industry. While not always acknowledged explicitly, an appreciation of these issues has driven much of the research associated with the contributors to this volume.

I have no doubt that the readers of the book will have gained an enormous respect for the way in which the various authors have met the challenges associated with tourism economics. These challenges came not only from the subject matter of what is, after all, an analytically demanding field of research, but also from the social and institutional context in which they were enmeshed. It is easy for those who have come to study tourism economics in more recent years to fail to appreciate the development of this area of thought that has culminated in the body of knowledge that presently exists. This, too, continues to evolve. The pioneers of the discipline, as illustrated in the contributions to this volume, have had to apply the concepts and techniques of economics to what was then a relatively unfamiliar context.

Given the peculiarities of tourism, with its subject matter more akin to "experiences" than the products and services typically dealt with by economists, the new breed of tourism economists has faced and met the difficult challenge also of making their work consistent with economic thinking while maximizing its policy relevance. Unfortunately, however, this work is gradually becoming less accessible to noneconomist tourism researchers and its policy relevance often neglected. Much of tourism economics today has followed the tradition in mainstream economic research to produce sophisticated analyses using statistical and econometric techniques. Given the developments in econometrics, we can expect increasingly sophisticated applications of new methods in tourism demand modeling and forecasting. It seems fair to say that the earlier work has been less quantitative than much of what is produced today and that it more firmly addressed policy issues. At the same time, it provides the very basis on which present-day researchers develop their models and frameworks. Changing global trends (economic, social, demographic, political, technological, and environmental) will continually pose challenges to economic theory and policy and the ways we analyze tourism activity.

Whatever the specific topics that researchers will address in the coming years, it is clear that tourism economics provides a fertile ground for research with the potential to inform policymaking to improve socioeconomic prosperity in all destinations worldwide. We are all richer for the contributions to knowledge made by the pioneers of tourism economics. In many cases, readers may have found parallels in their own career evolution. Others will have found words of wisdom to help them overcome barriers that await them in the future as they forge their careers as tourism economists.

A PERSONAL ASIDE

The other editors in the mini-series have each contributed a personal aside and so I hope to be forgiven for following tradition here. I was born and raised in Sydney, Australia. Parents, Tom and Iris, encouraged the education of myself, Wayne, and Alexis. I graduated high school from Waverley College, but did not do economics at school. I performed well at bat and ball games and was school tennis champion and, later, university table tennis champion. I was interested in astronomy, but my mother suggested that lonely nights looking into a telescope did not suit my gregarious personality and this seemed pretty convincing to me at the time. I went to the University of New South Wales to do a commerce degree. Mum encouraged me to enroll in industrial relations as she had read that lots of industrial matters were resolved on the golf course and it would be good to have a job that enabled time out of the office in the sunshine. Little did I realize then that would come to pass in an entirely different career. A year or so into my degree, there was a major labor strike that filled newspaper pages with commentary. I realized that I was not reading any of this material, indicating a lack of interest in industrial disputes or their resolution. So I switched my major to economics. I gained a good honors degree (Second Class Division 1). My thesis involved a cost-benefit study of the eastern suburbs railway proposed for Sydney and finally built in the 1980s over 100 years after it was first proposed.

Upon graduation, I worked as a marketing analyst for ESSO Standard Oil. I gained the position as a result of my commerce honors degree rather than any marketing knowledge (which was nil). I remember catching a crowded train to and from the city each day in my suit and tie, the boss telling me that my hair was too long and a general feeling that my life interests were not strongly associated with the profitability of a giant oil company. So I quit work after nine months. Two things then happened. I applied successfully for a tutorship in economics at the University of New South Wales (a very junior member of staff) and enrolled in philosophy degree part time at Sydney University with a view to becoming a philosophy academic. I enjoyed tutoring at this institution, but did not do any research in economics, devoting all of my readings to philosophy. I was admitted to the honors program at Sydney University and gained a first-class honors degree with a thesis on "Time Travel and Temporal Dualism." I went on to publish three papers in the philosophy journals. I once scanned some citations of my work and found the papers to be widely cited. One published article examined the views of four "Philosophers of Time" and I was rather bemused to find myself one of them. I had not realized that I had any well-structured views on the "Philosophy of Time" until I read that paper.

I was awarded a Commonwealth Scholarship to Canada to do a PhD in philosophy, tenable at any Canadian University. I chose the University of Western Ontario, since it had the best philosophy department in the country. I enjoyed my time in Canada enormously, both professionally and socially. I worked pretty hard by day on coursework (10 subjects plus 4 main philosophy theme areas) and thesis and went out carousing and partying at night. I had lots of girlfriends. I had a favorite nightspot called "Brass Tacks" that played music from the 1950s and 1960s with a highly popular dance floor. I was (and still am) a lousy dancer, but braved the floor in the anticipation of generating the required intimacy that lead to an extended night of passion. This activity was strategic in another sense: I was well aware that high productivity in my studies was crucially dependent on a satisfactory love life.

By the time I had selected a thesis topic, I had come to the view that I did not wish to become an academic philosopher. My colleagues enjoyed philosophical debate much more than I did and this dominated their discussion in much of their waking moments whether at the university or at leisure. My interests in life seemed to be less cerebral yet more eclectic. I was a wiz at pub trivia nights. The upshot was that I selected my thesis topic very strategically to span both philosophy and economics to broaden my future employment opportunities. I decided to explore the issues in the debate as to whether science can truly be value free, focusing on economics as the context of study. My epistemological stance was that science does not merely seek "truth" (since that would generate only analytical propositions), nor does it seek merely "interesting" truth (explanation and prediction). Rather it seeks "valuable" truths that are confirmed by successful action. It is the incorporation of "pragmatic" as well as "cognitive" utilities in the acceptance of economic facts and theories that infuses values into theory choice. Scientists (read "economists") cannot fail to make value judgements as an essential part of their scientific activity.

I returned to Australia with my PhD in philosophy, lived with mum and dad in their house on the water, applied for unemployment benefits and went surf skiing each day until some job turned up. One did arise, in the School of Economics at the University of New South Wales, where I returned to my role as tutor (bottom of pay scale, so I had gone backwards in my economics career over the preceding five years). However, I was promoted quickly to senior tutor thence lecturer. Peter Forsyth was on staff as a lecturer in economics and we became friends. Meanwhile, I published some material from my doctoral thesis in journals such as *American Journal of Economics and Sociology*, *Journal of Economic Issues*, *Australian Economic Papers*, *International Journal of Social Economics*, and *International Review of Economics & Ethics*. I then proceeded to look for an interesting research area in economics and thought that the economics of tourism might be the go. The little informal reading that I had done—mostly UNWTO and UNCTAD reports and Brian Archer's multipliers work (Archer 1977)—suggested that this area presented good possibilities to develop some interesting research products. This was at a time when (almost) none of my colleagues had the slightest interest in tourism economics. They seemed to be endlessly fascinated by reading and talking about articles on topics that were, to me, mind numbingly dull such as money, banking and finance, macroeconomic policy, and industry studies of automobiles, textiles, footwear, and other manufacturing. Having expressed to Peter Forsyth my interest in tourism economics, he asked me if I would like to be part of a research team under the auspices of the National Centre for Development Studies, at the Australian National University. The project involved a study of various aspects of South Pacific economies. The issues to be addressed included agriculture, trade, transport, banking and finance, investment, infrastructure, manufacturing, and so on, including tourism. Each researcher was required to produce a scoping study of the important issues for the South Pacific under each topic. I said "yes" to this invitation. Meanwhile, I had accepted a tenured position at Macarthur Institute of Higher Education (later incorporated into the University of Western Sydney). The dean of our faculty of Business and Technology had developed a theme for all research activity by staff. This was in the area of product innovation. Staff promotion would depend on their research outputs relevant to this theme, a position that had the backing of the CEO. Worried about this, I then contacted the National Centre for Development Studies to say that I had changed my mind and would not do the tourism study. Shortly thereafter Forsyth phoned me expressing his disappointment with my decision. He argued that deans come and go, and for me to give up on my research activity in tourism economics before it had even started was utter folly. He was right of course. I thence reversed my reversed decision. Luckily, they had not found a replacement for me and I proceeded to do the tourism overview. This was my first tourism research published as a book chapter in a collection of the research reports (Dwyer 1986).

I was subsequently invited to undertake some fieldwork in the region. I studied the extent of leakages from tourism expenditure in Fiji, Vanuatu, Tonga, and Samoa. For the research structure I found the study of hotel food imports in the Caribbean by Francois Belisle (1983) particularly helpful. I enjoyed my trips to these countries. In Samoa, I stayed at Aggie Greys hotel and met her personally. She was the inspiration for the "Bloody Mary" character in *South Pacific*. At the other end of town was the Tusitala hotel, affectionately known as the Tusi. The grave of the Tusitala or "Storyteller" (aka Robert Louis Stevenson) is located on a rise overlooking Apia township. Each night following my interviews, I would visit each of these watering holes to socialize with the patrons. I would drink local brew, thus minimizing the leakages while observing others to drink copious amounts of scotch, Jim Beam, Jack Daniels, and other imports. I prided myself that the import content of my expenditure was relatively low. In Tonga, I crashed a rented motorcycle twice trying to avoid pigs running in all directions across a coral road. My abrasions were sufficiently serious that I headed for the hospital to find myself treated personally by the King's physician. During my drive to hospital, youths would run out of the churches at the sound of my motorbike to display their anger at my violation of the Sabbath and to pelt me with mangoes. At any other time, I would have collected the mangoes, given a thumbs up, and sped off. Upon return to Australia, I published several papers based on the research (1988a, 1988b, 1989a, 1989b).

Early in 1990, I received a call from Neil Warren who was then a research adviser to The Committee for the Economic Development of Australia (CEDA), an organization that aims to facilitate better public policy and business outcomes for Australia's economy. Neil asked me if I would read a 200-page report on "Tourism in Australia" commissioned by CEDA to a foreign consultant and provide feedback to him by the end of the weekend. I read the report and phoned him on Sunday evening with the opening line "Do you want the bad news or the bad news?" My feedback confirmed his worst fears as to the quality of the report. He asked me if I could rewrite the report within six weeks given CEDA's pressing deadlines. I agreed but told him that this would require an entire restructuring of the text, deleting huge amounts of superfluous material while adding a discussion of several important issues omitted from the report. My life for the next six weeks was a misery. I worked on the redraft alongside my normal university teaching and other responsibilities, setting the alarm for 4.30 each morning to meet the CEDA deadline. I restructured the report as a SWOT analysis of Australian tourism to fit with the CEDA business management emphasis. Happily, CEDA liked the redraft and I then moved on to other research. Several months later I was informed that my report, now called *Tourism in Australia: Challenges and Opportunities* was to be published as a book with me as third author (Grey, Edelmann and Dwyer 1991). The book was officially launched by the then Prime Minister of Australia the Rt. Hon. R.J.L. Hawke at the Regent of Sydney. I met the Prime Minister who autographed my copy.

My next foray into tourism economics was again at the invitation of Peter Forsyth. He and Chris Findlay had been talking to the Federal Ministry of Tourism regarding the effects of foreign direct investment (FDI) on Australia's expanding tourism industry. At this time, early 1990, protest marches were being held in Queensland demonstrating against "selling the farm" to foreigners. The protesters often targeted the Japanese who were the largest foreign investors and racial tension was increasing. The government wanted less heat and more light to be thrown on the nature and potential of the costs and benefits associated with FDI in tourism as an input to possible policy implementation. The study involved desk research to understand what economists were saying about foreign investment, together with field research to interview tourism stakeholders and explore the implications for the industry. This required that Forsyth and I spend some time in the holiday destination of Cairns. Our partners, Libby and Joan were happy to accompany us. We prepared a report for the Federal Ministry of Tourism that argued essentially that this agency was net beneficial to the Australian tourism industry in terms of incomes and jobs generated and its positive effects on tourism flows.

We presented the report to Ray Spurr, a former ambassador to Syria and Lebanon and who was at that time the assistant secretary in charge of tourism policy in the relevant federal department. As is his want, Ray read the report forensically and quizzed us intensively on our findings, probing for clarifications and weaknesses and suggesting alternatives. The final report was much improved by his input. Ray subsequently became first assistant secretary of Australia's fledgling federal Department of Tourism that existed from 1992 to 1996. He then left Canberra to become a valued colleague of mine at the University of New South Wales. The FDI study was well received by both the federal department and the tourism industry. Bill Faulkner who was then head of the Bureau of Tourism Research (BTR), the research arm of the tourism ministry, published the report in two parts in its Occasional Paper series (Dwyer, Findlay and Forsyth 1990; Dwyer and Forsyth 1991). Forsyth and I also published a paper on FDI in tourism in *Annals of Tourism Research* (1994). This was our first joint publication in a collaboration that has lasted for almost 20 years and still ongoing. We published another paper in *Annals* at that time on the topic of the costs and benefits of inbound tourism (Dwyer and Forsyth 1993). Our thesis was (and still is) that if one is serious about teasing out the policy implications of tourism shocks, estimation of the net benefits is required. While we have been emphasizing for almost two decades that impacts are not benefits, the message still is not getting through. Needless to say, one of the *Annals*' reviewers recommended rejection of the paper, but Pauline Sheldon who was the coordinating editor for the paper liked it and recommended its publication. I had not met Pauline at that time, but she has since become a lifelong, greatly cherished friend who has been extremely supportive of my career journey. The paper has since become a much-cited article in the tourism economics literature and subsequently was selected by Clem Tisdell (2000b) for inclusion in his two volume collection of the outstanding papers in tourism economics. Since then Forsyth and I have published a substantial quantity of tourism articles ranging over topics such as costs and benefits of tourism promotion, taxation of tourism, tourism's economic impacts using CGE models, tourism's contribution as measured by tourism satellite accounts, tourism yield, evaluation frameworks for special events, MICE and cruise tourism, effects of climate change mitigation policies on tourism, carbon footprint of tourism, destination competitiveness, tourism–immigration linkages, and environmental effects of tourism. All of our work stresses the policy implications of our analyses.

It is appropriate that I here express my appreciation of the contribution that Peter Forsyth has made to my research effort, both as mentor and friend. Undoubtedly, my research record in tourism would not be nearly so substantial without his contribution. The great bulk of our joint research reflects the power and grunt of Peter's ideas. He is a prominent economist and many of his views have driven our best research across various issues. We are an odd pair. One of us is rather shy, formal, and reserved. The other is much more the extrovert and social animal, an irreverent person who nevertheless transforms acquaintances into friends rather easily. Our approach has been for one of us to draft a paper that is sent to the other who cuts and pastes and then returns in an iterative process. Neither of us ever feels so "precious" about his own words that we resist making appropriate changes. It has always been about content, never about ego, and this has been a crucial ingredient of whatever publishing success we have had.

I have, of course, collaborated with many other researchers over the years. Some have been economists (Andreas Papatheodorou, Trevor Mules, Albert Assaf, Nada Kulendran, Neelu Seetaram, Tanja Mihalic, Tien Duc Pham, Ray Spurr, Pauline Sheldon) while others have come from the broader tourism management and planning areas (Deborah Edwards, Nina

Mistilis, Margaret Deery, Leo Jago, Ljubica Knezevic, Emma Wong, Bruce Prideaux, Brian King, Alison Gill). My research in noneconomics areas has included planning for sustainable tourism, the influence of mega trends on management, the impact of unethical business practices on Australian tourism, strategic management of airlines, hotels and ecolodges, and triple bottom line reporting as a basis for sustainable tourism development. Another collaborator, Robert Mellor, deserves mention here. Despite Forsyth's success in convincing me to do the overview of tourism in the South Pacific, I did in fact pursue a parallel research agenda for many years while I was at the University of Western Sydney. This research addressed the then faculty theme of product innovation management. With coauthor Mellor, between 1990 and 1996, I published 10 or so articles in the technology management literature, including in top tier international journals. The upshot is that I find myself to have published articles in four different areas of thought: philosophy, economics, technology management, and tourism. Not exactly your narrow economist lost in the world of economic abstractions.

I received several promotions at the University of Western Sydney over the years, rising up the large number of steps from lecturer to full professor in a reasonably short time. In the initial years, I did not teach any tourism economics courses. That changed in 1992 when a new dean (yes, deans do come and go) asked me to develop a Bachelor of Commerce degree with a major in tourism management. This required replacing eight subjects in the existing undergraduate program with tourism-related subjects. I selected these subjects (one of which was tourism economics), did all of the required documentation, and steered the course development through various internal and external committees. This was a very time-consuming process. A short time after the course was eventually approved, the dean informed me that no funding was available to support the course and that it would not proceed. I then offered to teach all tourism subject "above load" to provide the teaching resources for the course. On this understanding, the dean allowed the first intake of students in 1993. The course proved very popular and eventually the dean allocated more resources to it. I was then able to hire other staff. This included Nina Mistilis, Deborah Edwards, and Martin Opperman who accepted an employment offer only to immediately accept a better one at Griffith University with Bill Faulkner. Following the success of the bachelor's degree the dean then requested development of an MBA (tourism management) which piggybacked on the generic MBA program. Over these years I was either head or *de facto* head of the tourism and hospitality group but my heart was never in administration. In my final months at UWS in 2002, I received a phone call from a staff member claiming that another had defamed him publicly by telling students that he wore his pants too tightly. He wanted me to sanction the defamer. I knew then that I had to escape.

Fortuitously, an advertisement appeared internationally for the Qantas professorship in travel and tourism economics at the University of New South Wales. I took up this chair in early 2003. A major purpose of the Qantas funding for the chair was to support research that improves our understanding of tourism economics and policy to achieve benefits for Australia's tourism industry and the wider economy. The funding from Qantas was channeled through the Sustainable Tourism Cooperative Research Centre (STCRC). Since the University of New South Wales was a member of the STCRC, I began to access a large amount of funded research, in a loose coalition of researchers under the banner of the Centre for Economic Policy. A major theme of this research was to develop economic models to assess the impacts of tourism demand shocks that could inform policymaking. I worked closely with Ray Spurr and Peter Forsyth and with modelers based at Monash University. Since then we have been joined by Tien Duc Pham based at the University of Queensland. Ray does an excellent job of maintaining team discipline and harmony calling upon all of his diplomatic skills. The STCRC, under the leadership of Terry Delacy and Leo Jago, was very supportive of our research effort and our work became well known internationally. We developed a number of reports and papers that argued for the superiority of CGE models over standard input–output modeling for economic impact analysis (Dwyer, Forsyth and Spurr 2004). A workshop that we convened in Sydney was attended by Thea Sinclair who soon after was to die tragically in a horseriding accident. A most charming person and excellent researcher, Thea would certainly have been invited to contribute her chapter to this volume but for her untimely death.

In our activities within the Centre for Economic Policy, we undertook several projects in addition to our CGE work. We developed a suite of tourism satellite accounts for each of the states and territories of Australia (Pambudi et al 2009). Other projects included measuring the contribution of tourism to regional economies (Pham et al 2009), estimation of the carbon footprint of Australian tourism (Dwyer et al 2010), measures of tourism yield (Dwyer et al 2007), megatrends affecting destination management (Dwyer et al 2009), and simulations of the effects on the tourism industry of a proposed emissions trading scheme (Hoque et al 2010).

Naturally, the Qantas professor was expected to fly Qantas. People assumed that I was continually flying around the world to conferences in first-class luxury. This was not entirely true, but I often let them think this, especially if they appeared to be discomforted by the thought. However, there is no such thing as a free lunch. The arrangement with Qantas was that I would pay an economy class fare, but was to be flagged for an "available upgrade." This meant that if there was a spare seat in business class, I would be upgraded. Qantas was not prepared to dump a full fare-paying passenger to accommodate me, nor would I have expected them to. I enjoyed a success rate of 70%, which was most welcome given that an upgrade meant a flat bed on those long haul trips to and from Australia. These days are now gone, regretfully, as the Australian government denied the STCRC further funding for an extended life. Given that the Qantas funding was tied to the center, the demise of the latter signaled the end of Qantas funding for the chair. My employment as professor with the University of New South Wales was not affected, however. My time as Qantas professor was highly valued by me and, so I have reason to believe, also by Qantas. It was a good flight with a smooth landing.

The BEST Education Network

I first heard of BEST (Business Enterprises for Sustainable Travel) when I received an invitation posted on TRINET by Michael Seltzer and Abe Pizam. The invitation was for researchers worldwide to participate in the development of teaching modules on sustainable tourism to be made available to instructors particularly in developing countries. The idea was to develop content on sustainable tourism that could be infused into the various subjects taught in business degrees. A Think Tank was to be held at Bongani Mountain Lodge, a five-star property adjoining Kruger National Park in South Africa. Funded by the Ford Foundation, if participants could pay their own transport to Johannesburg, all ground expenses for five days would be paid for by the Think Tank convenors. To be accepted, one simply made out a case for their value as a participant. It was easy for me to argue that economic expertise is required if one is to make any serious attempt to value the costs and benefits of different strategies of sustainable development. So I was invited to participate in what was a truly memorable event. Around 50 participated including Abe Pizam, Ginger Smith, Ray Spurr, Frederic Dimanche, Erik Cohen, Yoel Mansfield, Janne Liburd, Claudia Jurowski, Graham Miller, and Pat Long. Each day we set some hours aside for module development. Given the diversity in the group, this was tantamount to herding cats. The Mountain Lodge had views to die for, and we would eat sumptuous meals quaffed down with assorted beers and wines overlooking forests and plains where wild animals roamed. At dusk, we would go on safari either on foot or in vehicles that resembled army ducks looking for, and finding, Zebra, Elephant, Rhino, Lion, Buffalo, and a host of other wildlife. Partying at night, we were warned by Bongani management to make sure that a staff member, with fully loaded rifle, accompany us back to our rooms since leopards hunt in darkness. After one late night party, I remembered this stricture only when half way to my room in an open area. This realization certainly helped to concentrate my mind for the five agonizing minutes that it took me to complete my journey. Never had my room at any conference seemed so much a haven of safety.

Fun and adventure aside, the Think Tank delivered on its promise of module development. The next Think Tank was held in Hawaii, but since most of the Ford Foundation funding had dried up, most of the "Tanked Thinkers" were not seen again at any of the annual events. It was in Hawaii that Pauline Sheldon became involved in BEST, soon becoming chair of BESTEN Education Network. I served as chair of Knowledge Creation for some years. To date, there have been 10 Think Tanks held on four continents. For marketing purposes, we refer to them as Think Tank 2, Think Tank 3, etc., rather than second BEST Think Tank, third BEST Think Tank and so on. I am the only person to have attended all 10 to date. The outcomes of BEST now extend beyond module development to include the Tourism Education Futures Initiative, which seeks to provide vision, knowledge, and a framework for tourism education programs to promote global citizenship and optimism for a better world, and also the development of INNOTOUR a WEB 2.0 platform for education, research, and business development in tourism and is an experimental meeting place for academics, students, and enterprises. I now serve on the International Advisory Board of BEST, with Pauline Sheldon, Leo Jago, and John Tribe.

International Association For Tourism Economics

At an international conference on tourism economics in Mallorca 2007, it was decided to form the International Academy for the Study of Tourism (<www.tourism-economics.net>). The initiative came from staff at the University of Balaeric Islands. Eugenie Aguilo and Javier Lozano (and thence Vicente Ramos) were the first President and Secretary. I served initially as vice president, along with council members Andreas Papatheodorou, Andrea Saayman, Pauline Sheldon, Steve Wanhill, Francisco Pigliaru, Adam Blake, Carlos Gomez, Tim Tyrrell, and Michael McAleer. IATE is the leading forum for the discussion, exchange, and development of knowledge in the field of tourism economics. Its aims are to contribute to the development and application of tourism economics as a science and instrument for policy making, to improve communication and contacts among educators, researchers, and students in tourism economics all over the world, to improve communication and contacts between tourism economics and other fields in economics and in other disciplines, and to develop and encourage cooperation between university-level teaching institutions and research institutions so as to promote knowledge of the concepts and applications of economic analysis to tourism issues and policy analysis.

At the 2009 IATE conference in Chiang Mai, Eugenie Aguilo stood down and I assumed the presidency with Mondher Sahli as Secretary. I am confident that the association will continue to gain strength over the years and become a major association within the tourism discipline.

International Colleagues

One thing I cherish in my profession is the opportunity to meet colleagues from other countries and cultures. I have been overwhelmed by the hospitality offered to me by many colleagues. One of my earlier contacts was with staff at the Institute za Turizam, Zagreb. I spent six weeks there in 1997 at the invitation of Sanda Weber. The day after I arrived, I was driven by then director, Anton Radnic to the coast, mostly on the wrong side of the road as we overtook all cars ahead of us that were going slower than the speed of sound. We headed for a one-hut airport with grass tarmac and, to my horror, I was shown to my place in a three-seater plane. My concerns multiplied by orders of magnitude when the pilot arrived. I swear he was drunk. I do not speak Croatian but I suspected that I would still not have understood a word of what he was saying had he been speaking English (maybe he was). We took off on a fantastic voyage, surveying the islands of the Adriatic on a one-hour flight. My fear of dying was (almost) offset by the magnificent views on offer. It was the first time I had seen the Adriatic with its turquoise waters. We landed safely and disembarked. I suppose the pilot returned to the bar. We then drove to a seaport and boarded a large motor launch for more sightseeing and which took us to a portside restaurant for lunch. The night was spent at a comfortable hotel followed by meetings the next morning with local tourism officials in Mali Losing, before returning to Zagreb. I do not know if any innovative tourism development plans evolved from this visit, but it reinforced my growing conviction that there were worse jobs on the planet than being a tourism economist. I still maintain contact with Sanda and her colleague Renata Tomljenovic, popping into Zagreb occasionally to give guest lectures.

Another valued colleague in Croatia is Nevenka Cavlek, vice dean of the Faculty of Business and Economics at the University of Zagreb and a contributor to this volume. Each year Nevenka coordinates the International Tourism and Hospitality Academy at Sea (ITHAS). In 2007 ITHAS enrolled 140 students (108 female and 32 smiling males), plus staff from 5 countries in courses conducted during an 8-day cruise of the Danube. I was invited to give a lecture on evaluating cruise tourism and joined fellow instructors Bill Gartner and Julio Aramberri on board the SS Donau. This required giving the same two hour presentation to four groups of students. The rest of the time could be spent at the bar, swimming in the pool, lounging on deckchairs on the top deck watching the castles and towns along the Danube slip by or sleeping off a hangover. In fact I began writing my economics textbook at that time on the boats observation deck (Dwyer, Forsyth and Dwyer 2010). Stops were made in the great cities of Bratislava, Vienna, Budapest, and smaller towns. My partner Libby also joined the Love Boat only to be dragooned into judging student presentations at the final night festivities. I think it was around this time that Libby began to better appreciate my attitude that whatever your job, it is nice to spend some time out of the office. Our daughter Eve has certainly also enjoyed many of the travel experiences.

I enjoy my trips to Europe each year. Among the tourism economists I have ongoing associations with the University of Lalaguna in the School of Applied Economics, Raul Hernandez-Martin and also the University of Balearic Islands where Javier Rey-Maquieira and Vicente Ramos are based. For some years I have taught the Economics of Tourism to the Masters students at SKEMA at the invitation of Frederic Dimanche in France. I value my associations also with Tanja Mihalic and Ljubuca Knezevic in the Faculty of Applied Economics at the University of Ljubljana, and also with Snezana Besermenji at the University of Novi Sad, Serbia. Valued colleagues in Asia include Bob McKercher, Haiyan Song, and Chulwon Kim. These colleagues represent only some of those who have given me their friendship and hospitality over the years.

In 2007, I was elected as a fellow of the International Academy for the Study of Tourism. I was nominated by Geoffrey Crouch and Pauline Sheldon, and I am very grateful to them for their support. Although Geoffrey would consider himself to be a "marketer" by discipline, his meta-analysis of tourism demand is compulsory reading in the demand modeling literature. I have since been elected second vice president of the Academy under Pauline's presidency and we have introduced some innovations to enhance awareness of the activities of this august body.

While the international dimension of my research activity has always been important to me, I have remained active within the Australian tourism research community. I regularly attend the annual conference of the Council of Australian University Tourism and Hospitality Educators (CAUTHE). It's widely agreed that Australia, with a population of only 20 million, punches well above its weight on the world tourism research stage. The CAUTHE conference is in my view the most robust tourism conference held annually in the Southern Hemisphere and one of the world's more prestigious tourism conferences. In 2009, I was honored to be appointed as a founding fellow of CAUTHE for "outstanding" services to the organization, one of only eight persons to be accorded this honor. My research record aside, I suspect the honor was primarily for my contributions to workshops for PhD students during the CAUTHE conference over many years.

THE FUTURE

I have noticed certain changes in my attitude of late. I am less inclined to get enthused with the prospect of putting the hard yards involved in turning research into journal publications. I was approached by Michael Hall and Chris Cooper, on behalf of Channel View Publications, to write a textbook on tourism economics. I agreed and coopted Peter Forsyth and my brother Wayne as coauthors. Wayne, now retired, was a senior lecturer in economics at the University of Western Sydney and a specialist in managerial economics. The book took some time to finish, not simply because it is a mammoth 855 pages in length, but because we were continually distracted by requests from the STCRC to work on "hot topics" such as tourism's carbon footprint, climate change, and tourism and the effects of the global financial crisis on tourism. In the early days of writing, my enthusiasm was diminished by the knowledge that universities do not value staff publications of textbooks (indeed, any books) very highly compared to peer reviewed journal publications or grant monies. Thinking on this, I decided that at this stage of my career I should please myself. The book *Tourism Economics and Policy* was published in October 2010 (Dwyer, Forsyth and Dwyer 2010). It is to be launched officially at the CAUTHE Conference in February 2011 in Adelaide. In deciding who should be invited to speak at the launch, I asked myself: who has the most to lose from its success? Obviously this is John Tribe (2005) who currently enjoys the royalties associated with his best selling textbook due for its fourth edition in 2011. I invited John to speak at the book launch and he readily agreed. I do not know how many precedents there are for an author launching a rival text but it provides further demonstration of the level of collegiality that exists in our discipline (not to mention the opportunity it provides John to rain on my parade, so I won't mention that).

Another change of attitude is to choose conference participation on the basis of location rather than prestige factors. (I think my daughter and doctoral student Eve already realizes this!) I have been fortunate in receiving invitations to give keynote addresses at conferences and workshops in various locations worldwide, including Ouro Preto (Brazil), Kuala Lumpur (Malaysia), Faro (Portugal), Antibes (French Riviera), Alanya and Antalya (Turkey), Heraklion (Crete), Phnom Penh (Cambodia), Seoul, Jeju Island (Korea), Ljubljana (Slovenia), Novi Sad and Belgrade (Serbia), Zagreb (Croatia), Corsica, Auckland (New Zealand), Mallorca (Spain), and Hong Kong. My general conference participation alone has probably taken me to different cities in over 40 different countries. I remember my very first international tourism conference, the 26th annual Travel and Tourism Research conference in Acapulco. I had some funds for travel and selected this conference from some list primarily for its exotic location. I had never heard of this association at that time and was surprised to find a number of persons in attendance whose names were familiar to me from the journals. Some, like Chuck Goeldner and Pauline Sheldon have since become great friends. Still, it's a large planet and there are always new conferences to attend, destinations to explore, and new friends to meet.

I have always adopted a fairly lighthearted approach to academic research and will continue to do so. I am reminded by associate editor Leo Jago that we tourism researchers are not attempting to cure cancer or solve the Middle East crisis. This in no way implies a less rigorous approach to research, but it always intrigues me when I encounter colleagues puffed up with their own self importance when they assume the podium or when pontificating to others about their work. It is stating the obvious to say that we tourism economists swim in a very small academic pond. That said, we must all attempt to do what we can by our lights. Certainly the pioneers of tourism economics whose stories appear in this volume have "made a difference." If our concepts and theories can inform tourism stakeholders' decisionmaking to develop strategies which improve the human lot then that makes for a career journey with successful outcomes. But this point of view takes me back in time to the ideas espoused in my doctoral thesis before tourism research was even a blip on my radar. Little did I realize then that I would one day be writing an epilogue such as this as a tourism economist.

Larry Dwyer

References

Adams, W.A., and J.L. Yellen
1978 Commodity Bundling and the Burden of Monopoly. Quarterly Journal of Economics 90:475–498.

Alauddin, M., and C.A. Tisdell
forthcoming Quantitative Impacts of Teaching Attributes on University TEVAL Scores and Their Implications. International Journal of University Teaching and Faculty Development.

Archer, B.
1976 Demand Forecasting in Tourism. Bangor Occasional Paper in Economics, No. 9. Bangor: University of Wales Press.

Archer, B.H.
1977 Tourism Multipliers: The State of the Art. Bangor Occasional Paper in Economics, No. 11. Bangor: University of Wales Press.

Arita, S., C. Edmonds, S. LaCroix, and J. Mak
2011 The Impact of Approved Destination Status on Mainland Chinese Travel Abroad: An Econometric Analysis. Tourism Economics (forthcoming).

Arrow, K.J.
1951 Social Choice and Individual Values. New Haven: Yale University Press.

Artus, J.
1972 An Econometric Analysis of International Travel. International Monetary Fund, Staff Papers XIX(3):579–614.

Bandara, R., and C.A. Tisdell
2010 Economic Management and Evaluation of Human-Elephant Conflict. Köln, Germany: LAP Lambert Academic Press.

Baran, M.
2010 Online Agencies Lose Tax Hearings in San Diego. Travel Weekly, August 5 <http://www.travelweekly.com/article3_ektid21856.aspx> (last accessed on August 6).

Bardolet, E., and P. Sheldon
2008 Tourism Development in Archipelagos: Hawaii and Balearics. Annals of Tourism Research 35(4):900–923.

Baum, T.
1996 Managing Human Resources in the European Tourism and Hospitality Industry. A Strategic Approach. London: Chapman and Hall.

Baumol, W.
1967 Macroeconomics of Unbalanced Growth: The Anatomy of Urban Crisis. American Economic Review 57:415–429.

Belisle, F.

1983 Tourism and Food Production in the Caribbean. Annals of Tourism Research 10(4):497–513.

Bhagwati, J.N.

1984a Splintering and Disembodiment of Services and Developing Nations. World Economy 2(7):133–144.

1984b Why are Services Cheaper in Poor Countries. Economic Journal 94: 279–286.

Blackorby, Ch., R. Picard, and M. Slade

1986 The Macroeconomic Consequences of Expo 86. *In* The Expo Story, R. Anderson, and E. Wachtel, eds., pp. 231–256. Vancouver, BC: Harbour Publishing.

Blake, A.

2005 The Economic Impact of the London 2012 Olympics, Research Report 2005/5, Christel DeHaan Tourism and Travel Research Institute, Nottingham University Business School, UK.

Blair, R.D., and J. Mak

2008 Saving the Last 'American' Cruise Ship. The Milken Institute Review 10(4):50–57. Fourth Quarter.

Blair, R.D., J. Mak, and C. Bonham

2007 Collusive Duopoly: The Economic Effects of the Åloha and Hawaiian Airlines' Agreement to Reduce Capacity. Antitrust Law Journal 72(2): 409–438.

Bonham, C., E. Fujii, E. Im, and J. Mak

1992 The Impact of the Hotel Room Tax: An Interrupted Time Series Approach. National Tax Journal XLV(4):433–442.

Bond, M.

1979 The World Trade Model: Invisibles. International Monetary Fund, Staff Papers 26(2):257–333.

Boulding, K.E.

1985 Human Betterment. London: Sage.

Buhalis, D., and C. Costa, eds.

2006 Tourism Business Frontiers: Consumers, Products and Industry. Butterworth-Heinemann, Oxford: Elsevier.

Bushell, R., and P. Sheldon

2009 Wellness Tourism: Mind, Body, Spirit, Place. NY: Cognizant Communications.

Čavlek, N.

1998 Turoperatori i svjetski turizam. Zagreb: Golden marketing.

2000 The Role of Tour Operators in the Travel Distribution System. *In* Trends in Outdoor Recreation, Leisure and Tourism, W. Gartner, and D. Lime, eds., pp. 1–458. Oxton, UK: CABI Publishing.

2002 Tour Operators and Destination Safety. Annals of Tourism Research 29:478–496.

2006 Tour Operators and Destination Safety. *In* Tourism Security and Safety: From Theory to Practice, Y. Mansfeld, and A. Pizam, eds., pp. 335–353. Oxford: Elsevier.

Chapman, D., T. Mount, and T. Tyrrell

1972 Electricity Demand Growth and the Energy Crisis: An Analysis of Electricity Demand Growth Projections Suggests Overestimates in the Long Run. Science 178(4062):703–708.

Collins, D., and C.A. Tisdell

2002 Age-related Lifecycles: Purpose Variations. Annals of Tourism Research 29(3):801–818.

Cooper, C., J. Fletcher, A. Fyall, D. Gilbert, and S. Wanhill

2008 Tourism Principles and Practice (4th ed.). Canberra: FT Prentice Hall.

Council of Economic Advisers

1970 Economic Report of the President. Washington: Council of Economics Advisers.

De Keyser, R., and N. Vanhove

1994 The Competitive Situation of Tourism in the Caribbean Area – Methodological Approach. Revue de Tourism 49(3):19–22.

Dollery, B., and J. Wallis

1996 An Interview with Clem Tisdell: Essays in Honour of Clement Allan Tisdell, Part I. International Journal of Social Economics 23:20–48.

Dwyer, L.

1986 Tourism in the South Pacific. *In* Issues in Pacific Island Development, R.V. Cole, and T. Parry, eds. National Centre for Development Studies, Australian National University.

1988a Import Content of Tourist Hotel Food and Beverage Purchases in Western Samoa, Tonga, Vanuatu and Fiji. Islands/Australia Working Paper No. 88/1. pp. 1–32. Australia, Canberra: National Centre for Development Studies, Australian National University.

1988b Import Content of Tourist Hotel Food and Beverage Purchases in the South Pacific. Pacific Economic Bulletin 3(2):37–39.

1989a Hotel Food and Beverage Imports in Fiji and Vanuatu. Pacific Studies 13(1):99–120.

1989b Tourism-Agriculture Linkages in Western Samoa and Tonga. World Review (2). pp. 33–52.

Dwyer, L., and H. Clarke

1995 Problems in the use of Economic Instruments to Reduce Environmental Impacts of Tourism. Tourism Economics 3:256–282.

Dwyer, L., and P. Forsyth

1991 Impacts of Foreign Investment in Australian Tourism. BTR Occasional Paper No. 10. pp. 1–85. Canberra, Australia: Bureau of Tourism Research (July).

1993 Assessing the Benefits and Costs of Inbound Tourism. Annals of Tourism Research 20(4):751–768.

1994a Government Support for Tourism Promotion: Some Neglected Issues. Australian Economic Papers 33(63):355–374.

1994b Motivation and Impacts of Foreign Tourism Investment. Annals of Tourism Research 21(3):512–537.

2008 Economic Measures of Tourism Yield: What Markets to Target? International Journal of Tourism Research 10:155–168.

Dwyer, L., and P. Forsyth, eds.

2000 International Handbook on the Economics of Tourism. Cheltenham, England: Edward Elgar.

2006 International Handbook on the Economics of Tourism. Northampton, MA: Edward Elgar.

Dwyer, L., C. Findlay, and P. Forsyth

1990 Foreign Investment in the Australian Tourism Industry. BTR Occasional Paper No. 6. pp. 1–62. Canberra, Australia: Bureau of Tourism Research (May).

Dwyer, L., P. Forsyth, and H. Clarke

1995 Problems in the Use of Economic Instruments to Reduce Adverse Environmental Impacts of Tourism. Tourism Economics 1(3):265–282.

Dwyer, L., P. Forsyth, and R. Spurr

2003a Inter-Industry Effects of Tourism Growth: Some Implications for Destination Managers. Tourism Economics 9(2):117–132.

2004 Evaluating Tourism's Economic Effects: New and Old Approaches. Tourism Management 25:307–317.

2006a Effects of SARS Crisis on the Economic Contribution of Tourism to Australia. Tourism Review International 10:47–55.

2006b Assessing the Economic Impacts of Events: A Computable General Equilibrium Approach. Journal of Travel Research 45:59–66.

2007 Contrasting the Uses of TSAs and CGE Models: Measuring Tourism Yield and Productivity. Tourism Economics 13(4):537–551.

Dwyer, L., P. Forsyth, R. Spurr, and T. Ho

2003b Contribution of Tourism by Origin Market to a State Economy: A Multi-Regional General Equilibrium Analysis. Tourism Economics 9(4): 431–448.

Dwyer, L., M. Deery, L. Jago, R. Spurr, and L. Fredline

2007 Adapting the Tourism Satellite Account Conceptual Framework to Measure the Economic Importance of the Meetings Industry. Tourism Analysis 12(4):247–256.

Dwyer, L., P. Forsyth, L. Fredline, L. Jago, M. Deery, and S. Lundie

2007 Yield Measures for Australia's Special Interest Inbound Tourism Markets. Tourism Economics 13(3):421–440.

Dwyer, L., D. Edwards, N. Mistilis, N. Scott, and C. Roman

2009 Destination and Enterprise Management for a Tourism Future. Tourism Management 30:63–74.

Dwyer, L., P. Forsyth, and W. Dwyer

2010 Tourism Economics and Policy. Clevedon, UK: Channel View.

Dwyer, L., and C. Kim
2003 Destination Competitiveness: Determinants and Indicators. Current Issues in Tourism 6(5):369–413.

Eadington, W.R.
1991 Economics of Tourism. Annals of Tourism Research 18(1):41–56.

Elster, J.
1979 Ulysses and the Sirens: Studies in Rationality and Irrationality. Cambridge, UK: Cambridge University Press.

Fennel, D.A., and R.K. Dowling, eds.
2002 Ecotourism Policy and Planning. Wallingford, UK: CABI.

Forsyth, P.
1991 The Regulation and Deregulation of Australia's Domestic Airline Industry. *In* Airline Deregulation: International Experiences, K. Button, ed., pp. 48–84. London: David Fulton Publishers.

Forsyth P., L. Dwyer, and R. Spurr
2007 Climate Change Policies and Australian Tourism, Technical Report, CRC for Sustainable Tourism (December), Gold Coast, Qld, Australia.

Frechtling, D.
1974 A Model for Estimating Travel Expenditures. Journal of Travel Research 12(4):9–12.
1975 Travel Economic Impact Model, Volume I: Final Economic Analysis Methodology (with Stephen Muha et al.), p. 108. Washington, DC: U.S. Travel Data Center.
1991 A Proposed Work Program for Tourism Marketing and Economic Statistics. *In* World Tourism International Conference on Travel and Tourism Statistics, Ottawa, Canada, June.

Frechtling, D.C.
1981 Some Lessons Learned in Eight Years of Travel Research. *In* Proceedings of Twelfth Annual Conference on Innovation and Creativity in Travel Research and Marketing, pp. 101–107. Salt Lake City, UT: Travel and Tourism Research Association.
1994a Assessing the Impacts of Travel and Tourism – Introduction to Travel Impact Estimation. *In* Travel, Tourism, and Hospitality Research, J.R. Brent Ritchie, and C.R. Goeldner, eds. (pp. 359–365. revised ed.). New York: Wiley.
1994b Assessing the Impacts of Travel and Tourism – Measuring Economic Benefits. *In* Travel, Tourism, and Hospitality Research, J.R.Brent Ritchie, and C.R. Goeldner, eds. (pp. 367–391. revised ed.). New York: Wiley.
1994c Assessing the Impacts of Travel and Tourism – Measuring Economic Costs. *In* Travel, Tourism, and Hospitality Research, J.R. Brent Ritchie, and C.R. Goeldner, eds. (pp. 393–402. revised ed.). New York: Wiley.
1995a Common Definitions for a Common Goal, Implications of the UN/WTO Tourism Definitions for the U.S. Tourism Statistical System. Washington, DC: U.S. Travel and Tourism Administration.

1995b The U.S. Tourism Statistical System: Successes and Failures. *In* Global Tourism: New Rules, New Strategies, 26th Annual Conference Proceedings, pp. 370–375. Wheat Ridge, CO: Travel & Tourism Research Association.
2006 An Assessment of Visitor Expenditure Methods and Models. Journal of Travel Research 45(1):26–35.
2010 The Tourism Satellite Account: A Primer. Annals of Tourism Research 37(1):136–153.
Frechtling, D.C., and E. Smeral
2010 Measuring and Interpreting the Economic Impact of Tourism: 20–20 Hindsight and Foresight. *In* Tourism Research: A 20–20 Vision, D.G. Pearce, and R.W. Butler, eds., pp. 67–79. Oxford, UK: Goodfellow.
Frey, B.S.
1985 Umweltoekonomie (Environmental Economics). Goettingen, Germany: V&R.
Fujii, E., M. Khaled, and J. Mak
1985 The Exportability of Hotel Occupancy and Other Tourist Taxes. National Tax Journal 38(2):169–178.
Ghali, M.A.
1976 Tourism and Economic Growth: An Empirical Study. Economic Development and Cultural Change 24(3):527–538.
Galbraith, J.K.
1998 The Affluent Society. New York: Mariner Books.
Gerakis, A.
1965 Effects of Exchange Rate Devaluations and Revaluations on Receipts from Tourism. International Monetary Fund, Staff Papers No. 3. pp. 365–384, November 1965, Vol. XII. Washington, DC.
Gray, H.P.
1970 International Travel – International Trade. Lexington, KY: Heath.
1974 Towards An Economic Analysis of Tourism Policy. Social and Economic Studies 23(3):386–397.
1982 The Contributions of Economics to Tourism. Annals of Tourism Research 9:105–125.
Grey, P., K. Edelmann, and L. Dwyer
1991 Tourism in Australia: Challenges and Opportunities. Melbourne, Vic.: Longman Cheshire.
Grigalunas, T.A., J.J. Opaluch, and T.J. Tyrrell
1988 The Economic Damages Component of the CERCLA Type A Model System. Journal of Oil and Chemical Pollution 5(1):195–215.
Haites, E.E., J. Mak, and G. Walton
1975 Western River Transportation: The Era of Early Internal Improvements, 1810–1860. Baltimore, MD: Johns Hopkins University Press.
Harvey, A.C.
1989 Forecasting Structural Time Series Models. Cambridge: Cambridge University Press.

Hawaii' State Strategic Plan 2005–2015 <www.hawaiitourismauthority.com>

Hjallager, A.M.

1997 Environmental Economics in Tourism. Annals of Tourism Research (Book Review) 24(4):1020–1021.

Hoque S., L. Dwyer, P. Forsyth, R. Spurr, T. Van Ho, and D. Pambudi

2010 Economic Impacts of Greenhouse Gas Reduction Policies in the Australian Tourism Industry: A Dynamic CGE Analysis. Technical Report, CRC for Sustainable Tourism (June), Gold Coast, Qld, Australia.

Hunziker, W., and K. Krapf

1942 Grundriss der allgemeinen Fremdenverkehrslehre (The Outline of General Tourism Science). Zuerich, Switzerland: Polygraphischer Verlag.

<http://journals.elsevier.com/02615177/tourism-management/>

(last accessed on October 10, 2010). <http://www.un.org/millenniumgoals/>

Industries Assistance Commission

1989a Some Economic Implications of Tourism Expansion, Inquiry into Travel and Tourism. Discussion Paper No. 2. Canberra: AGPS.

1989b Travel and Tourism. Report No. 423. Canberra: AGPS.

Jainchill, J.

2010a Alaska Cruise Tax Slashed, but Capacity Gain not a Certainty. Travel Weekly, April 26 <http://www.travelweekly.com/cruise/article3_ektid213630.aspex> (last accessed on April 27).

2010b Greece Liberalizes Cruise Market. Travel Weekly, August 26 <http://www.travelweekly.com/cruise/article3_ektid219600.aspx> (last accessed on August 27).

Jennings, G.R.

2007 Advances in Tourism Research: Theoretical Paradigms and Accountability. *In* Advances in Modern Tourism Research: Economic Perspectives, A. Matias, P. Nijkamp, and P. Neto, eds., pp. 9–35. Heidelberg, Germany: Physica-Verlag.

Johnston, R.J., and T.J. Tyrrell

2003 Estimating Recreational User Counts. American Journal of Agricultural Economics 85(3):554–568.

2005a Estimating Recreational User Counts: Corrigendum. American Journal of Agricultural Economics 87(2):524–527.

Johnston, R., and T. Tyrrell

2005b A Dynamic Model of Sustainable Tourism. Journal of Travel Research 44(2):124–134.

Joint Economic Committee, U.S. Congress

1970a Housing Development and Urban Planning: The Policies and Programs of Four Countries (pp. 1–145). Washington, DC: Government Printing Office.

1970b Report of the Joint Economic Committee, Congress of the United States, on the January 1970 Economic Report of the President together with Statement of Committee Agreement, Minority, Supplementary and Dissenting Views (pp. 1–98). Washington, DC: Government Printing Office.

Kaspar, C.
1973 Fremdenverkehrsökologie – eine neue Dimension der Fremdenverkehrslehre (Tourism Ecology – New Dimension of Tourism Science). Festschrift zur Vollendung des 65. Lebensjahres von P. Bernecker. Beitraege zur Fremdenverkehrsforschung, pp. 139–143. Wien: Ender W.

Keir, G.
1973 Burns Would Veto Room Bill. Honolulu Advertiser (February 23):pp. A1 and A11.

Klein, L.R.
1971 Forecasting and Policy Evaluation using Large-Scale Econometric Models: The State of the Art. *In* Frontiers of Quantitative Economics, M. Intriligator, ed., Vol. 1, pp. 133–164. Amsterdam: North Holland.

Krippendorf, J.
1984 Ferienmenshen (The Holidaymakers). Zuerich, Switzerland: Orell Fuesli Verlag.

Kwak, S., and J. Mak
2009 Taxing Timeshare Occupancy in Hawaii. State Tax Notes (February 2):321–330.

Leiper, N.
1979 The Framework of Tourism: Towards a Definition of Tourism, Tourist, and the Tourist Industry. Annals of Tourism Research 6(4):390–407.

Linder, S.B.
1961 An Essay on Trade and Transformation. London: Wiley.

Liu, J.C., P.J. Sheldon, and T. Var
1987 Resident Perception of the Environmental Impacts of Tourism. Annals of Tourism Research 14(1):17–37.

Lodewijks, J.
2007 A Conversation with Clem Tisdell. Economic Analysis and Policy 37:119–143.

Loeb, P.
1982 International Travel to the U.S.: An Econometric Evaluation. Annals of Tourism Research 9(1):7–20.

Mak, J.
2004 Tourism and the Economy: Understanding the Economics of Tourism. Honolulu, HI: University of Hawaii Press.
2008 Developing a Dream Destination: Tourism and Tourism Policy Planning in Hawaii. Honolulu, HI: University of Hawaii Press.
2005 Tourist taxes. *In* The Encyclopedia of Taxation and Tax Policy, J. J. Cordes, R. D. Ebel, and J. G. Gravelle, eds. (pp. 441–443. 2nd ed.). Washington, D.C.: Urban Institute Press.

Mak, J., and E. Nishimura
1979 The Economics of a Hotel Room Tax. Journal of Travel Research 17 (4, Spring):2–6.

Mak, J., and K. White
1992 Comparative Tourism Development in Asia and the Pacific. Journal of Travel Research XXXI(1, Summer):14–23.

Mak, J., and J.E.T. Moncur
1980a The Choice of Journey Destinations and Lengths of Stay: A Micro Analysis. The Review of Regional Studies 10(2):38–47.
1980b Demand for travel agents. Journal of Transport Economics and Policy 221–231.
Mak, J., J.E.T. Moncur, and D. Yonamine
1977 Determinants of Visitor Expenditures and Visitor Lengths of Stay: A Cross-Section Analysis of U.S. Visitors to Hawaii. Journal of Travel Research 15(1):5–8.
Mak, J., S. Sunder, S. Abe, and K. Igawa, eds.
1998 Japan, Why It Works, Why It Doesn't: Economics in Everyday Life. Honolulu, HI: University of Hawaii Press.
Mak, J., L. Carlile, and S. Dai
2005 Impact of Population Aging on Japanese International Travel to 2025. Journal of Travel Research 44(2):151–162.
Mak, J., C. Sheehey, and S. Toriki
2010 The Passenger Vessel Services Act and America's Cruise Ship Industry. Research in Transportation Economics (26):18–26.
Mathematica, Inc.
1970 The Visitor Industry and Hawaii's Economy: A Cost-Benefit Analysis. Princeton, NJ: Mathematica, Inc.
Mathieson, A., and G. Wall
1982 Tourism: Economic, Physical, and Social Impacts. New York: Longman.
McKee, D.L., and C.A. Tisdell
1990 Developmental Issues in Small Island Economies. New York: Praeger.
Menges, G.
1958 Die touristische Konsumfunktion der Schweiz 1929 bis 1956. Schweizerische Zeitschrift für Volkswirtschaft und Statistik 329–334.
1959 Die touristische Konsumfunktion Deutschlands 1924 bis 1957. *In* Fremdenverkehr in Theorie und Praxis, Festschrift für Walter Hunziker (Hrsg.), pp. 124–139. Bern: Schweizerischer Fremdenverkehrsverband und Schweizer Reisekasse.
Mihalic, T.
2000 Environmental Management of a Tourist Destination: A Factor of Tourism Competitiveness. Tourism Management 21(1):65–78.
Mihalič, T., and C. Kaspar
1996 Umweltökonomie im Tourismus (Environmental Economics in Tourism). Bern, Switzerland: Paul Haupt.
Mitchell, F.
1970 The Value of Tourism in East Africa. Eastern Africa Economic Review 2(1):1–21.
Mok, C., and T.J. Iverson
2000 Expenditure-Based Segmentation: Taiwanese Tourists to Guam. Tourism Management 21(3):299–305.

Nash, D.
2007 The Study of Tourism: Anthropological and Sociological Beginnings Tourism Social Science Series. Amsterdam: Elsevier.
Nweze, A.
2006 Impact of Cabotage Act on Entrepreneurial Activities and Nigeria's Economic Growth. Dissertation submitted in partial fulfillment of the requirement for the award of the doctor of philosophy (in entrepreneurship) of the St. Clements University, Turks and Caicos Islands, July.
Pambudi, D., T.V. Ho, R. Spurr, P. Forsyth, L. Dwyer, and S. Hoque
2009 The Economic Contribution of Tourism to the Australian States and Territories 2007–08. STCRC Centre for Economics and Policy, Gold Coast, Qld, Australia, November.
Pearce, P.
2010 The Study of Tourism: Foundations from Psychology. *In* Tourism Social Science Series, J. Jafar, ed., Vol. 15, Elsevier.
Perdue, R., T.J. Tyrrell, and M. Uysal
2010 Understanding the Value of Tourism: A Conceptual Divergence. *In* Tourism Research: A 20–20 Vision, D.G. Pearce, and R.W. Butler, eds., pp. 123–132. Oxford: Goodfellow.
Pham, T.L., and R.S. Dwyer
2009 Constructing a Regional TSA: The Case of Queensland. Tourism Analysis 13(5/6):445–460.
Planina, J.
1961 Osnove turizma (Introduction to Tourism). Maribor, Slovenia: Višja komercialna šola Maribor.
1963 Ekonomika turizma (Tourism Economics). Ljubljana, Slovenia: Univerzitetna založba v Ljubljani.
Porter, M.
1990 The Competitive Advantage of Nations. New York: Free Press.
Prasad, B., and C.A. Tisdell
2006 Institutions, Economic Performances and Sustainable Development: A Case Study of the Fiji Islands. New York: Nova Science Publishers.
Quandt, R.
1970 The Demand for Travel: Theory and Measurement. Lexington, KY: Heath.
Rawls, J.R.
1971 A Theory of Justice. Cambridge: Harvard University Press.
Ritchie, J.R.B., and G.I. Crouch
1993 Competitiveness in International Tourism – A Framework for Understanding and Analysis. *In* Proceedings of the Association Internationale d'Experts Scientifiques du Tourismue: Vol. 35. Competitiveness of Long Haul Tourist Destinations, pp. 23–71. St. Gallen, Switzerland: Niedermann Druck.
Ritchie, J.R.B., and C.R. Goeldner, eds.
1994 Travel, Tourism and Hospitality Research: A Handbook for Managers and Researchers (2nd ed.). New York: Wiley.

Roy, K.C., and C.A. Tisdell
1998 Tourism in India and India's Economic Development. New York: Nova Science.
Sakai, M., J. Brown, and J. Mak
2000 Population Aging and Japanese International Travel in the 21st Century. Journal of Travel Research 38(3):212–220.
Schumpeter, J.
1942 Capitalism, Socialism and Democracy (2nd ed.). New York: Harper Brothers.
Sathiendrakumar, R., and C.A. Tisdell
1985 Tourism and Development in the Maldives. Masey Journal of Asian and Pacific Business 1(1):27–34.
1989 Tourism and the Economic Development of the Maldives. Annals of Tourism Research 16(2):254–269.
Schulmeister, S.
1978 Modellprognosen für den Reiseverkehr, Österreichisches Institut für Wirtschaftsforschung, Gustav Fischer, Wien.
Sharpley, R., and D. Telfer, (eds.)
2002 Tourism and Development: Concepts and Issues. Aspects of Tourism, 5. Clevedon, UK: Channel View Publications.
Sheldon, P.J.
1986 The Tour Operator Industry: An Analysis. Annals of Tourism Research 13:349–365.
1990 Tourism Expenditure Research Methodologies. *In* Progress in Tourism, Recreation and Hospitality Management, 2:150–162.
1993a Forecasting Tourism: Arrivals versus Expenditures. Journal of Travel Research (Summer).
1993b Destination Information Systems. Annals of Tourism Research 20(4):
1999 Tourism Information Technology. Oxford, England: CABI Publishing, 1997; second printing 1999.
2005 The Economics of Tourism Information Technology. *In* The International Handbook on the Economics of Tourism, L. Dwyer, and P. Forsyth, eds. Cheltenham, England: Edward Elgar Publishing.
Sheldon, P.J., and J. Mak
1987 The Demand for Package Tours: A Mode Choice Model. Journal of Travel Research XXV(3):13–17.
Sheldon, P.J., and T. Var
1985 Tourism Forecasting: A Review of Empirical Research. Journal of Forecasting 4(2):183–195.
Sheldon, P., D. Fesenmaier, and J. Tribe
forthcoming Tourism Education Futures Initiative (TEFI): Activating Change in Tourism Education. Journal of Teaching in Travel and Tourism.
Smeral, E.
1979 Ein Exportallokationsmodell für die westlichen Industrieländer (A Model of Export Allocation for the Western Industrialized Countries), Weltwirtschaftliches Archiv (Review of World Economics), No. 3. 450–466.

1988 Tourism Demand, Economic Theory and Econometrics: An Integrated Approach. Journal of Travel Research XXVI(4):38–43. Spring.

1993 What Can We Learn From Forecasting Models? Scope and Limits. *In* Spoilt for Choice – Decision Making Processes and Preference Changes of Tourists: Intertemporal and Intercountry Perspectives, R. Gasser, and K. Weiermair, eds., pp. 263–274. University of Innsbruck: Kultur Verlag, November.

1994 Economic Models. *In* Tourism Marketing and Management Handbook, St. Witt, and L. Moutinho, eds., pp. 497–503. Hemel Hempstead, England: Prentice Hall.

2001 Beyond the Myth of Growth in Tourism. *In* Tourism Growth and Global Competition, Th. Bieger, and P. Keller, eds., pp. 3–38. St. Gallen, Switzerland: AIEST.

2003 A Structural View of Tourism Growth. Tourism Economics 9(1):77–93.

2004 Long-term Forecasts for International Tourism. Tourism Economics 20(2):145–166.

2005 The Economic Impact of Tourism: Beyond Satellite Accounts. Tourism Analysis 10(1):55–64.

2006 Tourism Satellite Account: A Critical Assessment. Journal of Travel Research 45(1):92–98.

2007a World Tourism Forecasting – Keep it Quick, Simple and Dirty. Tourism Economics 13(2):309–317.

2007b The Productivity Puzzle in Tourism. *In* The Problem of Productivity in Tourism, Th. Bieger, and P. Keller, eds., pp. 27–39. Berlin: Erich Schmid.

2009a Growth Accounting for Tourism Industries. Journal of Travel Research 47(4):413–424.

2009b The Impact of the Financial and Economic Crisis on European Tourism. Journal of Travel Research 48(1):S. 3–S. 13.

2010a Impacts of the World Recession and Economic Crisis on Tourism: Forecasts and Potential Risks. Journal of Travel Research 49(1):S. 31–S. 38. February.

2010b How International Tourism Is Coping with the Consequences of the Financial and Economic Crisis. *In* Tourism Development after the Crisis: Coping with Global Imbalances and Contributing to the Millennium Goals, Th. Bieger, and P. Keller, eds. Berlin: Erich Schmidt Verlag.

Smeral, E., and A. Weber

2000 Forecasting International Tourism Trends to 2010. Annals of Tourism Research 27(4):982–1006.

Smeral, E., and M. Wüger

2000 The Use of Intervention Models to Assess the Effects of the EU Presidency on Revenues from International Tourism. Tourism Economics 6(1):61–72.

2005 Does Complexity Matter? Methods for Improving the Forecasting Accuracy in Tourism: The Case of Austria. Journal of Travel Research 44(1):100–110.

2006 Improving Marketing Efficiency through the Implementation of Advanced Forecasting Methods: A Short Term Approach. *In* Marketing Efficiency in Tourism, Coping with Volatile Demand, P. Keller, and Th. Bieger, eds., pp. 183–192. Berlin: Erich Schmid.

2008 Methods for Measuring the Effects of the EU Presidency on International Forecasting. Tourism Economics 14(2):313–324.

Smith, S.

1988 Defining Tourism a Supply-Side View. Annals of Tourism Research 15(2):179–190.

Smith S., ed.

2010 The Discovery of Tourism Tourism Social Science Series. Vol. 13, Amsterdam: Elsevier.

Solow, R.

1970 Growth Theory: An Exposition. Oxford: Oxford University Press.

Song, H., and G. Li

2008 Tourism Demand Modelling and Forecasting – A Review of Recent Research. Tourism Management 29(2):203–220.

Song, H., P. Romilly, and X. Liu

1999 An Empirical Study of Outbound Tourism Demand in the UK. Applied Economics 32:611–624.

Song, H., and S.F. Witt

2000 Tourism Demand Modeling and Forecasting: Modern Econometric Approaches. Oxford: Elsevier.

Song, H., S.F. Witt, and X.Y. Zhang

2008 A Web-based Tourism Demand Forecasting System. Tourism Economics 14(3):445–468.

Stabler, M.J., A. Papatheodorou, and M.T. Sinclair

2010 The Economics of Tourism (2nd ed.). London: Routledge.

State of Hawaii

1978 State Tourism Study, Public Revenue-Cost Analysis. Honolulu, HI: Office of Tourism, Department of Planning and Economic Development.

Surrey Research Group

1993 Scottish Tourism Multiplier Study 1992. ESU Research Paper No. 31. Guildford, UK: University of Surrey.

Tisdell, C.A.

1966 Some Bounds Upon the Pareto Optimality of Group Behavior. Kyklos 19(1):81–105.

1968 The Theory of Price Uncertainty, Production and Profit. Princeton, NJ: Princeton University Press.

1974 The Value of Demand For and Supply of National Parks – Economic Issues Raised by Recreational Use. Research Paper No. 4. Newcastle University, NSW: Board of Environmental Studies.

1977 National Parks: Economic Issues. *In* Leisure and Recreation in Australia, D. Mercer, ed., pp. 111–119. Melbourne: Sorrett Publishing.

1981 Science and Technology Policy. London: Chapman and Hall.

1982 Wild Pigs: Environmental Pest or Economic Resource?. Sydney: Pergamon Press.

1983a The Great Barrier Reef: A Regional Case of Tourism and Natural Resources. Australian Parks and Recreation, 37–42. Reprinted in the UN Wildlife and National Parks Management Bulletin, 10(4):1–6.

1983b Public Finance and Appropriation of Gains from International Tourists: Some Theory with ASEAN and Australian Illustrations. Singapore Economic Review 28:3–20.

1984a The Environment and Tourism in South East Asian and Australia: Experiences and Strategies Relevant to Tourism Development and Administration. Thai Journal of Development Administration 24(1):124–142.

1984b Seasonality in Tourism and the Desirability of Evening out Tourist Demand. Economic Activity 27(4):13–17.

1984c Tourism, The Environment, International Trade and Public Economics. ASEAN Australian Economic Papers No. 6. Kuala Lumpur and Canberra: ASEAN–Australian Joint Research Project.

1986a Australia's Antarctic Policy Options – A Review Article. Economic Analysis and Policy 16(1):76–85.

1986b Conflicts About Living Marine Resources in Southeast Asia and Australian Waters: Turtles and Dugongs as Cases. Marine Resource Economics 3(1): 89–109.

1987a Tourism, National Gains and Public Economics. Reference for Economic Study 92(June):31–45. Translated into Chinese by Yushi Mao.

1987b Tourism, the Environment and Profit. Economic Analysis and Policy 17(1):13–30.

1988a The Economic Potential of Wildlife on the Otago Peninsula, especially the yellow-eyed penguin for tourism. Economics Discussion Papers No. 8818. Dunedin, NZ: University of Otago.

1988b Sustainable Development: Differing Perspectives of Ecologists and Economists and Their Relevance to LDCs. World Development 16:373–384.

1988c Sustaining and Measuring Gains from Tourism Based and Natural Sites: Analysis with Reference to the Galapagos. *In* Economics of Tourism, C.A. Tisdell, G.J. Aislabie, and P.J. Stanton, eds., pp. 229–252. Australia: Institute of Industrial Economics, Newcastle University.

1991 Economics of Environmental Conservation (1st ed.). Amsterdam: Elsevier Science Publishers.

1993 Economic Development in the Context of China. London: Macmillan.

1996a Bounded Rationality and Economic Evolution. Cheltenham, UK: Edward Elgar.

1996b Ecotourism Economics and the Environment: Observations from China. Journal of Travel Research 34(4):11–19.

1997 An Abbreviated Autobiography: Saint or Devil or Neither?. International Journal of Social Economics 24:695–722.

1999a Biodiversity, Conservation and Sustainable Development: Principles and Practices with Asian Examples. Cheltenham, UK: Edward Elgar.

1999b Optimal Australian Dugong Populations and Conservation Plans: An Economic Perspective. Economic Analysis and Policy 29(1):59–69.

2000a Economics and University Life: The Further Reflections and Experiences of Clem Tisdell. International Journal of Social Economics 27: 669–698.

2000b The Economics of Tourism. Vol. 2, Cheltenham, UK: Edward Elgar.

2001 Tourism Economics, the Environment and Development: Analysis and Policy. Cheltenham, UK: Edward Elgar.

2003 Fostering Tourism to Diversify and Develop Small Economies: Brunei's Policies in a General Context. Pacific Tourism Review (6):83–94.

2005 Economics of Environmental Conservation (2nd ed.). Cheltenham, UK: Edward Elgar.

2006 Economics of Leisure. Vol. 2, Cheltenham, UK: Edward Elgar.

2007a The Evolution and Classification of the Published Books of Clem Tisdell: A Brief Overview. Economic Theory, Applications and Issues. Working Paper No. 44. Brisbane, Qld: School of Economics, The University of Queensland.

2007b The Economic Importance of Wildlife Conservation on the Otago Peninsula – 20 Years On. Economics, Ecology and the Environment. Working Paper No. 144. Brisbane, Qld: School of Economics, The University of Queensland.

2007c Valuing the Otago Peninsula: The Economic Benefits of Conservation. Economics, Ecology and the Environment. Working Paper No. 145. Brisbane, Qld: School of Economics, The University of Queensland.

2009 Wildlife Conservation and the Value of New Zealand's Otago Peninsula: Economic Impacts and Other Considerations. *In* Wildlife, Destruction, Conservation and Biodiversity, J.D. Harris, and P.L. Brown, eds., pp. 277–290. New York: Nova Science Publishers Inc.

Tisdell, C.A., and R. Bandara

2009 A Sri Lankan Elephant Orphanage: Does it Increase Willingness to Conserve Elephants? How Do Visitors React to It? *In* Wildlife, Destruction, Conservation and Biodiversity, , eds., pp. 253–276. New York: Nova Science Publishers Inc.

Tisdell, C.A., and J. Broadus

1989 Policy Issues Related to the Establishment and Management of Marine Resources. Coastal Management 47:37–53.

Tisdell, C.A., and K.C. Roy

1998 Tourism and Development: Economic, Social and Environmental Issues. New York: Nova Science.

Tisdell, C.A., and H. Swarna Nantha
2008 Conservation of the Proboscis Monkey and the Orangutan in Borneo: Comparative Issues and Economic Considerations. *In* Perspectives in Animal Ecology & Reproduction, V.K. Gupta, and A.K. Verma, eds., Vol. 5, pp. 225–250. Delhi: Daya Publishing House.

Tisdell, C.A., and C. Wilson
2002 Economic, Educational and Conservation Benefits of Sea Turtle Based Ecotourism: A Study Focused on Mon Repos. Wildlife Tourism Research Report Series No. 20. Gold Coast, Qld, Australia: CRC Sustainable Tourism, Griffith University.
2004 Economics, Wildlife Tourism and Conservation: Three Case Studies. Technical Report. Gold Coast, Qld, Australia: CRC for Sustainable Tourism Pty Limited, Griffith University.

Tisdell, C.A., G.J. Aislabie, and P.J. Stanton
1988 Economics of Tourism: Case Study and Analysis. Australia: Institute of Industrial Economics, Newcastle University.

Tisdell, C.A., H. Khan, S. Zaide Pritchard, J.A. Doeleman, M. Watson, M.O. Wirakartakusuma, and J.B. Marsh
1992 Marine Pollution and Tourism. *In* Resources and Environment in Asia's Marine Sector, J.B. Marsh, ed., pp. 381–419. New York: Taylor and Francis.

Tribe, J.
2005 The Economics of Recreation, Leisure and Tourism (3rd ed.). New York: Butterworth-Heinemann.

TSG
2007 Action for more Sustainable European Tourism. Report of the Tourism Sustainability Group. Brussels, Belgium: European Commission.

Tyrrell, T. J., and R. J., Johnston.
2001 A Framework for Assessing Direct Economic Impacts of Tourist Events: Distinguishing Origins, Destinations, and Causes of Expenditures. Journal of Travel Research (August).
2002 Estimating Regional Visitor Numbers. Tourism Analysis 7(1):33–41.
2003 Assessing Expenditure Changes Related to Welcome Center Visits. Journal of Travel Research (August).
2006 The Economic Impacts of Tourism: A Special Issue. Journal of Travel Research 45(1):1–5.

Tyrrell, T., and R. Johnston
2008 Tourism Sustainability, Resiliency and Dynamics: Towards a More Comprehensive Perspective. Tourism and Hospitality Research 814–24. Published online on 11 February 2008.
2009 An Econometric Analysis of the Effects of Tourism Growth on Municipal Revenues and Expenditures. Tourism Economics 15(4).

Tyrrell, T., and T. Mount
1982 A Non-Linear Expenditure System Using a Linear Logit Specification. American Journal of Agricultural Economics 64(3):539–546.
Tyrrell, T.J., P.W. Williams, and R.J. Johnston
2004 Estimating Sport Tourism Visitor Volumes: The Case of Vancouver's 2010 Olympic Games. Tourism Recreation Research 29(1):75–82.
Tyrrell, T., Paris, C.M. and Casson, M.
2009 Monetarizing the Triple Bottom Line. *In* TTRA Annual Conference, Honolulu, June 19.
2010 Evaluating Tourism Community Preferences. Tourism Analysis 15(2)
UN SD.
2010. National accounts main aggregates database. United Nations Statistic Division. Available at http://unstats.un.org/unsd/snaama/introduction.asp. Retrieved on August 2, 2010.
UNWTO,
2008 2008 International Recommendations for Tourism Statistics. New York: UNWTO.
U.S. Advisory Commission on Intergovernmental Relations (ACIR)
Revenue Diversification, State and Local Travel Taxes, M-189, Washington, DC: April 1994.
U.S. Bureau of the Census
1973 National Travel Survey, Travel During 1972. Washington, DC: Government Printing Office.
U.S. Travel Data Center
1974a National Travel Expenditure Study. Washington, DC: U. S. Travel Data Center.
U.S. Travel Data Center
1974b The 1973 National Travel Survey Annul Report. Washington, DC: U. S. Travel Data Center
U.S. Travel Data Center
1978 Travel Data Locator Index (2nd ed.). Washington, DC: U. S. Travel Data Center.
Vanhove, N.
1960 Torhout-Sociaal-Economischche Structuur en Ontwikkelingstendensen. Ghent: Serug.
1974. Het Belgisch Kusttoerisme-Vandaag en Morgen. Pro Civitate Award 1972, Recht en Local Economie (Translated into French "Le tourisme sur le littoral belge. Aujourd'hui et demain", Brussel).
1982 Interrelation between Benefits and Costs of Tourism Resources: An Economic Approach. Report to AIEST congress, ST-Gall: Editions AIEST.
1984. Tourism and the Architectural Heritage: Promotional, Economic and Fiscal Aspects. Report to AIEST congress, ST-Gall: Editions AIEST.
1994. Tourism and Economics: What Remains from a Long Research Tradition. Report to AIEST congress, ST-Gall: Editions AIEST.

1996 Globalisation of Tourism Demand. Report to AIEST congress, ST-Gall: Editions AIEST.
1999 Regional Policy. A European Approach. (3rd ed.). Aldershot: Ashgate. (The first (1980) edition, together with L. Klaassen, was translated into Greek and Chinese). There was a second edition in 1987.
2003 Externalities of Sport and Tourism Investments, Activities and Events. Report to AIEST congress, ST-Gall: Editions AIEST.
2005 The Economics of Tourism Destinations. Amsterdam, Elsevier: Butterworth-Heinemann.
2010 Tourism a Vehicle of Development? A Regional Approach. Report to AIEST congress. Berlin: Erich Schmidt Verlag.
2011 The Economics of Tourism Destinations (2nd ed.). Amsterdam: Elsevier.

Vanhove, N., and L. Klaassen
1980 Regional Policy. A European Approach. Guildford: Saxon House.

Vanneste, O., and G. Declercq
1955 Le littoral et son hinterland. Bruges, Belgium: Westtoerisme.

Veblen, T.
1932 The Theory of the Leisure Class. New York: Vanguard Press.

Victorian Auditor General
2007 State Investment in Major Events. Victorian Government Printer, Victoria, May.

Vukonić, B.
1987 Turizam i razvoj. Zagreb: Školska knjiga.
1990 Turizam i religija. Zagreb: Školska knjiga.
1993 Turizam u vihoru rata. Zagreb: Agencija za marketing Vjesnik and MATE.
1994 Turizam u susret budućnosti. Zagreb: Ekonomski fakultet and Mikrorad.
1995 Turizam kao područje istraživanja i edukacije na Ekonomskom fakultetu u Zagrebu. Acta turistica 7(1):3–23.
1996 Tourism and Religion. London: Elsevier – Pergamon.
1997 Tourism in the Whirlwind of War. Zagreb: Golden Marketing.
2000 Microeconomic Aspects of Macroeconomic Problems in Croatian Tourism. International Conference "Tourism and Transition", pp. 20–24. Dubrovnik, Croatia: Faculty of Tourism and Foreign Trade.
2001 "Uloga nastavne discipline Ekonomika turizma u obrazovanju hrvatskih turističkih kadrova". Second Professional Conference on the Theory of Economics for Faculties of Economics in Croatia, "Uloga povijesti ekonomske misli u nastavi na Fakultetima društvenih znanosti u Hrvatskoj" (The Role of Economic Thought in Teaching at Faculties of Social Sciences in Croatia), Conference Proceedings, pp. 211–230. Osijek, Croatia.
2002 Tourism at the Graduate School of Economics and Business, University of Zagreb 1962–2002. Rethinking of Education and Training for Tourism, pp. 1–12. Zagreb, Republic of Croatia: Graduate School of Economics and Business, University of Zagreb.

2003 Studij turizma: doprinos raspravi o visokoškolskoj nastavi u Hrvatskoj (The Study of Tourism: Contribution to the Debate on Higher Education Teaching in Croatia). Znanstveni skup Pristup strategiji ekonomskog razvoja Hrvatske (Professional Conference Approach to the Strategy of the Economic Development of Croatia), HAZU, Ekonomija, 10(1), 217–228.

2007 Ekonomika turizma: nesporazum i nerazumijevanje (Economics of Tourism: Misunderstanding and a Lack of Understanding). Acta Turistica Nova 1(1):5–20.

Vukonić, B., and Š. Tanković

1986 Snaga utjecaja pojedinih faktora na razvoj turizma. Turizam XXXV(3): 235–238.

Vukonić, B., and N. Čavlek, eds.

2001 Rječnik Turizma. Zagreb: Masmedia.

Wen, J.J., and C.A. Tisdell

2001 Tourism and China's Development: Policies, Regional Growth and Ecotourism. Singapore: World Scientific.

Witt, S.F., and C.A. Witt

1995 Forecasting Tourism Demand: A review of Empirical Research. International Journal of Forecasting 11:447–475.

World Bank

1975 Environment and Development. Washington: World Bank.

www.besteducationnetwork.org

www.tourismforecasting.net

www.tourism-economics.net

Xue, D., A. Cook, and C.A. Tisdell

2000 Biodiversity and the Tourism Value of Changbai Mountain Biosphere Reserve, China: A Travel Cost Approach. Tourism Economics 6:335–357.

Young, G.

1973 Tourism. Blessing or Blight? Aylesbury, England: Hazel Watson & Viney Ltd.

Author Index

Subject Index